About the Author

Dr Thomas Christie has a life-long fascination with films
and the people who make them. A member of the Royal Society of
Literature and the Society of Authors, he holds an M.A. in Humanities
with British Cinema History from the Open University of Milton Keynes,
and a Ph.D. in Scottish Literature awarded by the University of Stirling.

Thomas Christie is the author of *Liv Tyler, Star in Ascendance:
Her First Decade in Film* (2007), *The Cinema of Richard Linklater* (2008),
*John Hughes and Eighties Cinema* (2009), *Ferris Bueller's Day Off: Pocket
Movie Guide* (2010) and *The Christmas Movie Book* (2011), all of which are
published by Crescent Moon Publishing. A study of Mel Brooks
is forthcoming.

For more information about Tom and his books, visit his website
at www.tomchristiebooks.co.uk.

# Liv Tyler

# Star in Ascendance

# Liv Tyler

# Star in Ascendance

## Her First Decade in Film

Thomas A. Christie

CRESCENT MOON

Crescent Moon Publishing
P.O. Box 393
Maidstone
Kent
ME14 5XU, U.K.


First edition 2007.
© Thomas A. Christie 2007.

Printed and bound in Great Britain.
Set in Book Antiqua 10 on 14pt and Gill Sans.
Designed by Radiance Graphics.

*British Library Cataloguing in Publication data available for this title.*

*ISBN 1-86171-131-X*
*ISBN-13 9781861711311*

# CONTENTS

*"The world's a theatre,*
*the earth a stage,*
*which God and nature do with actors fill."*

John Heywood


*"We are all in the gutter,*
*but some of us are looking at the stars."*

Oscar Wilde

Liv Tyler in *The Lord of the Rings*, 2001,
© New Line Productions, Inc

# ACKNOWLEDGEMENTS

Having spent more time than I can realistically recall having worked on this book, there are inevitably many people to whom I would like to offer my sincere thanks for their help and assistance in all stages of the writing process (from early research to frenetic typing and everything in-between). I have great pleasure in doing so now.

First and foremost, I would like to thank my dear mother Sandra, my sister Julie and my aunt Mary, for their infinite patience with my research and also with my temporary absence from their company during my many repeated viewings of the films explored in this book. I am also very grateful to them for putting up with my frequent and prolonged disappearances into the background when it came to re-editing, reference checking, proofreading, and all of the other less glamorous tasks of authorship that never seem to get mentioned all that much.

My gratitude goes to Douglas J. Allen, my friend and one-time university dissertation supervisor, for his generosity with his time and advice as well as his wonderful foreword. His kind input was greatly appreciated. Additionally, I'd like to pay tribute to Dr Elspeth King, Margaret Job and Lesley Duncan, all of whom offered valuable advice and interesting discussions about literature the world over.

Thanks also to my old chum Ivy Lannon, with whom I have spent many a pleasant hour in conversation about (amongst many things) the international film industry and all of its ever-changing twists and turns. Her insight and enthusiasm with the subject of critical analysis continues to be a great inspiration. My heartfelt thanks to another pal, fellow researcher Alistair M. Dalrymple, for his very welcome input into this study; his involvement has been both lively and indispensable. Compliments as well are due to my friends Denham and Stella Hardwick for their passionate enthusiasm towards all things performance-related; their support is, and always has been, a real encouragement.

Sincere and profuse thanks are due to Diane Wright and her staff at Berwick-upon-Tweed Library for providing assistance which was above and beyond the call of duty. I am greatly indebted to them for their help in tracking down many articles, no matter how obscure or difficult to find; never once did they let me down.

A vote of thanks is also due to those great unsung heroes of the digital age, the many information and research websites of the Internet. Without these invaluable tools to confirm, compare and contrast facts and statistics, the process of my research would certainly have been greatly extended. Therefore, I would like to give a special acknowledgment to what must surely be the best of many Liv Tyler sites on the Internet today: the award-winning 'Lovely Liv Tyler' website (*http://www.lovelylivtyler.com*). As well as hosting a huge gallery of production photos taken from Liv Tyler's many feature film appearances, the site maintains an announcements section which outlines her latest movie news, and there is also an impressively comprehensive archive of press articles spanning the entire duration of Liv's film career (some of which are English translations of features which have originally been printed in foreign languages). It is difficult to imagine a more complete fan site than 'Lovely Liv Tyler', and their considerable dedication and commitment in chronicling Liv Tyler's ongoing career in the movies could not be more apparent.

# AUTHOR'S NOTE

As this is an analytical text by nature, many of the films discussed in subsequent chapters are accompanied by quite detailed examinations of individual storylines and plot elements. Therefore, any readers unfamiliar with a given film may find their enjoyment of the story spoiled by the accounts given of the events which take place in each film.

I have tried my best to avoid providing unnecessary detail about surprise plot twists wherever possible. However, as some of the performance analysis is based specifically upon just such story developments, it has not always been viable to steer clear of plot spoilers entirely (this is particularly true of the trick ending in *Silent Fall*, and the different cliff-hanger conclusions spread throughout *The Lord of the Rings* trilogy).

So if you aren't familiar with some of the films that are about to be discussed, but intend to watch them in the future, please read on with some degree of caution!

# FOREWORD

One of the great pleasures of a lifetime's tutoring in further education, adult education and the Open University has been the number of students I've met who somehow manage to fill in what is laughably known as their 'spare time' with all kinds of other activities. One of the most admirably energetic students in recent years is the author of this volume, Thomas Christie, and it is a pleasure to see the fruits of his 'off-duty' research and writing now ready to be presented to a wider public.

His pioneering account of Liv Tyler's film career to date is a truly impressive product, combining a wide-ranging knowledge of the film world with a strong, readable narrative style. In the age of the sensational, salacious celebrity biography, cut and pasted from newspaper headlines, it is good to see such a serious yet accessible account of a film career that has so far eluded biographers' attention. His meticulous approach has resulted in a work that is factually informative, while his judgements and opinions are scrupulously fair and even-handed.

For anyone looking for an authoritative account of Liv Tyler's film career, drawn from an impressively wide-ranging selection of international sources, moving easily between the worlds of high art and popular culture, this volume can be thoroughly recommended. Let us hope it is the first of many such sound explorations of unjustly neglected areas and personalities of the film world.

**Douglas J. Allen**


*Douglas J. Allen is Lecturer in Social Sciences at Motherwell College, Scotland. He has published widely in books, journals and magazines on the subject of film and television history.*

# INTRODUCTION

It seems difficult today to imagine a time when the name Liv Tyler (1977-) could be met with a lack of recognition. Yet scarcely a decade ago, it would have been difficult for anyone to have anticipated the sheer scale of her meteoric rise to worldwide fame in the film industry.

As we will see over the course of this book, Tyler's acting career has been remarkably diverse, encompassing a wide variety of different genres – prominent roles in seventeen films throughout the course of just over ten years. Thanks to her prolific and meticulously crafted body of work, she has clearly illustrated an increasingly versatile range of acting skills through her acute emotional observation and constant eagerness to experiment.

Her good humour, decisively down-to-earth attitude and apparent willingness never to take herself too seriously have made her not only one of the most popular young actresses in America, but arguably one of the most universally well-liked public figures of her generation. Yet in parallel to her oft-attributed reputation as one of the most straight-thinking and unpretentious performers working in the film industry today, it is significant to note that Tyler has constantly expressed a desire in press interviews to keep her personal life private and as separate as possible from her well-publicised appearances in films. As this book is not strictly speaking a biographical text, but rather an analytical survey of Tyler's evolving film career, I will not be making reference to any observations of her life outside of the film industry that have been made in the media at large. This is a study of Liv Tyler the public figure, and it seems apposite to concentrate on the public-facing professional persona that she has developed over the years rather than on the private face of the individual, wife and mother which lies behind it. Anyone seeking a fuller understanding of Tyler's early life and her first steps into acting need look no further than Bebe Buell's auto-biography *Rebel Heart*. The book outlines the beginnings of Tyler's career in professional modelling, and her subsequent move into acting, from the unique viewpoint of the woman who is not only her mother, but also her manager during the initial years of Tyler's emergence into the world of film.[1]

This is not to say, of course, that Tyler's life experiences have not informed the depth of her performances, or that she is reluctant to draw on authentic experience to strengthen her dramatic technique. Indeed, there have been a number of occasions where critics have praised her acting style for its delicately expressive emotional sensitivity – all the more remarkable for someone who had allegedly never undertaken formal acting training prior to her debut film performance.[2]

In this book, I have presented a chronological analysis of all of Tyler's films to date, from her first appearance in a motion picture in Bruce Beresford's *Silent Fall* (1994) to her recent role in Steve Buscemi's acclaimed *Lonesome Jim* (2005). For the purposes of this chronological approach, I have not discussed Tyler's cameo appearances in films thus far, in Oliver Stone's *U Turn* (1997) and the Harry Elfont/ Deborah Kaplan comedy *Can't Hardly Wait* (1998). Both of these appearances form rather brief vignettes within the films which, while admittedly entertaining to observe, add little to an overall understanding of her wider canon of performances. I have also omitted mention of her ultimately-excised cameo role in Woody Allen's 1997 musical *Everyone Says I Love You*, as well as her brief appearance (as herself) in Brendan Kelly's acclaimed short film *Franky Goes to Hollywood* (1999).

Following this film-by-film analysis of Tyler's performances up until the present time, I have provided a critical overview of her canon of film appearances which places her work in the wider context of contemporary American film. This summation will, I hope, illustrate some of the more remarkable aspects of a genuinely significant career, and one which still contains the constant ability to surprise.

Where possible, I have provided references to a variety of contemporary articles and reviews which discuss and examine Tyler's many film appearances from a range of different angles. These give some indication of each film's critical reception, as well as the manner in which Tyler's own image as an actress has developed and has come to gain considerable recognition over the years.

Respected by her peers and increasingly critically appreciated by reviewers, there seems to be little doubt that Liv Tyler is here to stay as a prominent fixture in popular film culture.

# I

# SILENT FALL (1994)

*Morgan Creek Productions / Kouf/ Bigelow Productions*

**Director**: Bruce Beresford
**Producer**: James G. Robinson
**Screenwriter**: Akiva Goldsman

MAIN CAST

| | |
|---|---|
| **Richard Dreyfuss** | Dr Jake Rainer |
| **Linda Hamilton** | Karen Rainer |
| **John Lithgow** | Dr René Harlinger |
| **J.T. Walsh** | Sheriff Mitch Rivers |
| **Ben Faulkner** | Tim Warden |
| **Liv Tyler** | Sylvie Warden |

Liv Tyler was born at Mount Sinai Hospital in New York City on Friday 1st July 1977. The daughter of Bebe Buell, a successful musical artist and model, and Steven Tyler, best known as the lead singer of legendary rock band Aerosmith, she grew up in Maine before relocating back to New York in her early teens. It was while living there that she began a modelling career, which quickly flourished. In spite of her near-instant success in this field, however, it took only a year of working in the modelling profession before she was to make the decision to diversify her talents and pursue an acting career.

*Silent Fall* marked Tyler's first appearance in a motion picture. Prior to this film, her experience of appearing in visual media had been contained to an appearance in Aerosmith's acclaimed music video for *Crazy* (1994), in which she appeared alongside a young Alicia Silverstone. *Crazy*, which has since become one of Aerosmith's best-known videos, featured the increasingly outrageous misadventures of two teenaged girls who shirk their prestigious school for a day in search of rather more diverting pursuits. Over the years, the video has developed into something of a cult classic in its own right.[3] *Crazy* was also responsible for introducing Tyler to an audience other than those who had become aware of her as a result of her modelling career. Now ready to make the transition to the big screen, Tyler rose to the occasion with characteristic enthusiasm, and her performance was to have an immediate impact upon critics and filmgoers.

*Silent Fall* was filmed during a particularly prolific period in the career of director Bruce Beresford. A highly significant figure in the cinema of his native Australia, Beresford consistently produced a number of critically successful films throughout the 1970s, the pinnacle of which, arguably, was the Oscar-nominated *Breaker Morant* (1980). Beresford made a relocation to Hollywood in the early 1980s, and as the decade progressed he was to lend his hand to films which were critically acclaimed (*Tender Mercies* (1983)), high-profile (*Her Alibi* (1989)), and universally successful (the multiple Academy Award-winning *Driving Miss Daisy*

(1989)). Technically refined, his films have covered a wide variety of challenging subject matter over the years, and his output rarely, if ever, retreads old ground.

By the time of *Silent Fall*, some of Beresford's films were starting to be received variably by critics. He had directed four films since the beginning of the 1990s, none of which had matched the massive international success of *Driving Miss Daisy*, but he had nonetheless retained his ability to move effortlessly between different genres with much stylistic flair. His historical dramas *Mister Johnson* (1990) and *Black Robe* (1991) met with general critical approval, whereas the domestic drama *Rich in Love* (1993) and satire *A Good Man in Africa* (1994) fared less well, receiving an uneven reaction from reviewers. *Silent Fall* was to signify another genre shift in this period of Beresford's oeuvre; a psychological thriller, the film contains echoes of the intensity of his earlier work whilst continuing the theme of familial tension that had been addressed in *Rich in Love*.

The film concerns the brutal murder of a prominent American businessman and his wife, who are violently stabbed to death at home in their bedroom. Their teenaged daughter Sylvie (Liv Tyler) and nine-year-old autistic son, Tim (Ben Faulkner), are both found at the scene of the crime. Sylvie is discovered unconscious in a closet, and claims to have no memory of the murderer's appearance, whereas Tim's condition means that he is unable to relate his side of the story through any conventional method. Mitch Rivers, the investigating officer (J.T. Walsh), contacts an old associate, Dr Jake Rainer, to assist in the criminal enquiry and – if possible – uncover Tim's eye-witness account of the murder.

Rainer (Richard Dreyfuss), we discover, was once a respected child psychologist in the area. However, following a tragic accident which led to the death of an infant in his care, he has become a practicing adult therapist who shuns children whenever possible. Although reluctant to become involved in the case, Rainer is concerned that Tim – having been found covered in blood and gripping a kitchen knife when the police arrive at the crime scene – will be convicted for the murder when forensic evidence indicates that he was not to blame. Fighting against the clock, and an imperious, heavy-handed rival psychologist who disagrees with Rainer's methodology, the case gradually unfolds as Jake tries desperately to piece together the fragmentary evidence and establish the truth of the events which led up to the murder.

It cannot be denied that Tyler gives a remarkably assured supporting performance in *Silent Fall*; her debut role leaves little doubt of her natural screen presence. This is particularly note-worthy given the august range of acting luminaries who surround her. Richard Dreyfuss gives a suitably studied performance as the grave, often distant analyst who must struggle with the demons of the past while fighting his way towards some very uncomfortable truths as his investigation continues. The always-watchable character actor John Lithgow is likewise impressive as the unctuous Dr Harlinger. Lithgow makes the most of every moment of his brief screen time as his character battles Rainer's person-centred approach to child psychology in order to champion his own particular style of therapy: for Harlinger, only a stark bedside manner and an abundance of strong medication can win the day. Linda Hamilton also turns in a sensitive and believable performance as Rainer's put-upon wife, a lawyer who initially sees the investigation as a means for her husband to expunge his feelings of self-blame, but ultimately begins to have misgivings when he appears to grow closer to Sylvie, the only person with whom Tim will interact. Hamilton is highly effective in the role of Karen Rainer, but like Lithgow her development of the character is stymied by the brevity of her appearance. However, her anxieties about her husband's gradual self-imposed retreat from the outside world do contrast effectively with Rainer's concern about Tim, whose condition inhibits him from interaction with the world outside of his own indissoluble psychological shell.

To an extent, the fact that these accomplished actors take a subsidiary position in the storyline gives Tyler a golden opportunity to shine, and she seizes it with considerable aplomb. The character of Sylvie requires many shifts in disposition; as Rainer perceptively notes near the conclusion of the film, she presents a different personality to almost everyone with whom she interacts during the course of the investigation. There are clear, emergent reasons for Sylvie's chameleonic behaviour (like Rainer, she too has suffered major personal trauma in the past, though of a very different kind), and it is an undeniable mark of Beresford's skill as a director that he came to put so much confidence in Tyler's relatively untried abilities at such an early stage in her career. If casting her in a role of such complexity was a gamble, then it was one which paid considerable dividends.

It is probably fair to say that there are some areas of her debut performance which are stronger than others. Her on-screen chemistry with Ben Faulkner's Tim is very convincing, and Sylvie's care and attention towards her troubled brother throughout the course of the film is very representative of the kind of emotional sensitivity that Tyler would come to greatly refine in the years to come. Conveying the close bond between the siblings is, given Tim's condition, largely demonstrated through Sylvie's protectiveness towards him – in particular, this is effectively realised in her reaction when Tim is accidentally injured while in Rainer's care. Likewise, Tyler's interactions with Linda Hamilton's character convey a great deal of subtle tension, with a very restrained air of conflict running throughout their relationship as Karen begins to suspect that Sylvie may have more than a professional interest in her husband. Indeed, it is only in Sylvie's later attempt to seduce Rainer that Tyler fails to fully convince; the scene seems more awkward than tense, and neither she nor Dreyfuss seem entirely engaged in any real possibility of intimacy between their characters. That said, the uncomfortable platonic relationship which develops between them during the film is very skilfully realised by both actors; Tyler portrays well the apprehension of the troubled Sylvie in her initial reluctance to trust Rainer, whereas the understated Dreyfuss is very persuasive in communicating his character's morbid introspection and disinclination to interact with others. The grudging development of their bond of trust is accomplished effectively, which makes Sylvie's eventual shocking betrayal all the more striking when it arrives.

The common denominator between all of the main characters, of course, is Tim. His inability to communicate his account of the murder is central to the storyline, and it is his reliance on Sylvie – and, in turn, Sylvie's pseudo-reliance on Rainer – that provides one of the film's major sources of conflict, as the psychologist struggles to draw his own conclusions in the face of growing pressure from the police to achieve quick results. Interestingly, however, one of the major problems identified by critics was the film's depiction of autism, and the manner in which the disorder is reflected in Tim's character. Although once a relatively little-known condition, by the time of *Silent Fall*'s release autism was becoming increasingly well-established in the public consciousness. One such factor in this heightening of public awareness was the remarkable success of Barry Levinson's *Rain Man* (1988). Levinson's film had drawn wide-scale attention to autism, largely due to the astonishing performance of Dustin Hoffman as the protagonist Raymond Babbitt, and by the mid-1990s the nature of autism had received a good deal of press and media coverage which had better informed the general public of its nature. Indeed, J.T. Walsh's character even goes so far as to refer to *Rain Man* during the course of his investigation.

Some critics argued that the treatment of autism presented in Akiva Goldsman's screenplay for *Silent Fall* was at times exaggeratedly sensationalised, conveniently handling the attributes of this complex condition to drive the plotline in a manner which appeared somewhat at odds with the increasingly acute perception of the behavioural condition that existed at the time. Subsequently, the film's general approach to the complaint – while undoubtedly placing autism at the very centre of the storyline – has been dismissed by some critics as somewhat overwrought in its handling of the subject matter.[4] It is important to note, however, that this analysis was far from unanimous,[5] with a number of reviewers giving fulsome praise for the way in which Ben Faulkner's performance presents a believable depiction of a distressed autistic youth involved in harrowing outside events which, although involving him directly, remain almost entirely outwith his control.[6]

It must be observed that Goldsman does not solely employ autism as a plot device – indeed, far from it. His script applies much exposition on the nature of autism as a unique and exceptional condition, mostly articulated through Rainer's discussions with Sylvie as they try to encourage Tim to reveal his account of his parents' murder. It is to Beresford's credit that these extended interactions never fully divest the film of momentum, and indeed they are critical in augmenting the viewer's understanding of Tim's sometimes baffling behaviour. As the features of his condition are gradually fleshed out, we discover that unlike *Rain Man*'s Raymond Babbitt, Tim's autism does not manifest itself in the form of incredible mathematical acuity, but instead through the talent of total recall expressed through pitch-perfect vocal mimicry. This provides a turning-point in Rainer's investigation, as he relies on Tim's disconnected, stream of consciousness-like reconstruction of a verbal exchange that took place at the time of the murder in order to pinpoint the true identity of the killer.

This ultimately gives Rainer the breakthrough that he needs, and when his research eventually draws close to uncovering the real murderer – Sylvie, seeking vengeance against her father for the lifetime of silent abuse that he had subjected her to – he sparks a resultant change of behaviour in her character which sees her transform from a solitary, distressed teenager into a calculating and resourceful predator. Her desire for self-preservation is well-served by the concurrent gear-shift in Tyler's performance, injecting a growing air of desperation as she fights to protect herself and her brother from the inevitable consequences that begin to close in on them. It is only through Tim's unexpected intervention – and Rainer's quick thinking – that her plan is foiled, and the full truth behind the gruesome killings is finally revealed.

Given the disturbing *modus operandi* which is eventually identified as the driving force behind the Wardens' double-murder, it is interesting to note that Beresford and Goldsman decide to end the film on a reasonably upbeat note. In spite of her actions, we find that Sylvie, through incarceration, has been allowed the opportunity to atone for what she has done, and does appear at the film's conclusion to have embraced this chance at redemption for her actions. Tim, meanwhile, remains happy in the care of the Rainers, providing Jake with the closure that he has long desired and restoring his faith in himself and his abilities.

Bruce Beresford was nominated for a Golden Berlin Bear award for *Silent Fall* at the 1995 Berlin International Film Festival. It has, however, come to be regarded as a lesser work in the filmography of a world-class director. Despite some dizzying convolutions in the plot, the film does have much to recommend it, including some highly effective cinematography which proficiently renders an atmospheric, autumnal environment that slowly cools into a harsh winter as the investigation continues towards its conclusion. But for a few less plot acrobatics and unlikely coincidences, the film may have become something of a modern classic in the thriller genre. As it stands, however, *Silent Fall* has been eclipsed by Beresford's earlier triumphs, and also by his more recent success with films such as *Paradise Road* (1997).

Today, *Silent Fall* is perhaps most noteworthy as the motion picture which marked the introduction of Liv Tyler into popular film, and it formed a strong beginning for her acting career. Her performance in this demanding, multifaceted role was impressively confident, though not without the occasional rough edge inherent in any first-time supporting appearance. Her mature and charismatic performance was certainly impressive enough to mark her out amongst critics as a talent worth watching.

## FURTHER READING

Because of *Silent Fall*'s place at the very beginning of Tyler's career, her part in the film was not nearly as heavily publicised in the media as her later appearances would come to be.

Tyler talks about the challenges she faced in her acting debut in an interview with Kim Lockhart for *Sassy* magazine in April 1995.[7] She also discusses the strengths and weaknesses of her performance in *Silent Fall* with James Ryan in the April 1995 edition of *Details* magazine.[8]

Tyler briefly discusses her first film in an interview with Malissa Thompson in the June 1996 issue of *Seventeen* magazine,[9] as well as conversing about the wider issues of her early career in general. She takes a rather more retrospective look at her break into acting in an interview with Karen Schoemer for *Elle* magazine in May 2001.[10]

# 2

# **HEAVY** (1995)

*Available Light Productions*

**Director**: James Mangold
**Producer**: Richard Miller
**Screenwriter**: James Mangold

MAIN CAST

| | |
|---|---|
| **Pruitt Taylor Vince** | Victor Modino |
| **Shelley Winters** | Dolly Modino |
| **Liv Tyler** | Callie |
| **Deborah Harry** | Delores |
| **Joe Grifasi** | Leo |
| **Evan Dando** | Jeff |

Tyler's next acting role was to be something of a contrast to her first cinematic appearance in a high-profile, issue-based action thriller. *Heavy*, an independent feature helmed by first-time writer-director James Mangold, was very distinct in tone from the tense *Silent Fall*, and was to present Tyler with a chance to display an entirely different spectrum of her acting range.

Already an experienced and accomplished writer in the entertainment industry prior to his directorial debut, Mangold's impressive first film is both nuanced and thoughtful. It is a work which draws the audience into a living, breathing world, where time passes slowly and a sense of hopeless despondency gradually and relentlessly begins to radiate from the dejected cast of characters as we are drawn into their dingy environment. Yet *Heavy* is no overwrought tragedy; its slice-of-life depiction of essentially isolated people lingering on the outer fringes of mainstream American society may be downbeat, but it is never entirely depressing in its outlook. Like the reality that it so painstakingly seeks to depict, individuals go about their lives with an agenda beyond that of simply driving the film's plot, and the major strength of *Heavy* lies in its ability to convey so much of these characters' feelings and insecurities without the use of laboured foregrounding or expository dialogue.

*Heavy* takes place in a shabby diner situated in upstate New York, which is operated by widowed Dolly Modino (Shelley Winters) and her overweight son Victor (Pruitt Taylor Vince). It is obvious from very early on that this diner has become something of a land where time stands still. It is too cheerless to be homely, too impersonal to be familiar. The diner's jaded waitress Delores (Deborah Harry) is a long-term employee of many years standing, and the only regular customer with whom the staff appear to have built up any kind of lasting rapport is Leo (Joe Grifasi), a near-permanent fixture at the bar who seems to have turned his regular drinking habit into a workable alternative to life.

It rapidly becomes clear that all of these characters, despite their apparent interconnection, are all essentially inaccessible to each other on an emotional level. Despite the fact that customers like Leo have a tendency to talk without really saying much, there is little doubt that real communication between people in this world is at a premium. The garrulous Dolly still remains wistful over the ways of her long-since-departed husband Pete, and we soon learn that she essentially does all of Victor's talking for him by proxy, rendering him something of a lonely, near-mute cipher as he haplessly labours at the back of the diner's kitchen. Delores is cool and cynical, craving affection but resistant to emotionally connect with anyone. She is also defiant in the face of Leo's apparent interest in her, though neither he nor Delores seem too concerned in pursuing the matter too forcefully due to an seemingly mutual apprehension of commitment.

This claustrophobic, slightly entropic environment is radically shaken by Dolly's sudden recruitment of a new waitress, Callie (Liv Tyler), who instantly has an effect on all of the diner's denizens. Dolly appears to be delighted with the injection of new blood into her workplace, but Delores is resentful of the youthful Callie's good looks and sweet nature, perhaps drawing a contrast with her own fading youth and aimless existence but never going so far as to make her disdain completely explicit. Yet undoubtedly the person most significantly affected by Callie's arrival is Victor, who immediately finds himself infatuated with the beautiful newcomer. Within a short time, his interest begins to border on the obsessive. Callie, however, has other things on her mind. She has recently dropped out of further education, and her long-term plans are fuzzy at best. She seems almost completely oblivious to the shockwave that her unexpected arrival has caused, being content to gain experience from her new job and, in spite of her uncertainties, to try to take pleasure in the world around her.

Victor, meanwhile, finds his moribund life turned upside down by the strength of his feelings for Callie. He starts to become increasingly self-conscious about his excessive weight, and tries unsuccessfully to diet. His long-suppressed ambitions towards gaining professional qualifications in food preparation begin to surface. Yet, as has been the case throughout his life, it is his symbiotic relationship with Dolly which stymies his aspirations, and his comparative emotional immaturity ultimately strengthens his ties to the diner, keeping the outside world frustratingly outwith his reach.

Pruitt Taylor Vince turns in an excellent performance as Victor. He creates a character who is edgy but difficult to dislike, and effectively conveys in Victor a nascent passion which is thwarted by his own subconscious acknowledgement that Callie will almost inevitably remain inaccessible to him. Yet Victor nonetheless continues to find her aesthetically fascinating, gazing lovingly at photographs of her and daydreaming of elaborate scenarios where he daringly rescues her from certain peril. In a sense, his desire for the escape that she represents comes to form the very purpose that his life has been missing for so long.

Tyler's performance in *Heavy* is subtle and nicely underplayed, very much in keeping with the general tone of the film itself. The soulful and affable Callie is a world away from the manipulative, traumatised Sylvie Warden of *Silent Fall*, and the disparity provided early evidence of Tyler's broad acting range. Beresford's fast-paced, plot-intensive earlier film had proven Tyler's proficiency in a mainstream action-thriller, but *Heavy* presented her with a very different challenge. Mangold's stately, measured approach to storytelling, combined with the fact that so much of the characters' stories is suggested by inference rather than words, meant that the film would rely greatly on the cast's ability to convey their feelings indirectly, often through gesture and expression. In addition to Vince's studied and commendable performance, Shelley Winters and Deborah Harry both present a subtle, understated rendering of their respective characters, perfectly capturing the sense of disillusionment and atrophy eating away at Dolly's diner. Tyler's Callie, however, is the very personification of a breath of fresh air blown into a world of broken dreams. She could all too easily have been objectified as the embodiment of the positive factors which lie tantalisingly outwith the confines of the other characters' domestic drudgery. Yet Tyler manages to transcend this overly-convenient juxtaposition, and works hard to add an extra dimension to the character.

Callie's breeziness and general enthusiasm to interact with the staff and patrons of the diner is tempered by personal difficulties of her own. We learn little of her family or circumstances beyond the fact that she has chosen to leave college, but we are introduced to her boyfriend (Evan Dando), a rather ambivalent and occasionally combative character who is uneven in his emotional treatment of Callie. But it is not only Callie's inter-personal relationships that are tenuous; her long-term future is largely uncertain, and Tyler manages to suggest the initial stages of a weary acceptance forming within the character such that, had the film's events transpired slightly differently, one can almost imagine the diner's potent will-sapping qualities gnawing away at Callie until she reaches the point that, in years to come, she would take on the mantle of purposelessness and lethargy which is so amply borne by Delores. As it stands, by the film's conclusion we are still unsure about whether her escape from the confines of the diner will only lead to another form of emotional incarceration elsewhere.

Mangold, however, does not provide any comfortable or straightforward certainties in his narrative. Instead, the film's events are shaped by the death of Dolly – or, more precisely, by the other characters' reaction to it. The reclusive Victor, reticent and inarticulate even at the best of times, fails to share the news of his mother's death with the others. Yet the truth, when it does finally surface, is remarkable precisely because of its muted impact on the diner's residents. There are no overwrought histrionics or relationship-shattering dynamics between the regulars; after the initial flaring of emotions when the news ultimately breaks, we are left in little doubt that business will eventually resume as normal, that Delores will return to one side of the bar and Leo to the other, and Victor will once again dutifully return to his kitchen never to emerge into the world outside… although the film's climax does suggest a faint glimmer of hope that perhaps, just maybe, there could be a future for Victor beyond the diner after all.

If the effect of the delayed news of Dolly's death is ultimately stifled when it impacts upon the diner's regulars, however, the consequences for Callie's friendship with Victor are rather more significant. When Victor reveals the truth to her, in a somewhat unorthodox fashion, she feels both shocked and betrayed by his silence, and their fragile platonic connection is damaged beyond repair. Yet in spite of Callie's departure from the diner, and the apparent resumption of the status quo *sans* Dolly, it is testimony to Mangold's skill that we are by no means certain at the end of the film whether Callie has altered Victor's life so profoundly that his entrenched existence will indeed change for the better, or if he is doomed to the same fate as Pete and Dolly, bound to the diner until the bitter end.

*Heavy* would not be the last time that Tyler would play a character who is presented as the personification of others' desires, and here – as would also be the case later in her career – she never allows her character to be objectified, but rather develops the role acutely enough to suggest a troubled, multi-layered individual functioning behind the seemingly lackadaisical exterior. Her management of Callie's relationship with the other characters, particularly Victor, is central to the film, and she appears to take great care in the development of an underlying vulnerability which suggests that Callie, too, is subject to the same kind of internal forces which are so relentlessly bogging down the lives of the diner's patrons and staff. Whether Callie ultimately comes to be the prisoner of such forces, albeit beyond the confines of the diner, is left to the audience to decide.

*Heavy* performed well with critics,[11] and won James Mangold the Special Jury Prize at the 1995 Sundance Film Festival. Mangold would later go on to further success with films such as

*Cop Land* (1997), the award-winning *Girl, Interrupted* (1999), and the recent, highly-acclaimed Johnny Cash biopic *Walk the Line* (2005).

The small-budget, independently-produced *Heavy* had proven Tyler's ability to perform effectively outwith the format of the traditional conventions of commercial film-making, particularly due to Mangold's deliberate, often protracted pacing and the onus on the small central cast to interpret the film's complex and subtly understated nuances to the audience. Having now proven that she was in possession of a notable repertoire of dramatic skills, Tyler's next film would provide a welcome break from the tone of her first two features, and would present her with a well-deserved opportunity to let her hair down by utilising her comedic talents instead.

## FURTHER READING

As was the case with *Silent Fall*, *Heavy*'s relatively early position in Tyler's career means that media coverage of her part in the film was less extensive than would be the case with most of her later features.

An interesting article about Tyler's early performances, with particular emphasis on *Heavy*, is Richard Corliss' 'One Life to Liv – But Can She Act?' in the 17 June 1996 issue of *Time* Magazine.[12] In the article, Corliss discusses Tyler's promising critical reception and expounds upon the possible reasons for her popularity amongst commentators.

Tyler's interview with Kim Lockhart for *Sassy* magazine in April 1995 also touches on some of her experiences during the filming of *Heavy*.[13] Likewise, her thoughts on the character of Callie are discussed in her interview with James Ryan in *Details* magazine's April 1995 issue.[14] Another article of interest is Claire Connors' 'Evan Can't Wait' in the February 1995 issue of *Dolly* magazine, where the production of *Heavy* – and Tyler's performance – is discussed from the perspective of her co-star, musician Evan Dando.[15]

# 3

# EMPIRE RECORDS (1995)

*Warner Brothers/ Regency Entertainment/ New Regency Pictures/ Monarchy Enterprises*

**Director**: Allan Moyle
**Producers**: Tony Ludwig, Arnon Milchan, Michael Nathanson, Alan Riche
**Screenwriter**: Carol Heikkinen

MAIN CAST

| | |
|---|---|
| **Anthony LaPaglia** | Joe Reaves |
| **Maxwell Caulfield** | Rex Manning |
| **Debi Mazar** | Jane |
| **Rory Cochrane** | Lucas |
| **Renée Zellweger** | Gina |
| **Liv Tyler** | Corey Mason |

After the baleful chills of *Silent Fall* and the absorbing psychological reflection of *Heavy*, Tyler's next choice of film was to significantly lighten the tone of her canon of performances thus far. *Empire Records* was to place different demands on Tyler's acting skills, with her comic talents taking the forefront in her performance in place of the soulful dramatic renderings that audiences had become accustomed to thus far.

*Empire Records* occupies an interesting place in the history of the teen comedy genre. It arrived well after the heyday of the hugely successful John Hughes films of the 1980s, which included *The Breakfast Club* (1985) and *Ferris Bueller's Day Off* (1986), and some time prior to the rather less restrained offerings of later years, such as Paul Weitz's smash hit *American Pie* (1999) and Todd Phillips' *Road Trip* (2000). It must be said that *Empire Records* never quite seems much like part of an evolutionary phase bridging these two ends of the teen comedy spectrum, and in tone is not particularly similar to either.[16] Instead, its general mood most closely resembles earlier works in the filmography of its director Allan Moyle, such as *Times Square* (1980) and *Pump Up the Volume* (1990). It is arguable whether either of these two previous features could truly be considered as straightforward comedies, given that both of them attempt to deal with dramatic subject matter in a rather more purposeful manner than *Empire Records* ever attempts to. Instead, *Empire Records* is rather more upbeat in the treatment of its themes, offering snappy dialogue, abundant musical accompaniment and a quirky, likeable ensemble cast.

The film concerns an unfeasibly busy day in the life of an independent music shop, the eponymous Empire Records, and its eclectic staff. Its manager, the long-suffering Joe Reaves (a marvellously world-weary performance from Anthony LaPaglia), has a problem. A problem of considerable proportions. $9000 has been 'borrowed' from the store's safe by night-manager Lucas (Rory Cochrane), who – following a period of zen-like enlightenment – decides to gamble the day's takings in Atlantic

City. Success, he hopes, will allow Joe to buy the store from its owner, oily yuppie Mitchell Beck (Ben Bode), who plans to sell it off to a major multinational called Music City. Lucas' winning streak is short-lived, however, and Joe finds himself not only facing the threat of an imminent take-over, but the difficulty of having to explain away the disappearance of the nightly deposit.

To make matters worse, the store is hosting an autograph session with Rex Manning, a washed-up TV actor turned cheesy-listening star (Maxwell Caulfield, who steals the show with his performance as the sleazy, mildly bewildered fading star). Manning's appeal has declined so far that even his own personal assistant is becoming openly contemptuous of his talents. However, as coincidence would have it, he is also the long-time idol of Corey Mason (Liv Tyler), another of the store's employees. Corey has just been accepted to study in the Ivy League, but her talents have been hot-housed by her overbearing father to such an extent that she has become reliant on amphetamines to help her cope with the pressure. This is a matter of considerable concern to her best friend Gina (Renée Zellweger), who has a heart of gold but an appetite for pastimes rather more diverting than study.

During the course of this very long day in the life of Empire Records, the staff also have to cope with a shoplifter, reflections on their individual futures (ranging from deliberations over a failed suicide attempt to finding just the right name for an embryonic band), and even an armed hold-up. In the end, however, every disadvantage is ultimately turned into an advantage, the store is saved at the eleventh hour from sliding into corporate hell, and Joe discovers not only that his livelihood has been secured, but that he has found himself a hot date into the bargain.

The main success of *Empire Records* lies in the film's propensity never to take itself too seriously. This is probably just as well, given that the entire narrative takes place over a single unbelievably eventful day which – had Moyle been aiming for anything even remotely approaching straight drama – would have stretched credibility far beyond breaking point. But for all its comedic credentials, *Empire Records* never descends into farce. It has few pretensions beyond telling an entertaining story well, and as comedies go it is geared more towards raising knowing smiles than producing raucous laughter. And in this, it succeeds well. The large ensemble cast are mostly an amiable, idiosyncratic bunch whom it is difficult to dislike. There are no affected statements on the human condition; genre clichés such as the quasi love-triangle between Corey, Rex Manning and cashier AJ (Johnny Whitworth) are played out with tongue firmly planted in cheek, barely suppressing a knowing wink at the audience. Carol Heikkinen's script is both sharp and well paced, with the good-humoured dialogue and effectively rendered characterisation compensating for the occasionally hackneyed plot development – after all, was anyone in the audience really in any doubt of a happy ending? Or, indeed, the occurrence of a wild party at some point in the proceedings? Strangely enough, this predictability strays close to a kind of arch self-awareness at times, though the film stops well short of a truly post-modern inclination towards its narrative (this in spite of the occasional straight-to-camera soliloquy from Lucas).

This is not to say that *Empire Records* is entirely without the occasional stab at social commentary; if one is inclined to look hard enough, the film does at times attempt to deal with monopoly capitalism, illegal drug use, and at a few significant points even grapples with the nature of life and death. What ultimately matters is that these issues are handled sparingly, usually unpretentiously, and are never superimposed over the action to the point where they become overly distracting. There is no laboured philosophising, nor is there a contrived moral behind the story – the production generally seems to be having too much fun to bother with one.

Tyler's performance fits rather nicely into the film's multi-character jigsaw. Although most of the ensemble has at least one exaggerated character attribute, Tyler displays a lightness of touch in her portrayal which never allows her rendering of Corey to slide into mawkish sentimentality. This is particularly note-worthy, given the nature of the character. For most comedies, issues such as the burden of shouldering excessive parental expectations and dalliances with illegal substances could be considered potential disaster areas, yet *Empire Records* never labours these points excessively, and Tyler manages to avoid the kind of heavy-handedness which would otherwise push her performance too close to melodrama.

Instead, Corey remains likeably kooky throughout, with only the occasional flicker of her underlying anger and frustration manifesting itself here and there, and Tyler manages to retain her character's distinctiveness right the way through the course of the narrative. This is no small feat in a film where the sheer size of the cast means that other characters seem to be almost competing for a fair slice of screen time.

Corey is developed into something of a creature of contra-dictions. Her elation at the news of her acceptance to Harvard is balanced with her reluctance to leave the familiarity of her friends and her workplace. Her disappointment over her shattered expectations of Rex Manning ultimately leads to the evolution of her friendship with AJ, which develops from platonic into romantic by the film's conclusion. Her tiff and subsequent recon-ciliation with Gina ultimately deepens the bond of closeness between them. And, as AJ decides to eschew a life of selling albums in order to attend an art college in Boston, his dedication to the romance blossoming between Corey and himself hints at a happy ending which lurks somewhere beyond the confines of the end credits reel.

If these sound like overly profound developments for a knockabout teen comedy, it is testament to Tyler's handling of Corey that her character arc never seems particularly forced – and this despite the admitted predictability of many of the film's plot twists. Ultimately, the success of *Empire Records* lies not in the innovation of its storyline, but in the appeal of the cast's keenly-observed approaches to their characters. In Joe, for instance, Anthony LaPaglia avoids a stereotypical rendering of a put-upon boss in blood-pressure overload, providing many well-disposed moments of touching sincerity amongst the general chaos that he is nominally in charge of. Despite having once been a promising musician, Joe is disappointed at the direction his life is taking, yet is still able to connect meaningfully with his much younger staff, including less social members such as the troubled Debra (Robin Tunney). Special mention must also be made of Rory Cochrane's memorable Lucas, whose Buddha-like pronouncements mark him out as a slightly absurd oasis of calm in the madness that surrounds him.

In summation, *Empire Records* is an interesting side-step in Tyler's acting career, entirely different from the performances which had preceded it, but also building upon her assuredness of character development and emotional awareness that were in evidence in her earlier films. Here, amongst a much larger cast than either *Silent Fall* or *Heavy*, she not only acquits herself well but also delivers a distinctive performance which would provide a useful benchmark for more comedic roles later in her career.

*Empire Records* may not have been as successful with critics or audiences as Allan Moyle's earlier Christian Slater vehicle *Pump Up the Volume*,[17] but over time it has acquired something of a cult following due to its impressive soundtrack and affable, eccentric cast of characters. It is also worth watching due to its significance in the early careers of many members of its young ensemble – most notably Renée Zellweger, who would later go on to enormous critical and box-office success with films including Sharon Maguire's comedy adaptation *Bridget Jones' Diary* (2001) and Anthony Minghella's Academy Award-winning epic *Cold Mountain* (2003).

Whilst no-one would mistake *Empire Records* for high art, it is a breezy, witty, good-natured piece of cinema which – if not as ice-cool as it perhaps aims to be – is certainly far from half-baked.

And, if nothing else, it even boasts a choking-on-a-pretzel joke which impressively managed to predate the George W Bush administration by some six years.

## FURTHER READING

Kim Lockhart's interview with Tyler in April 1995's *Sassy* magazine brushes lightly against her expectations of *Empire Records* prior to filming.[18]

A similarly brief retrospective view of Tyler's experiences with *Empire Records* is included in her interview with Ingrid Sischy in the January 1997 issue of *Interview* magazine.[19]

Tyler discusses her approach to the character of Corey Mason in her interview with James Ryan in the April 1995 issue of *Details* magazine.[20]

# 4

# STEALING BEAUTY (1996)

*Union Général Cinématographique/ Recorded Picture Company/
Jeremy Thomas Productions/ France 2 Cinéma/ Fiction*

**Director**: Bernardo Bertolucci
**Producer**: Jeremy Thomas
**Screenwriter**: Susan Minot, from a story by Bernardo Bertolucci

MAIN CAST

| | |
|---|---|
| **Liv Tyler** | Lucy Harmon |
| **Sinead Cusack** | Diana Grayson |
| **Donal McCann** | Ian Grayson |
| **Jeremy Irons** | Alex Parrish |
| **Jean Marais** | Monsieur Guillaume |
| **Rachel Weitz** | Miranda Fox |

It would be no exaggeration to say that *Stealing Beauty* was the definitive turning point in Tyler's early career. Even although she had gained general critical approval for her previous performances, *Stealing Beauty* was to mark out once and for all her affirmation as a genuine talent in the eyes of international commentators. Although the reception of the film itself was to vary widely amongst critics, it undoubtedly remains one of Tyler's most distinctive and impressive performances to date.

Bernardo Bertolucci has long been one of Europe's best-known and most controversial directors. A distinctive and skilful Italian film-maker of long standing, he has enjoyed great critical acclaim as well as occasionally evoking considerable debate. His aptitude as a published poet is evident in his stylish, prolific film-making, which is often excruciatingly acute in its depiction of his characters' emotional awareness and inner turmoil. For many years, Bertolucci was perhaps best known to international audiences for his notorious *Last Tango in Paris* (1972), though in recent years even this *tour de force* has arguably been eclipsed by his epic *The Last Emperor* (1987), which depicted sixty turbulent years of Chinese political history and met with huge critical approval on release. The film was to gain a remarkable nine Oscars at the 1988 Academy Awards (including Best Picture and Best Director), three BAFTA film awards, and a wide range of other prestigious honours across Europe and North America.

The ambitious *The Last Emperor* deservedly won major praise amongst critics, and was followed by the similarly wide-canvas *The Sheltering Sky* (1990), which explored (amongst other things) the clash of cultures between the West and the developing world. This theme of cultural disparity was also evident in his next film, *Little Buddha* (1993), where North American mores were viewed through the unfamiliar lens of Bhutanese Buddhism. Yet Bertolucci was to investigate the relationship between the American ethos and the wider world in an entirely different manner with *Stealing Beauty*; the film centres its focus on his native Italy in an intensely intimate examination of the fate of a young visitor from the United States, who is visiting a diverse community of European artists in rural Tuscany.

Following the suicide of her mother, nineteen year-old American Lucy Harmon (Liv Tyler) travels to the Tuscan home of family acquaintance Ian Grayson (Donal McCann). Lucy has been sent there for the summer by her father in an attempt to help her recover from her sudden loss. An artist and sculptor, Ian has agreed to paint her portrait, but Lucy has more pressing goals. Her late mother's journals are full of cryptic poetry which suggests that Lucy was conceived in that very same Tuscan hillside estate two decades previously. Furthermore, they hint that the man who she considers to be her father, who has remained in the States, was not responsible for her conception.

Ian and his wife Diana (Sinead Cusack) were old friends of Lucy's mother, who in life had been a free spirit and highly successful poet. Amongst the other eclectic guests and occupants at the Graysons' home are the knowing designer Miranda Fox (Rachel Weitz) and Alex Parrish (Jeremy Irons), an ailing English playwright who is nearing the final stages of an undisclosed terminal illness. Lucy is also searching for Niccoló Donati (Roberto Zibetti), a young Italian she met four years previously and with whom she is eager to kindle a budding romance.

Almost immediately, Lucy's comparative naivety is thrown under the spotlight of the older, rather more jaded majority of the community's denizens; they take an almost compulsive interest in her burgeoning sexuality, and at one point appear almost ready to take bets on where and when Lucy will lose her virginity. This is a question never far from Lucy's own mind, however, and the viewer is drawn into her contemplation and uncertainty regarding the issue as the film progresses.

The cynicism of the elder occupants is not all-encompassing, however. Alex is particularly affected by Lucy's beauty and relative innocence; the fact that her vibrancy and zest for living contrasts with his own rapidly failing health is not lost on him. She forms a particularly close bond with him during his last days, as the pair discuss their experiences of life's journey; Lucy at the beginning of the trek, Alex nearing the end of it.

It is not surprising that *Stealing Beauty* has come to be considered Tyler's breakthrough film; as Lucy Harmon, she delivers a deeply personal performance that is full of passion and emotional fervour. From Lucy's gawky, exuberant first appearance disembarking from an Italian train to her thoughtful, emotionally transformed self-awareness on her return to America, Tyler's engaging, honest approach to the part lends Lucy the kind of much-needed integrity that avoids her character becoming objectified by the desire of the potential suitors – young and old – who almost constantly surround her throughout the narrative.

In many ways, the dilemma faced by Lucy is similar to that of *Heavy*'s Callie. She, too, was the unwitting catalyst of change in an otherwise dormant environment, a force of change affecting both men who longed for her and women who either felt threatened by her, or who craved the youth and vitality that she represented. The major difference between the two characters, of course, was that whereas Callie remained largely oblivious of the profound affect that her presence had on those around her, Lucy is all too aware of the power of her blossoming sexuality. Whereas Callie was essentially ignorant of the hapless Victor's doomed advances in *Heavy*, Lucy comes to develop a growing appreciation of the male admiration that she attracts. It is the manner in which Lucy comes to handle this interest that so acutely defines her character; during her numerous sittings for Ian's portrait, for instance, Tyler excels in articulating Lucy's relaxed sensuality, radiating a kind of sexual purity that is devoid of knowingness or predatory wiliness.

It is this sophistication in Tyler's performance that highlights the essential innocence of Lucy's character, and the manner in which this innocence is slowly eroded by the scorn and cynicism of the ageing intelligentsia who cluster anticipatorily around her, personified in the predatory veteran war correspondent, Monsieur Guillaume (Jean Marais). It is testament to Tyler's handling of Lucy that her strength of character is so effectively expressed; the

Lucy who leaves Tuscany is a profoundly different young woman from the one who arrived there at the beginning of the summer, and in finding the answers that she sought – and, indeed, uncovering a few that she wasn't even aware she was looking for – she ultimately discovers that she is more than she initially thought herself capable of being. It is thanks to Tyler's development of the character that this emotional evolution is so fundamentally believable, having been achieved progressively and convincingly.

By the conclusion of the film, we become aware of just how profoundly Lucy has touched the lives of those around her. The Graysons, long cocooned in their Italian retreat, begin to consider their future. A dying Alex, leaving for the last time on a stretcher, sardonically regales his onlookers with a mock-cheerful ditty. And even one of Lucy's youthful suitors finds himself contemplating his long-term expectations after she draws closer to him. All told, even the most jaded and worn-out of the community's residents cannot resist being affected in one way or another by her irresistible appeal, and just as she leaves Italy a changed woman, so too has the Graysons' Tuscan home been left altered in her wake.

Critical opinion of *Stealing Beauty* was fairly entrenched in its division, with some commentators hailing it a major reinvigoration of Bertolucci's filmic style whilst others disapproved of what they perceived to be the film's essentially anticlimactic deficiency of clear and unambiguous resolution.[21] There was, however, near unanimous praise for Bertolucci's tremendous showcasing of the stunning Tuscan countryside, and general approval of the lead performances – even if a few of the characters themselves were criticised by some as being lifeless or superfluous. Others observed that this may in fact have been entirely intentional, the blandness of some of the less sympathetic supporting characters communicating their relative charmlessness and lack of purpose in opposition to characters such as Ian, Alex and of course Lucy, whose artistic flair and emotional depth shines like a beacon in comparison.

After Bertolucci's grand-scale epic in *The Last Emperor*, the wide open spaces of *The Sheltering Sky* and the sweeping social and religious observations of *Little Buddha*, *Stealing Beauty* marked a striking change of pace in Bertolucci's oeuvre. Its focus on the keenly-drawn interplay between a spirited, emotionally raw American teenager and older, unconventional but world-weary Europeans was to build on his previous works concerned with cultural disparity, whilst suggesting an expressive intimacy of psychological interaction which does undeniably add considerable richness to the narrative. Despite the critical polarisation over the film's reception, *Stealing Beauty* was to become Bertolucci's best-known work of the 1990s amongst audiences, and achieved a resonance with the public that he would not match until the release of his remarkable and contentious film *The Dreamers* in 2003. *Stealing Beauty* has since attracted cult interest in its own right, its breathtakingly beautiful Italian scenery and enigmatic, artfully eccentric narrative benefiting greatly from repeated viewings.

*Stealing Beauty* remains one of Tyler's best-known performances, and as has been discussed earlier, was undoubtedly a major catalyst in her rise to prominence with the public and in the eyes of the critics. Although commentators were far from unanimous in their appraisal of Bertolucci's film, most were impressed with Tyler's highly personal approach to Lucy's cathartic spiritual journey, and her deft handling of the character throughout the occasionally impenetrable nuances of Susan Minot's erudite and refined narrative. *Stealing Beauty* is a film that is laced with ambiguities and subtle suggestions, relying on the audience's own perceptions to interpret the subtlety of the underlying subtexts, and it is to Tyler's credit that Lucy's emotional awakening is not subordinated to the film's understated but compelling flow, but instead remains very much at the centre of the narrative where it belongs. Given that it is the first film in which she appears squarely in the central role, it is difficult to imagine how Tyler could have performed more memorably than she did in *Stealing Beauty*.

## FURTHER READING

Bernardo Bertolucci's worldwide acclaim has led to a considerable amount of published commentary on his works and technique. One particularly valuable reference work worth consulting is *Bernardo Bertolucci: Interviews*,[22] edited by Fabien S. Gerard, T. Jefferson Kline and Bruce Sklarew, which contains a wide variety of detailed discussions with Bertolucci over the course of his career. Of especial interest is Allen Olensky's previously unpublished interview 'Tiptoeing in Tuscany',[23] which deals specifically with Bertolucci's experiences during the filming of *Stealing Beauty*.

Graham Fuller's article in the July 1996 issue of *Interview* presents a detailed commentary on Bertolucci's work on *Stealing Beauty* by placing his films in comparison to the work of the highly influential French director Eric Rohmer.[24]

David Cavanagh's feature in the September 1996 edition of *Empire* magazine discusses Tyler's growing star status following *Stealing Beauty*, and is well worth reading.[25] Another interesting article about Tyler's escalating popularity in the wake of her appearance in Bertolucci's film can be found in Bruce Newman's commentary, which appears in the 23 June 1996 edition of the *Milwaukee Journal Sentinel*.[26]

Another discussion of Tyler's rising fame at the time can be read in Stephen Schaefer's article 'Liv Tyler'[27] in the 24 June 1996 issue of the *Boston Herald*, which discusses Tyler's experiences at that year's Cannes Film Festival. A fascinating tangential story regarding this particular appearance at Cannes can be found in Suzanne Lowry's article 'Young pretender to Liz Taylor's throne'[28] in the 17 May 1996 issue of the *London Telegraph*, which emphasises the sheer level of potential that some commentators considered to exist in Tyler's acting career following her *Stealing Beauty* performance.

# 5

# **THAT THING YOU DO!** (1996)

*20th Century Fox/ Clavius Base/ Clinica Estetico Ltd.*

**Director**: Tom Hanks
**Producers**: Jonathan Demme, Gary Goetzman, Edward Saxon
**Screenwriter**: Tom Hanks

MAIN CAST

| | |
|---|---|
| **Tom Everett Scott** | Guy Patterson |
| **Liv Tyler** | Faye Dolan |
| **Johnathon Schaech** | Jimmy Mattingly |
| **Steve Zahn** | Lenny Haise |
| **Ethan Embry** | The Bass Player |
| **Tom Hanks** | Mr White |

Tyler's appearance in *That Thing You Do!* was to prove an interesting shift in tone to her breakout role in *Stealing Beauty*. As we have seen, her acting talents had by now elevated her to a position of prominence in the public eye as a rising star in the film industry, and the impressiveness of her performance in Bertolucci's film had promoted her in the eyes of many critics from a talent with considerable potential into a genuinely gifted performer with the aptitude for a promising career. Her filmography was growing impressively, and with effective appearances in both comedic and dramatic roles now under her belt, there was sincere interest surrounding which film she would appear in next.

That film was to be directorial debut of Tom Hanks, one of the most instantly-recognisable performers in modern American film. A hugely successful actor in television roles and then on the big screen from the early 1980s, Hanks had enjoyed considerable fame in popular comedies and comedy-dramas such as Ron Howard's *Splash!* (1984), Nicholas Meyer's *Volunteers* (1985) and Tom Mankiewicz's *Dragnet* (1987). Towards the end of that decade, Hanks was to alternate with greater frequency between dramatic and comedic roles, winning an Academy Award nomination in 1989 for his performance in Penny Marshall's *Big* (1988) and then picking up Oscars for Best Actor in a Leading Role over two successive years for his appearances in Jonathan Demme's acclaimed *Philadephia* (1993) and Robert Zemeckis' box-office hit *Forrest Gump* (1994).

By the mid-1990s, in addition to his many acting achievements, Hanks had also started to branch into directing, helming episodes of television series such as *Tales From the Crypt* and *Fallen Angels*. *That Thing You Do!* was to mark his first time behind the camera on a major motion picture, and he was also to pen the film's screenplay in addition to making a noteworthy appearance in a supporting role. Given his impressive public profile, there was much curiosity amongst critics as to whether Hanks' directorial talent could match the long (and continuing) winning streak that his acting career had accomplished.

The film is set in the summer of 1964, and begins in the town of Erie, Pennsylvania. Guy Patterson (Tom Everett Scott) divides his time between assisting in his father's electrical goods shop and drumming with a band that has been formed with some college friends (having been recruited after their original drummer was unexpectedly injured). The band includes guitarist Lenny Haise (Steve Zahn) and singer/ songwriter Jimmy Mattingly (Johnathon Schaech), along with Jimmy's devoted girlfriend Faye Dolan (Liv Tyler), whose enthusiasm for her friends' music means that she is never far away from the band's rehearsal sessions. It is Faye who devises the band's name, the Wonders (originally spelt the 'One-ders', but changed when virtually everyone they encounter ends up mispronouncing it).

The band's members unexpectedly find themselves on the up, thanks to winning a college talent contest, and are soon performing gigs in nearby venues. Guy decides to cut a record of their catchy trademark song, *That Thing You Do!*, and shortly after selling copies locally the Wonders find themselves recruited by talent scout Phil Horace (Chris Ellis). Phil takes the band under his wing, secures them live performances in larger venues within the state, and keeps a promise to obtain radio airplay for *That Thing You Do!* This leads to one of the film's most memorable scenes as Faye – hearing the song broadcast for the first time on radio – races ecstatically to Guy's family's appliance store only to converge with all the other members of the band. Virtually every radio set in the shop is soon turned up to maximum volume as they celebrate their success.

Following a less-than-impressive performance in Pittsburgh, Phil introduces the Wonders to the enigmatic Mr White (Tom Hanks), who represents the thriving Play-Tone Records company. Despite their lacklustre live appearance, White sees the potential of their song, and swiftly persuades the band to sign up to the Play-Tone stable. Their fate, under White's tutelage, is then transformed out of all proportion. Their new manager is brusque, his demeanour often decidedly chilly, but he is a highly competent and experienced professional who briskly has the band equipped with new instruments and costumes (including, memorably, outfitting Guy with a gimmicky pair of sunglasses and rechristening him 'Shades' – a stratagem which works unexpectedly well).

While travelling from state to state between gigs, their single begins to do well nationally, and White wastes no time in flying the Wonders over to California. There, they make an appearance in an extraordinarily tacky but high-profile beach movie, and also briefly meet with the head of Play-Tone Records – a bloated, boorish vulgarian – for a publicity appearance. This less than inspiring encounter begins to enlighten the band to the fact that Play-Tone really has little interest in any potential new output from the Wonders, and is content to promote the foot-tapping *That Thing You Do!* for every last ounce of mileage left in it.

The final blow comes with the band's appearance on a family TV show. Jimmy, incensed when a superimposed caption suggests that he and Faye have become engaged, treats her appallingly and ends their long-running relationship before firmly turning his back on White's regimented stage-management. Lenny, who has been shamelessly enjoying every moment of the Wonders' ephemeral fame, unexpectedly disappears off to Las Vegas and elopes. The band's bass player (Ethan Embry), in receipt of his call-up papers for the U.S. Marine Corps, heads out for training. And Guy, disillusioned by his transient experience of stardom, has a chance encounter with a jazz legend that he has long admired, and is reminded of exactly why he loves music so much in the first place.

The four band members decide to go off on their separate ways, and Faye realises that her faith in the band was not entirely in vain when she discovers that another of the Wonders – someone who had been holding a torch for her – values her wisdom and dedication more greatly than Jimmy ever had. And as the band dissolves with only one hit to its name, Mr White surreptitiously melts into the background as he quietly continues to keep the cogs turning in the well-oiled Play-Tone machine.

The major strength of *That Thing You Do!* lies in its impeccable attention to period detail. Every nuance of the mid-1960s is captured faithfully, from the nostalgic collection of refrigerators and televisions in Guy's father's shop to the band's ever-evolving fashions – notable as their wardrobe develops from small town into big league. Hanks' enthusiasm for the period is obvious, and it is particularly notable that the major negative aspects of that era – the Vietnam War and the assassination of John F Kennedy – are largely underplayed throughout the film, encapsulated mostly in infrequent casual glances at the odd newspaper headline. Indeed, the bass player's departure for the Marine Corps forms perhaps the most visible evocation of the growing Vietnam tensions of the time (we later learn, in the epilogue, that he served with distinction). This is a film, then, where nostalgic whimsy and youthful dreams are briefly allowed to supplant the harsh realities of commercialism that were to come later in the decade that is depicted. *That Thing You Do!* also greatly benefits from an excellent score from composer Howard Shore, who would later go on to enormous critical acclaim with his soundtracks for the *Lord of the Rings* trilogy (2001-03). The score is peppy and gently reminiscent of the period, and also contains a number of original songs written by Hanks himself, though the eponymous *That Thing You Do!* itself is credited to songwriter Adam Schlesinger.

The film is also supported by an affable cast of characters, and it is precisely because most of them are so likeable that their path to fame becomes so engaging to the viewer. Lenny, for instance, has such unabashed enthusiasm for every step of the band's success that, at times, it is difficult not to raise a smile at his zeal. Even Johnathon Schaech's Jimmy, for all the character's mild arrogance and pretensions of artistic integrity, is never entirely alienated from the audience until his final ego-driven bust-up with Faye and the band. The key performance, however, belongs to Tom Everett Scott as Guy, whose breezy, easy-going temperament and penchant for jazz keep him anchored in reality even during the fastest-moving phases of the band's meteoric rise to fame.

Faye is, in many ways, the conscience of the band. She is involved from its very inception, and has a clear-sighted detachment which allows her an unwaveringly objective view of the Wonders' fortunes from the elation of their song's initial radio airing right through to the band's sudden but inevitable fracturing. Tyler infuses Faye with an appealing, committed loyalty, first to her friends, and secondly to the band. Faye never pursues the trappings of fame herself, nor does she capitalise on the achievements of the Wonders for her own gain. Instead, she's happy to be along for the ride, enjoying a once-in-a-lifetime trip through the echelons of the music industry whilst remaining all too aware that it will inescapably prove transient.

The film also featured some significant upcoming talent, including Giovanni Ribisi as Chad, the Wonders' unfortunate original drummer, and future Academy Award-winner Charlize Theron, who plays Guy's jaded girlfriend Tina (unimpressed with Guy's musical interests prior to his band's big breakthrough, she runs off with a brawny dentist). However, the most notable supporting role belongs to Hanks himself as the inscrutable Mr White. A creature of contradictions, White remains irresolutely shadowy throughout the film; he is gruff and irritable, but also slick and even-handed. There is no doubt that White is a businessman, not an artist, and in many ways his reliance on attention-grabbing publicity apparatus and manufactured gimmickry marks him out as a grim harbinger of the music industry yet to come. Yet he is never painted as a straightforward cliché, for to see him as a commercial antagonist in direct contrast to the band's unsullied creative drive would be to overstate the matter considerably. White may be cool and detached, but he is not entirely uncaring; his efficient professionalism communicates much to both Guy and Jimmy during their band's short-lived collision course with fame, and once the Wonders have outlived their usefulness to Play-Tone, his severance from the group –

whilst characteristically brisk – is neither as brutal or as hard-hearted as might be expected. Ultimately, we do not blame White for the band's downfall because he is not responsible for it, either directly or indirectly; although he and his horrendous mogul boss are eager to exploit new talent in order to keep cramming cash into the Play-Tone coffers, we are led to understand that the kind of heavily-marketed success enjoyed by the band is inevitably transient at best, and the eventual fragmentation of the Wonders – though foreseeable due to their disillusionment and the mounting conflict between individual members – is ultimately depicted as the fault neither of the system or of the band, but rather as an unavoidable by-product of their momentary prominence. Nevertheless, Guy – and by extension, the audience – is left in little doubt that ageing jazz marvel Del Paxton (Bill Cobbs) is correct in his astute reflection that while bands rise and fall, the need for good music remains a constant factor.

Tyler shares the spotlight with an accomplished and amiable cast, and it is to her credit that she uses her every moment of screen time to bring Faye Dolan to life. Hanks' screenplay makes it abundantly clear that Faye is no casual groupie; her devotion to the band's success, and to her friends, makes her as much an integral part of the Wonders as its performing members. Indeed, her support is so ardent – and valued by the band – that even the taciturn Mr White finds a grudging respect for her tenacity, tolerating her presence along every step of the band's path to success in spite of his otherwise hard-nosed regime.

Tyler shines throughout the film, from Faye's early quiet encouragement and her astonishment at the band's rise to fame right through to her disenchantment with the trappings of success and dawning realisation that celebrity does indeed have its pitfalls. Many critics were in agreement that her charismatic performance reached its zenith with her heartfelt speech near the film's climax, where Faye's suppressed frustration at Jimmy's wintry aloofness – and the band's fate in general – is vented with touching sentiment. As the film's only female character of any real substance (particularly as Tina fades into obscurity fairly early into proceedings), Tyler's optimistic, expressive rendering of the sensitive Faye is vital in underscoring the character's integral importance to the Wonders – she is by far the most level-headed of all the group, and even when the other band members become overwhelmed by the suddenness of their rise to fame, Faye manages to keep both feet firmly on the ground. This is in no small part thanks to her understanding that a band is nothing without its members and, in the end, that it was their shared friendship and ability to work together which brought the Wonders to prominence in the first place. It is perhaps because she manages to keep this realisation in mind throughout the band's rise to fame that she finds its inexorable collapse all the more disappointing, even painful. Whilst Tyler articulates this disenchantment well, even better is her expression of Faye's growing maturity at the end of the film, which leaves the viewer in no doubt that the band's experiences – far from embittering her – have emotionally prepared her for better and more fulfilling things to come.

*That Thing You Do!* met with general approval from critics, who praised Hanks' subtle self-assurance behind the camera as well as his performance in front of it.[29] At the time best known for roles in which he played genial everymen or good-natured eccentrics, the frosty efficiency of Mr White offered Hanks the opportunity for a change of pace, and it is one which he seized with relish. White's moral ambiguity and cold objectivity are ably fleshed out by Hanks, who never neglects the reserved humanity lurking beneath White's sleek corporate surface. Hanks' scriptwriting skills were also well received by most commentators, with particular praise for his careful avoidance of overt truisms despite an otherwise conventional narrative.[30] As a number of reviewers observed, *That Thing You Do!* is less concerned with making a point about the commercialisation of art than it is with providing a snapshot of a more innocent bygone age. Indeed, it is perhaps in this goal that the film is most successful; its fond evocation of the late, lamented post-Camelot America is considered, painstakingly accurate, and crafted with obvious affection.

Although *That Thing You Do!* has been the only film helmed by Tom Hanks to date, he has since directed instalments of acclaimed television series including *Band of Brothers* (2001), as well as appearing in a large number of high-profile acting roles including Sam Mendes' *The Road to Perdition* (2002) and Steven Spielberg's *The Terminal* (2004). Additionally, he was nominated for a further two Academy Awards for Best Actor in a Leading Role, for his performances in *Saving Private Ryan* (1998) and *Cast Away* (2000). He retains his reputation as one of the hardest working and most critically acclaimed performers in America.

As for Tyler, her touching and gently understated performance as Faye Dolan had earned her additional critical praise from commentators, building on the acclaim that she had recently earned from the success of her *Stealing Beauty* appearance whilst again proving her ability to adapt to roles with widely diverse demands.

## FURTHER READING

Jeff Gordinier's detailed report from the set of *That Thing You Do!* in the 11 October 1996 issue of *Entertainment Weekly*[31] is well worth a look. In addition to a behind the scenes look at the filming process, the article includes a number of quotes from the cast and crew, including Tom Hanks (who discusses the film from his perspective on both sides of the camera) and Tyler herself.

Tyler discusses her approach to Faye Dolan's character in an interview printed in the June 1996 issue of *Paper* magazine.[32] She also speaks briefly about *That Thing You Do!*, amongst other subjects, in Kevin Sessum's article 'Liv For the Moment', which appears in the May 1997 edition of *Vanity Fair*.[33] She takes a look back on her experiences of filming *That Thing You Do!* in an interview conducted by Lucy Kaylin for the August 1998 issue of *GQ* magazine.[34]

# 6

# INVENTING THE ABBOTTS
## (1997)

*20th Century Fox/ Imagine Entertainment*

**Director**: Pat O'Connor
**Producers**: Brian Grazer, Ron Howard, Janet Meyers
**Screenwriter**: Ken Hixon, from a story by Sue Miller

MAIN CAST

| | |
|---|---|
| **Liv Tyler** | Pamela Abbott |
| **Joachin Phoenix** | Doug Holt |
| **Billy Crudup** | John Charles 'J.C.' Holt |
| **Jennifer Connelly** | Eleanor Abbott |
| **Joanna Going** | Alice Abbott |
| **Barbara Williams** | Joan Abbott |

Tyler's experience of period roles was to continue with *Inventing the Abbotts*, a bleaker and rather more contemplative reflection on America's recent history than the generally upbeat *That Thing You Do!* had offered. Although more introspective than Tom Hanks' film had been, this homage to the bygone social mores of the 1950s presents a muted nostalgia all of its own, a melancholic wistfulness that shines out from beneath the regrets and broken dreams of its characters.

Irish-born director Pat O'Connor had previously helmed features for both television and cinematic presentation, including *Cal* (1984) and *January Man* (1989), though prior to the filming of *Inventing the Abbotts* he was perhaps best known for the critically well-received *Circle of Friends* (1995), a big-screen adaptation of the popular Maeve Binchy novel which featured Chris O'Donnell and then-upcoming British talent Minnie Driver. That film was to share a number of features with *Inventing the Abbotts*, including the theme of transition between youth and adulthood, a mid-1950s setting, and a focus on three young women as the fulcrum of the narrative.

*Inventing the Abbotts* concerns two working-class brothers, JC and Doug Holt, and their complicated relationship with the beautiful, well-heeled Abbott sisters, Alice, Eleanor and Pamela, in the leafy town of Haley, Illinois. The brothers, we soon find, are separated by more than their difference in age (JC, at seventeen, is two years older than Doug), and the bond between them often proves to be tempestuous. JC (Billy Crudup) is good-looking, intelligent and bursting with the impetuous arrogance of youth. Doug (Joachin Phoenix), although similarly striking, is quieter and more contemplative; although he lacks his brother's natural academic flair and allure with women, he is somewhat more grounded and accepting of his life and those around him. However, one factor which unites the two is their fascination with the three daughters of local self-made steel magnate Lloyd Abbott (a magnificently cold, unyielding performance from Will Patton).

Lloyd was a close friend of their father, who was killed during

JC's infancy (and before Doug's birth) in a tragic accident. Everyone is in agreement over the circumstances of the late John Holt's demise – he drowned in his car when, late on a winter's night, he accepted a $20 wager with Abbott that he could drive his car across a frozen lake to a small island and back. Unfortunately, the ice had not been as substantial as Holt had anticipated, and he was never to return to claim the winnings from his bet.

Much dissension, however, came to surround the events following Holt's death. Lloyd Abbott was later to grow rich after exploiting the patent for a desk drawer design, ensuring the future of the steel factory where he worked (once the World War II contracts had dried up in the mid-1940s, the factory was to make a highly successful shift from developing ordnance to manufacturing steel desks). However, JC is convinced that the patent originally belonged to his father, and that Abbott had swindled Holt's widow Helen (Kathy Baker), a local schoolteacher, out of the design after his death. Worse still, Abbott's concern for Helen's wellbeing following the demise of Holt caused him to visit her regularly in the months following the accident, leading to unfounded accusations from his wife Joan (Barbara Williams) that Lloyd and Helen were having an affair. Despite the baseless nature of Joan's finger-pointing, the Abbotts' growing stature in the community led to the ostracism of Helen by other locals, the gossipy allegations of infidelity rendering her as something of a pariah despite her hard-working, honest nature.

JC has grown up embittered, incensed at the injustice of Lloyd Abbott's rise to wealth and influence while his own family struggles to survive. Doug, on the other hand, is largely oblivious to the demons which drive his brother. To him, the Abbotts are neither better nor worse than his household; they are simply more materially well-off. To further complicate matters, Eleanor (Jennifer Connelly), the Abbotts' stunning middle daughter, has caught the eye of JC – who, in spite of himself, is smitten. The coquettish Eleanor toys with JC's affections, flirting with other men before finally making herself available to him. However, when their affair becomes known to Abbott he is infuriated and demands that she break it off immediately. Convinced that JC intends to marry his way into Abbotts' wealthy family (the very method that Lloyd himself took when instigating his loveless marriage to Joan), he is determined to thwart Eleanor's relationship with JC.

While we are never entirely sure just how serious Eleanor's affections for JC actually are – even he suspects that she is seeking excitement by courting someone unacceptable to her snobbish parents – she persistently defies her father's attempts at keeping them apart, finally leading Lloyd to deal with the problem by sending her off to a ambiguous-sounding clinic in Wisconsin followed by a school for stewardesses in Chicago. Abbott places the blame for Eleanor's departure entirely on JC, and thus the animosity between them heightens.

Jennifer Connelly's excellent performance as Eleanor is one of the highlights of the film; she perfectly captures the character's arch playfulness and frank sexuality whilst (especially in her appearances nearer the end of the film) imbuing Eleanor with a growing humanity and strength of character that is never quite as apparent in her supercilious mother Joan.

Doug, meanwhile, is finding that his long-held friendship with the youngest Abbott daughter is deepening. The attractive Pamela (Liv Tyler) has been able to maintain some level of freedom thanks to her low profile in her parent's attentions, due mostly to their focus on the pre-marital grooming of her beautiful but insipid eldest sister Alice (Joanna Going) and the hushed histrionics surrounding Eleanor's exploits and departure. Although Pamela and Doug have, against all odds, shared a bond of friendship since childhood, he begins to feel increasingly awkward about their intensifying affection. Despite the fact that they both genuinely care for each other, JC's raging conflict with Lloyd Abbott has made Doug progressively more class-conscious. This threatens to fracture the relationship between Doug and Pamela, which is profoundly hurtful to her. She is gentle and sensitive, quite unlike the palpably self-confident Eleanor or the slavishly conventional Alice. However, when Pamela later confronts Doug with the fact that she can hardly be held responsible for being born into wealth and influence, he begins to re-evaluate his feelings for her, and their attraction gradually continues to grow.

There is a terrific onscreen chemistry between Tyler and Joachin Phoenix, who make the relationship between Doug and Pamela both touching and tenderly realistic. They manage to encapsulate well the awkwardness and fragility of young love, putting particular emphasis on their uncertainty of the evolution of their friendship into something more profound. Ken Hixon's insightful screenplay establishes the rawness of Doug and Pamela's developing romance with astonishing sensitivity, contrasting very effectively with the conquests of the calculating lothario JC.

Doug and Pamela's relationship is, however, to be further complicated by JC's machinations. Now studying at a prestigious university in Philadelphia, the elder Holt brother makes full use of a summer break back in Illinois to make a move on Alice Abbott, who is suffering from marital difficulties. Alice has separated from her brutish husband Peter Vanlaningham (Alessandro Nivola), whose marriage had been actively encouraged by the Abbott parents due to the Vanlaningham family's highly successful steel firm. Now the mother of a small daughter, Alice is brittle and emotionally vulnerable; JC naturally wastes no time in moving in on her.

After a turbulent attempt to seduce Alice, JC finds that his manoeuvrings have once again been thwarted by Lloyd Abbott, who makes his position on JC's continued interference with his family abundantly clear. Alice, in spite of her resentment at her father's manipulation of her life, finds herself unable to turn her back on years of docile obedience to her parents' will, and ultimately turns her back on JC only to resume her affectionless marriage.

With JC's continued campaign against Abbott having

seemingly burnt out, Doug moves on to the same Philadelphia university as his elder brother, having been awarded a scholarship in stage design. While there, he unexpectedly meets Pamela, from whom he had drifted apart following their families' heightened animosity surrounding JC's abortive approaches to Alice. Studying at a nearby college, Pamela is now free from the meddling of her overbearing parents, and Doug is keen to rekindle the connection between them. However, Pamela seems uncomfortable and evasive around him. This vexes Doug, and despite his continued attempts at rapprochement she remains cool and distant towards him.

Later, to his shock and disgust, he discovers that JC had taken advantage of Pamela at a party where, having had rather too much to drink, she had succumbed to his advances. Although Doug is incandescent at his brother's betrayal, JC seems satisfied that his ostensible revenge against Lloyd Abbott is finally complete, having damaged the lives of all three of his privileged daughters. Doug rushes to reassure Pamela that his affection for her remains undiminished, but it is too late; she has fled college for an unknown location.

Doug and JC remain estranged for some time, until the unexpected death of their mother forces them back together. United in grief, the two brothers uncover some unexpected revelations about their late father's business dealings which cast a new light on the dealings which supposedly took place between their parents and the Abbotts. Doug finally decides to take the bull by the horns and confront Lloyd Abbott personally. Somewhat taken aback by the directness of Doug's approach, Lloyd finally decides to talk frankly about the resentment that exists between his family and the Holts, and his candour offers Doug one final chance to find Pamela and work towards the happy ending that he is so desperately seeking.

If there is one major observation that could be made about *Inventing the Abbotts*, it is that the film excels in its uncompromisingly realistic approach to class conflict, and the script's depth of characterisation amply articulates the discomfiture that comes with living on 'the other side of the tracks' – whether in the case of Doug, who struggles to achieve by merit what birthright has denied him, or Pamela, whose disenchantment with her family awakens her to the notion that material gain is only a means to an end, and certainly no guarantor of happiness. This dichotomy is tellingly explored in Lloyd Abbott's final discussion with Doug, when he admits that he had envied the late John Holt due to the genuine devotion shown to him by his wife-to-be, Helen. In comparison to Lloyd's dissatisfaction with his own wife, whom he has married out of expediency and ambition and for whom he appears to have little genuine affection, the viewer is left in no doubt that in the town of Haley, as in the world at large, the privileges of wealth are not necessarily all-encompassing.

As mentioned earlier, Doug and Pamela's growing affections form a touching counterpoint to JC's Machiavellian romances, and their relationship – based on sincere love and mutual respect – is the one that holds our interest the longest. Of all the three sisters, Pamela is the only one who is sympathetic enough to encourage true empathy with the audience; the smart-mouthed Eleanor, with her smouldering, flirtatious manner, appears almost as manipulative as JC at times, whereas the bland Alice is too wishy-washy and in thrall to her parents' will to elicit any real compassion (her ineffectual snootiness is very effectively expressed by Joanna Going, whose studied performance elevates the character far beyond any kind of potential stereotyping). O'Connor imbues the film with a contemplative, dignified pace, which lends itself well to a complex narrative that pulls no punches in its depiction of emotional pain and moral confusion. The subtle shifts in time which artfully move the storyline forward are deftly handled by the use of a narrator – a powerfully reflective performance from an uncredited Michael Keaton.

Another prominent feature of *Inventing the Abbotts* is the undeniable talent of its young cast. Among the many actors who would go on to even greater future success were Billy Crudup, who would come to gain critical praise for his appearances in Cameron Crowe's *Almost Famous* (2000), Gillian Armstrong's *Charlotte Gray* (2001) and Tim Burton's *Big Fish* (2003). Joaquin Phoenix would later be nominated for both a BAFTA and an Academy Award in 2001 for his performance as Emperor Commodus in Ridley Scott's *Gladiator* (2000), and would also appear in M. Night Shyamalan's prominent films *Signs* (2002) and *The Village* (2004). Perhaps most noteworthy of all, the always-impressive Jennifer Connelly – already a well established actress by the time of *Inventing the Abbotts* – was later to appear in a variety of well-received films including Alex Proyas' *Dark City* (1998) and Darren Aronofsky's *Requiem For a Dream* (2000) before winning the Academy Award for Best Actress in a Supporting Role in 2002 for her performance in Ron Howard's acclaimed *A Beautiful Mind* (2001).

The critical appraisal of *Inventing the Abbotts* proved to be uneven. There was near-unanimous approval of the film's impeccable attention to period detail, with its painstaking evocation of 1950s America – both urban and suburban – proving worthy of considerable praise.[35] Commentators differed, however, when it came to the subject of the film's pacing, which was judged to be rather too stately for some tastes. A number considered the narrative too protracted and unhurried, subordinating action to introspection, whereas others commended the film for its deliberate and measured approach to storytelling, enabling a more focused depiction of character interaction than is conventional in modern films.[36]

Although *Inventing the Abbotts* remains one of Pat O'Connor's best-known films, along with *Circle of Friends*, he would also later go on to direct the successful *Dancing at Lughnasa* (1998) and *Sweet November* (2001).

*Inventing the Abbotts* offered Tyler the opportunity to widen her dramatic range still further; although she had played characters with romantic entanglements previously, most notably in *Heavy* and *That Thing You Do!*, the role of Pamela Abbott presented a character with an emotional sensitivity greater even than Lucy Harmon in *Stealing Beauty*. Whereas Lucy had been actively seeking to broaden her emotional awareness, and did so largely on her own terms, Pamela is uncertain and fearful of the consequences of her desire. Like *That Thing You Do!*'s Faye Dolan, Pamela is sweet-natured and supportive, but her dysfunctional family and heightened appreciation of class conflict profoundly affects her approach to building a relationship with Doug, complicating matters in a way that had never been the case for Faye. As in earlier performances, Tyler excels at articulating emotional sensitivity and complex, conflicting feelings. She shines most brightly when portraying Pamela's awkwardness in matching Doug's passionate affections, and the hurt she feels at his clumsy self-consciousness regarding the bond that has grown between them. The rawness of Pamela's subtle, understated ardour for Doug contrasts effectively with his initial mock-casual approach to their relationship, and it is also to the credit of Joachin Phoenix that he carefully balances the dynamic between Doug and Pamela to create a rounded, believable relationship between two young lovers who, in spite of all the obstacles strewn in their path – both social and emotional – still manage against all odds to build a lasting love in the face of overwhelming adversity.

## FURTHER READING

Sue Miller's original short story 'Inventing the Abbotts' (formerly entitled 'The Lover of Women'), upon which the film was based, makes for interesting comparative reading. It is available in an anthology, *Inventing the Abbotts and Other Stories*, which contains a number of Miller's other short works.[37] She has also written a number of full-length novels.

Perhaps the most enlightening interview with Tyler regarding *Inventing the Abbotts* can be found in Ingrid Sischy's article 'Inventing the Future', which appeared in the April 1997 issue of *Interview* magazine.[38] The interview is conducted not only with Tyler but also with co-star Joachin Phoenix, and they discuss their experiences of the filming process as well as their friendship during the production.

Kevin Sessums' article 'Liv for the Moment', which was printed in *Vanity Fair's* May 1997 edition,[39] contains various reflections from Tyler on *Inventing the Abbotts*, as well as her thoughts on her film career up until that point.

# 7

# ARMAGEDDON (1998)

*Touchstone Pictures/ Jerry Bruckheimer Films/ Valhalla Motion Pictures*

**Director**: Michael Bay
**Producers**: Michael Bay, Jerry Bruckheimer, Gale Anne Hurd
**Screenwriters**: Jonathan Hensleigh and J.J. Abrams, from a story by Robert Roy Pool and Jonathan Hensleigh.

MAIN CAST

| | |
|---|---|
| **Bruce Willis** | Harry S. Stamper |
| **Billy Bob Thornton** | Dan Truman |
| **Ben Affleck** | A.J. Frost |
| **Liv Tyler** | Grace Stamper |
| **Will Patton** | Charles 'Chick' Chapple |
| **Steve Buscemi** | Rockhound |

With *Armageddon*, Tyler was entering uncharted waters. She had built her acting career largely on the strength of challenging parts in dramatic roles, with the singular exception of her brief detour into comedy with *Empire Records*. But with Michael Bay's new film she was to face something entirely new to her career – a large-scale action film, produced for international mainstream consumption, which was to prove to be a marked departure from the more intimate character-driven dramas in which she had appeared thus far. This transition was to place new demands on her established acting skills, and – as we shall see – she would have to deploy her understanding of emotional articulation in a different manner from her previous performances in order to meet these new requirements.

By the time *Armageddon* was being produced, director Michael Bay was already well-known in the film industry for his frenetic, spirited action movies, such as *Bad Boys* (1995) and *The Rock* (1996). Both of these films had performed successfully with audiences, featuring big-name talent and explosive special effects, and as such a good deal of media attention surrounded the impending release of *Armageddon*, his first directorial foray into space-based action adventure.

In the closing years of the Twentieth Century, the American government finds itself in the middle of an unexpected crisis. On a routine maintenance mission in Earth orbit, NASA astronauts unexpectedly detect an incoming meteor shower – a phenomenon which, on entering the planet's atmosphere, promptly causes major devastation in New York City. Worse still, NASA scientists discover that this was merely the vanguard for worse to come; the meteors herald the arrival of an enormous asteroid which is mere days away, and on a collision course with Earth.

The asteroid, they discover, is roughly about the same size as the American state of Texas, and on impact will destroy every living thing on the planet down to the microbial level. While the American military futilely conjecture about possible nuclear missile strikes on the approaching asteroid, which will almost certainly fail due to its enormous mass, NASA administrator Dan Truman (Billy Bob Thornton) and his head researcher, Dr Ronald Quincy (Jason Isaacs), devise a daring plan which has a greater guarantee of success. By drilling far enough into the asteroid's crust, they speculate, a nuclear device could be implanted far enough inside it to trigger a massive tectonic shift, effectively splitting the asteroid in half and altering its trajectory so that it misses the planet altogether. Their plan has only one drawback; none of their astronauts have the necessary expertise in deep-core drilling to confidently make the scheme work.

Fortunately for NASA, Harry S Stamper (Bruce Willis), the world's foremost deep-core oil driller, is tracked down and persuaded to lend his skills to aid their plan. Harry is reluctant to assist, particularly as he has enough to deal with in keeping his beautiful daughter Grace (Liv Tyler) apart from his amorous protégé AJ Frost (Ben Affleck). However, when he discovers what is at stake, he quickly rounds up a hand-picked team of offbeat but trusted expert drillers to assist him in the work that lies ahead.

Initially, NASA are only seeking Stamper's expert advice, but when he discovers that the astronautics team have no prior experience of drilling he grudgingly comes to another arrangement with Truman. He and his team agree to undertake a rudimentary crash-course in space flight and, together with a crack team of NASA pilots, will travel to the asteroid personally to resolve the situation.

Leaving Grace behind with Truman at the NASA control room, Stamper, Frost and his team head into space on a pair of space shuttles loaded with specialised drilling gear. Following a tense journey via an international space station, they execute a complex slingshot manoeuvre around the Moon before managing to land on the asteroid itself. But facing a constantly ticking clock, major equipment malfunctions, and the military poised to take control of the mission from him at the first sign of trouble, Stamper finds that he must make every possible kind of sacrifice before he will be able to detonate the nuclear device and secure the future of the Earth.

What is immediately noticeable about *Armageddon* is how markedly different it seems from any film that Tyler had previously appeared in. In fact, it is about as far from contemplative drama or independent cinema that it is conceivably possible to reach. *Armageddon* is not a film that is concerned with an in-depth exploration of character motivation or complex psychological ambiguity; it is a larger than life, comic-book style romp designed to entertain audiences with breathlessly fast-paced action and perilous high drama. It doesn't seek to be taken seriously as anything other than an entertaining popcorn movie, and aims to succeed on this level by providing audiences with all the ingredients necessary for a summertime blockbuster; a cast of accomplished performers, excellently realised special effects, and plenty of rapid-fire excitement.

The film does contain many appealing attractions, not least its wonderfully bombastic opening narration from Hollywood legend Charlton Heston. The catastrophic effects of hundreds of meteorites striking New York is brilliantly realised with disturbingly realistic special effects, and this achievement is mirrored near the film's conclusion when the city of Paris is completely destroyed by the impact of falling space debris.

The cast is also first-rate, and features many big names. By the time of *Armageddon*, Bruce Willis was already an action star in Hollywood thanks to his appearances in the highly successful *Die Hard* trilogy, comprising *Die Hard* (1988), *Die Hard 2: Die Harder* (1990), and *Die Hard: With a Vengeance* (1995). He had also earned recent critical acclaim for his appearances in Quentin Tarantino's *Pulp Fiction* (1994) and Terry Gilliam's *Twelve Monkeys* (1995), amongst others, and as such was a suitably heavyweight actor to cast as *Armageddon*'s irascible but courageous hero. Willis portrays Stamper as a gleefully arrogant, hugely self-assured character – someone who is at the top of his game and knows it. Although the script allows little time for development beyond this portrayal, there are a few cursory glimpses of a deeper, more spiritual side to Stamper (during his visit to his father, for instance, or his occasionally proffered spoken prayers), which – though often less than subtle – do add some measure of poignancy to the final decision that he makes at the end of his mission.

As Stamper's daughter Grace, Tyler appears to be slightly less comfortable with her performance than had been the case in her other films. It is difficult to believe that the material she is provided with in *Armageddon* does not bear responsibility for this; in terms of character, Grace Stamper is comparatively meagre in stature when weighed against the more profound dramatic roles that Tyler had previously engaged with. However, this is not to mean that Tyler's efforts with her character are ever in vain; it is more the case that once her father and friends on the drilling crew get into space, there is little for Grace to do but stay at NASA headquarters and pensively stand watch at various different monitor screens.

Tyler does, however, manage to articulate Grace's feeling of helplessness without ever letting her performance seem one-note. *Armageddon*'s screenplay, though admittedly seeming rather impersonal given the sheer number of different people involved in its construction, does contain a certain amount of knowing irony with regard to its subject matter, and Tyler makes the most of this (particularly in the first act of the film) to render Grace as an intelligent and increasingly independent woman, rather than simply the foil of either Stamper or Frost. This is largely achieved through the establishment of her multilingual skills, her apparent business acumen, and the fact that Stamper relies on her as a valued employee as well as a daughter.

Given that one of Tyler's major strengths has been her ability to portray characters in an emotionally sensitive, low-key manner, it is laudable indeed that she manages to bring some measure of subtlety to Grace, eschewing *Armageddon*'s general enticement towards an inflated, more explicitly emotive performance. She provides Grace with more dimension than may otherwise have been expected – a particularly important point, given that she is the most prominent female character in the film by quite a considerable margin.

It is significant to note that *Armageddon* was hardly the exception to the Hollywood rule when it comes to characterisation; it would not be the first time that an action blockbuster would subordinate character development to the needs of the plot. Fortunately, the main ensemble of actors who dominate the film are skilled enough to put a strong, identifiable stamp on their characters. Most notable are Will Patton as grizzled drilling veteran Chapple and Michael Clarke Duncan as gentle giant 'Bear' Kurleenbear, though Steve Buscemi steals the show with his memorably eccentric performance as Rockhound, an oddball genius and unlikely Casanova figure. Billy Bob Thornton must also be commended for his remarkably controlled rendering of the constantly-beleaguered Dan Truman, while comic relief was ably provided with a brilliant turn from Peter Stormare as the slightly space-crazy Russian cosmonaut Lev Andropov.

From the point of view of Tyler's performance, the key supporting character is Ben Affleck's Frost, with whom Grace has fallen deeply in love. Affleck was most definitely a rising star in Hollywood at the time of *Armageddon*, having a string of acting appearances to his name before really hitting his stride in Gus Van Sant's *Good Will Hunting* (1997), which he also co-wrote with that film's star, Matt Damon. Affleck turns on the charm to portray Frost as an old-fashioned square-jawed hero, supportive of Stamper despite the older man's resentment of Frost's interest in his daughter. This is, we learn, the result of a wider issue; namely that Stamper loves Grace profoundly and is pained to admit that she has come of age and is moving on with her life. Willis and Affleck both do a creditable job with this tug-of-love scenario, but ultimately the emotional sub-plot becomes less dominant as the film progresses and the danger to the planet intensifies. The climax of this 'love triangle', where Stamper and Frost resolve their differences near the end of the mission, is handled efficiently rather than touchingly.

Ben Affleck and Tyler were to be nominated jointly for Best On-Screen Duo in the 1999 MTV Movie Awards, which emphasises the resonance that their pairing in the film was to have with young audiences. However, the chemistry between Frost and Grace sometimes suffers from the brevity with which their romance is portrayed. Tyler and Affleck make much of the few romantic moments that their characters are provided with, particularly in the 'animal crackers' scene, but other sequences work less well. The pre-launch scene, where Frost serenades Grace with a rendition of 'Leaving on a Jet Plane', for instance, is so heavily choreographed that it fails to engage on an emotional level quite as fully as might have been hoped. It did, however, coincidentally turn out to be one of the more iconic scenes in the film. Given *Armageddon*'s high profile, the sequence quickly penetrated the public consciousness, and came to be emulated and parodied in the popular culture of the time – perhaps most notably in the pastiche that appeared in Britney Spears' music video *Crazy*, which followed some time later.

On the subject of music, many cultural commentators were quick to note that a memorable part of *Armageddon*'s soundtrack, the song 'I Don't Want to Miss a Thing', was performed by Aerosmith – the band responsible for Tyler's initial screen breakthrough with their music video for *Crazy* back in 1994. Tyler's father, Steven Tyler, was to deliver a highly distinctive performance of the song, ensuring that 'I Don't Want to Miss a Thing' would become one of Aerosmith's best-regarded and most popular works in recent years.

If *Armageddon* was principally designed for audience-pulling, then it can certainly be judged a success; the film proved to be a major box-office hit, with cinemagoers across the world flocking to see it in theatres over the summer of '98 and beyond. Its critical reception was, however, chilly at best. Most commentators in newspapers and magazines didn't doubt the competence of the film's complex visual effects, but many found *Armageddon*'s characterisation to be sketchy and shallow, lamenting the fact that such a talented cast appeared not to have been as dramatically engaged as they potentially could have been.[40] Some considered the film's overt, flag-waving patriotism to be somewhat overwrought,[41] whilst others criticised the film's rather blatant use of cliché in certain parts of the storyline.[42] In all fairness, some of this disparagement may well stem from the fact that the film went on general release at around the same time as Mimi Leder's similarly-themed *Deep Impact* (1998). Another film which dealt with the threat of an asteroid strike on Earth, *Deep Impact* generally came to be more sympathetically regarded by most critics both at the time and, indeed, retrospectively. That said, some critics freely admitted the fact that *Armageddon* was produced for entertainment purposes, not consumption by contemplative art-house audiences, and chose to judge the film by its crowd-pleasing merits instead.[43]

Michael Bay was to continue his run of success in the film industry with his next film, *Pearl Harbor* (2001), a historical drama based around the eponymous battle during World War II. *Pearl Harbor* would have a similarly patriotic flair as *Armageddon*, and also starred Ben Affleck – this time in the central role.

*Armageddon*'s major financial achievement was reflected in its performance at awards ceremonies, where the film gained worthy recognition for the refinement of its audio-visual presentation. It was nominated for many technical prizes internationally, winning a good number of them outright, but principal among them were the 1999 Academy Awards, where the film was nominated for four Oscars: Best Sound Effects Editing, Best Visual Effects, Best Original Song, and Best Sound. Trevor Rabin's stirring soundtrack was nominated for several honours, winning the BMI Film Music Award, whereas the highly successful 'I Don't Want to Miss a Thing' did well for Diane Warren, being conferred a Golden Satellite Award as well as a number of other nominations.

The increased public visibility of Tyler's performance was to pay dividends, as her appearance as Grace Stamper also won award nominations. These were the Blockbuster Entertainment Award for Best Actress in a Science Fiction Presentation, and the MTV Movie Award for Best Female Performance (together with Best On-Screen Duo, which she shared with Ben Affleck). This marked her first major nominations for awards since being shortlisted for the YoungStar Award in 1997, in appreciation of her appearance in *Stealing Beauty*. This further recognition was to provide additional proof that not only was Tyler becoming an increasingly bankable celebrity name, but also that in the eyes of her peers, her star remained in ascendance.

## FURTHER READING

Tyler gives a short interview with Cindy Pearlman in the August 1998 issue of *React* magazine, where she briefly discusses her reaction to watching the completed *Armageddon* on the big screen.[44]

A rather more detailed article dealing with the filming of *Armageddon*, which includes quotes from both Tyler and director Michael Bay, can be found in Lucy Kaylin's feature in the August 1998 edition of *GQ*.[45]

Tyler talks about her experiences working on *Armageddon*, as well as giving her reaction to the film's massive success with audiences, in an interview with Bruce Westbrook in the 2 July 1998 issue of the *Houston Chronicle*.[46]

For an interesting overview of summer blockbusters released in 1998, and *Armageddon*'s place among them, Dan Webster's article in the 30 August 1998 edition of Spokane's *The Spokesman Review* is well worth checking out.[47]

# 8

# PLUNKETT AND MACLEANE
## (1999)

*Working Title Films/ Arts Council of England/ Gramercy Pictures/*
*Stillking Films*

**Director**: Jake Scott
**Producers**: Tim Bevan, Eric Fellner, Rupert Harvey
**Screenwriters**: Robert Wade, Neal Purvis and Charles
McKeown; original screenplay by Selwyn Roberts

MAIN CAST

| | |
|---|---|
| **Jonny Lee Miller** | Captain James Macleane |
| **Robert Carlyle** | Will Plunkett |
| **Ken Stott** | Mr Chance |
| **Liv Tyler** | Lady Rebecca Gibson |
| **Alan Cumming** | Lord Rochester |
| **Michael Gambon** | Lord Chief Justice Gibson |

*Plunkett and Macleane* was to offer more fertile ground for Tyler's ever-evolving film career, and was a definite change of pace from the major studio influences which had dominated *Armageddon*. A British-made historical adventure, it was to offer audiences an abundance of fast-paced action and sharp dialogue, but not at the expense of detailed character development. *Plunkett and Macleane* was unusual in that it was a historical drama produced in a very modern, stylised way; a film where distinctive pre-Enlightenment architecture and the social customs of the late Eighteenth Century were to rub shoulders with current dance music and intentionally anachronistic turns of phrase. Tyler, her reputation as an international star buoyed by the worldwide success of *Armageddon*, was to find herself joining forces with some of Britain's top acting talent.

*Plunkett and Macleane* was to mark the feature film debut of director Jake Scott. Although he had previously helmed a variety of music videos and short films, and had also worked in television, he was perhaps equally well-known for his acclaimed work as a conceptual artist on David Fincher's *Alien3* (1992). He is also the son of highly praised director Ridley Scott, the man behind influential, award-winning films such as *Alien* (1979), *Blade Runner* (1982) and *Gladiator* (2000), amongst numerous others.

A crime-wave has gripped the grimy streets of London in 1748. One fateful night, providence is to bring together Will Plunkett (Robert Carlyle), an accomplished highwayman, and James Macleane (Jonny Lee Miller), an impoverished gentleman who is languishing in a debtor's prison. Plunkett is being hunted down by the sadistic Mr Chance (Ken Stott), the head of the London militia, who kills Plunkett's co-conspirator in a fierce pursuit. Macleane manages to escape his incarceration, only to find himself unwillingly recruited by a desperate Plunkett, who needs him to disembowel his deceased comrade in order to uncover an expensive ruby that he had swallowed on one of their recent raids. The pair find the misplaced stone, but their victory is short-lived – a large party of armed militiamen arrive soon after and take them into custody.

Plunkett, a fiercely intelligent but socially unrefined man, soon devises a plan to evade their sentence at the brutal Newgate Prison. Using Macleane as a 'respectable' front-man, he bribes the prison governor with the precious ruby that he had acquired and buys their freedom. With the two men liberated, Plunkett suggests an alliance with Macleane. His plan is to use Macleane's knowledge of social airs and graces to infiltrate high society, and then – once he has determined the most lucrative targets to pursue – Plunkett will use his criminal expertise to rob the appropriate stagecoaches. The two men have a shared objective; Plunkett wants to raise enough capital to leave for the New World, whereas Macleane merely wants to be rich enough to be taken seriously in the upper echelons of society. He therefore agrees, albeit reluctantly, to assist in Plunkett's plan.

The pair rent stylish accommodation in a well-to-do part of the city, and Plunkett shells out the capital from his previous raids to have Macleane outfitted with the best and most fashionable finery. Plunkett's plans exceed expectations, with their scheme quickly claiming the monetary scalps of numerous society high-flyers. The masked Macleane's unusual politeness towards the victims of his raids quickly earns him the title of 'the Gentleman Highwayman', lending the pair notoriety amongst London's upper classes.

This infamy is far from lost on the establishment, however, which quickly rounds on Lord Chief Justice Gibson (Michael Gambon). He in turn leans hard on his subordinate, Mr Chance, to resolve the situation, but Plunkett and Macleane continue to evade his best attempts at detection. Chance is enraged at the failure of his men to capture the rogue highwaymen, yet even his cruel and unorthodox attempts to motivate his company of men cannot increase their efficiency any further.

The situation is complicated further when Macleane finds himself falling in love with the beautiful Lady Rebecca (Liv

Tyler), Gibson's niece. This brings him into conflict with Lord Gibson himself, who is desperately seeking to marry her off to an appropriately well-placed bachelor (regardless of her own wishes in the matter), and also Chance, who harbours a dark desire of his own for Rebecca. Nevertheless, the independently-minded young woman only has eyes for Macleane, and she is able to determine his criminal alter-ego long before the authorities manage to.

Eventually, Plunkett and Macleane's luck begins to run out. Chance, emboldened by a vote of confidence from the Prime Minister's office, deposes Gibson and offers him the opportunity either to voluntarily leave the country or else face the consequences. Chance is also planning to keep Rebecca for himself, against her will. Macleane desperately seeks to rescue Rebecca (and, if possible, 'liberate' her uncle's valuables in the process), but Plunkett – ever aware that the law is catching up with them – has decided that the Land of the Free is beckoning at last, and is reluctant to take what he regards to be an unnecessary risk. With the noose beginning to tighten around their throats, the pair must resolve their differences and call on every last ounce of their initiative if they are to thwart Chance's conspiracies and escape with both Rebecca and their lives.

Tyler is well cast in the role of Lady Rebecca. She brings to the role a kind of penetrating intelligence and knowing playfulness which chimes perfectly with the film's generally ironic, tongue-in-cheek approach to its subject. Rebecca is far from the conventional genteel, subservient lady of the time; she is forthright and independent, as is evidenced in her continual rebuffing of her uncle's attempts to find her a marriage partner irrespective of her own desires. She also sparkles in her scenes with Jonny Lee Miller's Macleane, her drollness of delivery (particularly in her first, almost ethereal appearance in the ballroom scene) proving her to be more than a match for Macleane's silver-tongued charm.

*Plunkett and Macleane* is a film with definite stylistic flair, and Scott succeeds in offering a new twist on a long-established genre. His vigorous medley of visual styles are combined with a lively modern soundtrack, which brings a progressive edge to the film's detailed Eighteenth Century locales. The screenplay is both witty and tightly-paced, and the central characters are well delineated. This is particularly true of the basic dichotomy between the two leads; Plunkett's lack of patience with Macleane's pretensions of gentrification are mirrored in Macleane's repulsion at the classless Plunkett's lack of sophistication and social finesse. Yet it is the two men's growing reliance on each other, in spite of their differences, which drives the film so compellingly.

Both Robert Carlyle and Jonny Lee Miller had appeared in Danny Boyle's hugely successful *Trainspotting* (1996), one of the major triumphs of 1990s British cinema. *Trainspotting* had been a droll yet harrowing film, adapted from Irvine Welsh's bestselling novel about Scottish drugs culture. Although Carlyle and Miller had been commended for their appearances in *Trainspotting*, both men had considerable onscreen experience beforehand, and indeed both had continued to receive critical praise for their performances since. Miller had appeared in Alan Rudolph's Oscar-nominated *Afterglow* (1997) and Gillies MacKinnon's First World War drama *Regeneration* (1997), based on the acclaimed Pat Barker novel. Carlyle had been equally well-regarded for his performances in Ken Loach's moving *Carla's Song* (1996) and Peter Cattaneo's Oscar-winning *The Full Monty* (1997). The pair appear to relish their onscreen reunion in *Plunkett and Macleane*, the basic incompatibility between the smooth, upwardly-mobile Macleane and gruff, pragmatic Plunkett creating a memorable clash of personalities right throughout the film. Yet they are also developed convincingly as rounded characters – particularly in the case of Plunkett, whose revelation of his pre-crime life as an apothecary, and the traumatic death of his wife, provides much more dimension to the character than his crusty exterior may initially suggest. Carlyle brilliantly communicates the character's practical intelligence, just as Miller nicely underscores the fact that Macleane's exaggerated charm obscures a deeper, more profound character which lies beneath. Both actors capitalise fully on their every moment of shared screen time, to great effect.

If the titular partnership of the film can be considered a success, then special mention must also be reserved for the central antagonist – the scene-stealing, eyeball-gouging Mr Chance, as portrayed by top Scottish actor Ken Stott. Stott, well-known to audiences for his prolific appearances in films as diverse as *Franz Kafka's It's a Wonderful Life* (1993), *Shallow Grave* (1994) and *Fever Pitch* (1997), confirms his reputation in *Plunkett and Macleane* as one of Britain's foremost character actors. Chance is vividly brought to life as a palpably evil character; a sadistic, brutal, totally uncaring man with absolutely no redeeming features whatsoever. Stott is highly effective in his portrayal of Chance, ably articulating the character's vice-ridden depravity through a malevolent demeanour and his omnipresent, barely-contained rage. Chance's violent bursts of anger, when they come, are chillingly realised, and Stott squeezes every ounce of malice out of this immoral but ambitious fiend, from Chance's impotent fury at his inability to track down the Gentleman Highwayman through to his gleefully treacherous ousting of Lord Gibson.

It must be noted that Tyler is particularly effective in her scenes with Ken Stott. Rebecca's initial contempt for Chance's flesh-crawling advances turns to outright revulsion at his eventual sexual violence. Chance's sinister obsession with Rebecca is all the more repugnant for the fact that Lord Gibson, when he becomes aware of the abhorrent violation of his niece, does nothing to stand in Chance's way in order to protect his own venal interests. It is this combination of hypocrisy and casual maltreatment which stresses the fact that, in this film, the law does not necessarily mean justice – something that is abundantly clear when Macleane is framed for Gibson's murder near the film's climax. It is the sheer duplicity and disinterest of the establishment in *Plunkett and Macleane* that makes the goal of the two protagonists, for all its unabashed criminality, almost a sympathetic one.

On a lighter note, *Plunkett and Macleane* also featured cameo appearances from some of Britain's most prominent young comic actors. Foremost among them was Alan Cumming, who was well on the way to becoming a major star on the strength of appearances in films such as Pat O'Connor's *Circle of Friends* (1995) and Martin Campbell's James Bond film *GoldenEye* (1995). Cumming dazzles in the role of the foppish Lord Rochester, whose flamboyant, outrageously garish costumes sparkle amongst the drabness that surrounds him. An old friend of Macleane's, the ostentatious Rochester proves to be a valuable ally in the struggle against Chance and his men, and eventually comes to play a pivotal role in assisting Plunkett and Macleane's final stand.

Other notable appearances included Alexander Armstrong and Ben Miller as society toffs Winterburn and Dixon – both men had been best known for their work together on Channel Four's *Armstrong and Miller* show. Two acquaintances of Rochester's, Winterburn and Dixon help to highlight the gross hypocrisy of pre-Enlightenment high society; they are quick to pull a knife on a dishevelled Macleane immediately following his release from Newgate Prison, but are just as swift to embrace him when he enters into 'polite' society. The film was also to feature cameo appearances by Matt Lucas and David Walliams in the roles of Sir Oswald and Viscount Bilson. Lucas and Walliams would later go on to massive national success with their surreal comedy sketch show *Little Britain* on the BBC.

Given the highly distinctive style of *Plunkett and Macleane*, critical opinion of the film would transpire to be somewhat polarised. A number of commentators approved of the film's exuberance and innovative qualities,[48] while others criticised it as a triumph of style over substance.[49] It was perhaps inevitable that such an inventive film would divide analytical judgment, and indeed the robust entrenchment of opinion on both sides of the argument was ultimately to make *Plunkett and Macleane* one of the more noteworthy 'love it or hate it' British films of the late 1990s.[50]

Jake Scott, his reputation as a director enhanced by the film's high profile in Britain, would go on to helm a variety of prominent music videos in the following years before making a return to the big screen in 2004 with the good-natured family comedy *Tooth Fairy*.

*Plunkett and Macleane* is a film well-suited to Tyler's growing mastery of emotional observation. The role of Rebecca Gibson demanded both subtlety and empathy in the development of the character's romance with Macleane, which Tyler was to achieve admirably. Similar sensitivity is evident in the way she articulates Rebecca's growing disillusionment with her churlish, overbearing uncle and the frigid, devious society that he represents. Most notably, her rendering of Rebecca's growing hatred for Chance is most intricately refined; her disdain at his growing fixation with her is almost tangible. Her English accent is well realised too, though it would be employed to even greater effect in Martha Fiennes' *Onegin* later that same year.

## FURTHER READING

Tyler talks about *Plunkett and Macleane*, as well as discussing her packed filming schedule at the time, in her interview with Jamie Diamond in the August 1999 issue of *Mademoiselle* magazine.[51]

She also converses about her role as Rebecca Gibson, including the difficulties involved in perfecting an authentic English accent, in an interview conducted by Helena Christensen in the April 1999 edition of *Nylon* magazine.[52]

*Plunkett and Macleane*'s star Jonny Lee Miller discusses the film, and other motion pictures he was involved in at around the same time, in conversation with Elizabeth Weitzman in *Interview* magazine's January 1998 issue.[53]

# 9

# COOKIE'S FORTUNE (1999)

*Elysian Dreams/ Kudzu/ Moonstone Entertainment/ Sandcastle 5
Productions*

**Director**: Robert Altman
**Producers**: Robert Altman and Etchie Stroh
**Screenwriter**: Anne Rapp

MAIN CAST

| | |
|---|---|
| **Glenn Close** | Camille Dixon |
| **Julianne Moore** | Cora Duvall |
| **Liv Tyler** | Emma Duvall |
| **Chris O'Donnell** | Jason Brown |
| **Charles S. Dutton** | Willis Richland |
| **Patricia Neal** | Jewel Mae 'Cookie' Orcutt |

With *Cookie's Fortune,* Tyler was to collaborate for the first time with long-standing Hollywood veteran Robert Altman. A true legend of the American film world, Altman had been involved in directing since the early 1950s, working both in television and the big screen until finally hitting the critical jackpot with his acerbic anti-war film *MASH* in 1970. He was to continue to switch between visual media with ease, helming films in the 1970s which were both challenging and generally well-received by critics – most notably *Brewster McCloud* (1970), *McCabe and Mrs Miller* (1971) and *Nashville* (1975) – whilst also directing features for television. This continued into the 1980s, where he remained prolific in both media, before he experienced a major revival when achieving considerable critical praise in the early 1990s for his films *The Player* (1992), *Short Cuts* (1993) and *Kansas City* (1996). By the time of filming *Cookie's Fortune*, Altman had been nominated for the Best Director Academy Award on no less than four occasions.

Although not evident in all of his films, Altman has perhaps become best-known for his distinctive skill in orchestrating large ensemble casts to convey intricate, interweaving stories, deftly drawing together diverse story-threads to create complex but satisfying character tapestries. In terms of his recent films, this was perhaps most evident in *Short Cuts,* which interlinked the incidents of several Raymond Carver short stories to great effect, though his memorable appraisal of the modern film industry in *The Player* (based on the Michael Tolkin book) was similarly accomplished. With the generally light-hearted *Cookie's Fortune,* he was to turn his attention to the Deep South – a subject which he had treated very differently in his most recent project, an evocative film adaptation of John Grisham's legal drama *The Gingerbread Man* (1998).

Easter is coming to the small Mississippi town of Holly Springs. In the local church, the overbearing Camille Dixon (Glenn Close) is orchestrating a rather drab, melodramatic production of Oscar Wilde's *Salome*, which stars her affable but slow-witted sister Cora

Duvall (Julianne Moore). The play also, incidentally, features most of the rest of the town's population.

One townsperson who isn't involved in the play is elderly Jewel Mae Orcutt (Patricia Neal), better known as Cookie to the people of Holly Springs. Eccentric but relatively well-off, Cookie owns a large house that is taken care of by her close companion and sometime-handyman Willis Richland (Charles S. Dutton), and has no interest in the over-the-top pretensions of her niece Camille. In fact, it soon becomes clear that Willis is more of a family member to her than any of her immediate relatives, with the exception of her great-niece Emma Duvall (Liv Tyler), for whom she has a soft spot.

Emma, as it turns out, has fled the town some time earlier to escape from her aunt Camille's judgmental nagging. Willis, however, finds that she has recently returned to Holly Springs and is now working as a catfish cleaner for the slightly creepy Manny Hood (Lyle Lovett). Emma is hard-working and level headed, rejecting the self-important posturing of her aunt (which, to a lesser extent, her easily-led mother is also guilty of) and preferring spirited independence to false airs and graces.

Everything is to change in the town, however, when Cookie – who greatly misses her long-departed husband Buck – suddenly decides that she has grown tired of life, and resolves to commit suicide. Alone in the house, she makes out a final parting note to Willis before using one of Buck's guns to fire a single shot through her head.

Camille, who later visits Cookie's house to reclaim an old punch bowl, is shocked when she discovers the body. However, dreading the stigma that may come from having a suicide in the family, she uses her amateur skills of theatrical direction to remove the evidence and restage the scene to make it look as though Cookie had been murdered by an intruder. Swearing Cora to secrecy, Camille eats Cookie's suicide note, hides the 'murder weapon' in the house's expansive back garden, and then alerts the police.

Given that Cookie was a well-known figure in Holly Springs, the local sheriff's team are thunderstruck by the possibility of a murder in their sleepy town. Willis becomes their prime suspect due to his fingerprints being on the gun used to kill Cookie – but as he had been cleaning an entire cabinet's-worth of vintage firearms the day before, his prints are on every handgun in the house. Nobody really believes that Willis is to blame for the crime, particularly as he is a close acquaintance of many of the local police force who can vouch for his good character, but with no other apparent leads they are left with no alternative but to put him into custody.

Outraged at the treatment of her long-time friend, Emma joins Willis in his cell. The sheriff's team, however, are so obviously certain of Willis' innocence that his cell door is left permanently open and unlocked, and he is often to be found playing board-games with his unconventional lawyer Jack Palmer (Donald Moffat) and veteran officer Lester Boyle (Ned Beatty), both of whom are his regular fishing partners. In the meantime, investigator Otis Tucker (Courtney B. Vance) is dispatched from a nearby town to get to the bottom of the case, only to be confounded by the locals' laid-back quirkiness.

With Camille and Cora moving their possessions into Cookie's house (still festooned with crime scene tape) while the entire local sheriff's department try to uncover the real story behind the old woman's demise, the townsfolk are soon to find that a number of revelations are still to be uncovered before the case can be solved. But if the law are convinced that Cookie's death was not caused by suicide, and they are also certain that Willis was not to blame, then who will ultimately be found guilty for pulling the trigger?

*Cookie's Fortune* is a deceptively simple story which is told both skilfully and engagingly. Anne Rapp's screenplay brings Holly Springs to life with a large cast of likeable, offbeat townsfolk, and Altman carefully adds fine detail to the individual foibles and peculiarities of even the most minor of supporting characters. Donald Moffat, for instance, stays in the memory as the town's bicycling lawyer, who represents virtually everyone who lives in Holly Springs and is a formidable repository of useless knowledge. Lyle Lovett is also noteworthy as the harmless but vaguely disturbing Manny, who quietly (and totally fruitlessly) lusts after Emma. Sheriff's deputy Wanda Carter, played by Niecy Nash, displays a remarkable line in flirtatiousness to hilarious comic effect as she tries in vain to catch the eye of smooth, snappily-dressed investigator Tucker. And Patricia Neal is both wacky and touchingly melancholic in her short but nonetheless pivotal appearance as Cookie.

If the film belongs to anyone, however, it is Charles S. Dutton for his warm, hugely dignified portrayal of Willis Richland. A gentle and caring soul, Willis is more distraught over the death of his close friend Cookie than by his own imprisonment, and never seems to doubt the good intentions of the townspeople during his incarceration. It is testament to his popularity in Holly Springs that such effort is made to confirm his innocence, and Dutton communicates well the kind of convivial amiability that makes Willis such a trustworthy and approachable soul. Although he interacts convincingly with his reluctant jailers, bringing solidarity to a patently absurd situation, his most memorable moments are spent near the end of the film with Tyler, where Willis and Emma discover that a more profound connection lies between them than either had hitherto suspected.

Glenn Close comes near to stealing the show as the domineering Camille Dixon; her performance brilliantly articulates the character's hysteria and haughty, dictatorial manner. Her building histrionics near the conclusion of the film are so convincingly handled that Close easily reminds audiences of the reason why she had received Oscar nominations five times prior to *Cookie's Fortune*. Julianne Moore (herself an Academy Award nominee) is similarly excellent as the pleasant but obtuse Cora. Often to be seen portraying highly intelligent and capable characters, Moore is cast against type to great effect as Camille's well-intentioned sister, whose choices in life are endlessly predetermined by her sibling with the same kind of ruthless efficiency used to direct her hopeless stage plays.

Tyler seems much more at ease in the gentle comedy-drama of *Cookie's Fortune* than she had appeared in the quick-fire wit and occasional slapstick of *Empire Records*, and this allows her natural comic talents to come to the fore in a much more satisfying way. The role of Emma Duvall was, however, also to prove something of a major shift for Tyler; her hair was severely cropped for the part, and the character's appearance throughout is unglamorous but practical. Emma prefers to wear utilitarian clothing, eschewing her mother's affected Southern Belle fashion style, and she carries herself in an unpretentious, no-frills manner. This is a profound change from the sophisticated glamour that Tyler had become known for in some of her previous appearances, and she carries it off with effortless sincerity. She is perhaps at her most effective in her scenes with Willis, with whom Emma shares a strong emotional bond, and also rookie officer Jason Brown (Chris O'Donnell), an old flame of Emma's who is keen to rekindle their past romance. Emma and Jason are at first mildly uncomfortable around each other, their unspoken tensions due to Emma's earlier unannounced flight from town, but they are quickly to achieve rapprochement and resume their passionate relationship (much to Willis' amusement).

As is the case with many of Altman's films, *Cookie's Fortune* contains a number of powerful subtexts which run subtly beneath the surface of the central plot. Most prominent here is the Easter staging of *Salome*, the main themes of which include suicide, betrayal and murder (thus lending more relevance than might be expected to Camille's decision to share the credit for the play with Oscar Wilde). Likewise, the issue of racial equality is touched upon without such concerns ever being stated explicitly, and the theme is developed throughout the film in a very delicately refined way. For instance, we see from Willis' early visit to a local bar that the audience, enraptured by Josie Martin's (Ruby Wilson) excellent singing talents, is predominantly composed of other

African-American customers, whereas the simultaneous rehearsal of *Salome* – somewhat dreary by comparison – has a largely white cast. Any suggestion of segregation here is quickly contrasted by the fact that when Willis later appears to break into Cookie's house, we are quickly made aware that this is regular procedure for him when paying late-night visits (so as not to alarm his elderly friend), and Cookie quickly greets him not with hostility but with the offer of a drink. When Willis is later imprisoned for a crime that everyone believes he did not commit, the sheriff's team (and the external investigator's party) is made up of a mixed-race group, all of whom are professionals who work closely together and are obviously reliant on each other's skills. Furthermore, everyone (regardless of racial origin) is equally committed to freeing Willis and tracking down the real culprit. Even Camille, by far the least sympathetic character in the film, is shocked at Willis' incarceration, and when she fails to speak up on his behalf it is not out of disregard for his fate, but rather because she wants to avoid revealing her own complicated entanglement in an increasingly convoluted case. It seems that this heartfelt acceptance of racial parity in the town means that the fictional Deep South of *Cookie's Fortune* is not the same place that was depicted in films such as, for instance, Alan Parker's *Mississippi Burning* (1988) or Joel Schumacher's *A Time to Kill* (1996).

Altman appears to render Holly Springs as a kind of latter-day utopia, where a quiet effort is made by the townsfolk to avoid any conflict (racial or otherwise), and harmony is not taken for granted, but is instead something which must be cherished and maintained. Together with the expansive cast of eccentric characters and the relaxed pace of the film's plot, this combines to create an effective and multi-faceted film which is both proficient and appealing.

Tyler seems very relaxed and at ease in refining Emma into an offbeat and congenial character, and nicely conveys the fact that beneath Emma's fiercely independent personality lies a deeply caring and sensitive individual. Her antipathy with her monstrous aunt and ineffectual mother is neatly realised, and contrasts well with her obvious concern for Cookie and Willis. By the film's conclusion, we are left in little doubt that Emma has abandoned her temporary wanderlust, returning fully to the embrace of Holly Springs and its denizens. The closing sequence, where she joins Willis, Jack Palmer and Lester Boyle for one of their frequent fishing sessions, suggests that she has indeed come back for good (something made all the more obvious as she gently hints at her growing feelings for Jason).

*Cookie's Fortune* was generally well-received by the critics,[54] and went on to be nominated for numerous prizes including the Edgar Allan Poe Awards (for Anne Rapp's screenplay), several Independent Spirit Awards, and a Golden Berlin Bear at the 1999 Berlin International Film Festival (Altman himself was to win the Prize of the Guild of German Art House Cinemas at this same Festival). The film's success was to continue Altman's long-running winning streak which had lasted throughout most of the 1990s. His next film, *Dr T and the Women*, was to be his first feature of the new millennium, and – like *Cookie's Fortune* – was also to feature Tyler in a prominent role.

Tyler talks about her appearance in *Cookie's Fortune*, and her experiences of working with Robert Altman, in an article by Sheila Johnston which appears in the 13 August 1999 issue of *The Evening Standard*.[55]

Another interview where she discusses the film, and some of her other roles which took place at around the same time, can be found in Geoffrey Macnab's 'Liv and Kicking', which appears in the 1 August 1999 edition of *The Sunday Herald*.[56]

Tyler gives an in-depth interview about her film career at the time of the release of *Cookie's Fortune* with Graham Fuller and fellow actress Drew Barrymore, in the April 1999 issue of *Interview* magazine.[57]

# 10

# ONEGIN (1999)

*Seven Arts International/ Baby Productions/ Canwest/ Rysher Entertainment/ Starz!*

**Director:** Martha Fiennes
**Producers:** Simon Bosanquet and Ileen Maisel
**Screenwriters:** Peter Ettedgui and Michael Ignatieff, based on the verse novel by Alexander Pushkin

MAIN CAST

| | |
|---|---|
| **Ralph Fiennes** | Evgeny Onegin |
| **Toby Stephens** | Vladimir Lensky |
| **Liv Tyler** | Tatyana Larina |
| **Lena Headey** | Olga Larina |
| **Martin Donovan** | Prince Nikitin |
| **Alun Armstrong** | Zaretsky |

Tyler was to make her return to costume drama with *Onegin*, though it would prove to be a very different historical story to the modernised, surreally anachronistic Eighteenth Century of *Plunkett and Macleane*. *Onegin* was a film adaptation of Alexander Pushkin's famous 1831 verse novel *Eugene Onegin*, and came about through an artistic collaboration between star Ralph Fiennes, who also served as executive producer, and his sister Martha, the film's director. It is fair to say that *Onegin*'s approach to its subject matter strongly bears the imprimatur of Ralph Fiennes' own performance style: it is powerful, refined and elegant, whilst always remaining capably understated.

*Onegin* was to mark the feature film debut of Martha Fiennes, who was already a skilled director in other media. By adapting one of Pushkin's best-known works for a modern audience, she was to face a considerable challenge. Pushkin was, after all, a Russian literary figure of equivalent stature to the likes of Chekhov, Dostoevsky and Tolstoy, and *Eugene Onegin* was one of his most notable masterpieces. The story had last appeared on the big screen in Roman Tikhomirov's acclaimed 1959 version, an adaptation of Pyotr Tchaikovsky's famous opera *Yevgeni Onegin*. However, other adaptations had appeared even earlier than that; silent versions of the tale had been screened in 1911 (Visili Goncharov's *Yevgeni Onegin*) and 1919 (Alfred Halm's *Eugen Onegin*). Thus Martha Fiennes was faced with the prospect of creating a new version of Pushkin's story which would be both faithful to the original text and relevant to contemporary viewers.

In the Russia of the early Nineteenth Century, a well-to-do St Petersburg socialite named Evgeny Onegin (Ralph Fiennes) finds that he has been bequeathed a large country estate in the will of his recently-departed uncle. As Onegin has squandered most of his own fortune on gambling and high living, he decides to move out into the country in order to visit his uncle's estate and claim his inheritance.

Initially, Onegin finds rural life to be somewhat jarring in comparison to his high-flying urban lifestyle. He initially finds what he considers to be a provincial lack of cultural refinement distasteful in comparison to his life in St Petersburg. However, he finds the inhabitants of the neighbouring estates to be welcoming and hospitable, meeting young poet Vladimir Lensky (Toby Stephens), and subsequently the family of Lensky's fiancé, the Larins. Madame Larina (Harriet Walter) is a gentle, courteous widow who wishes only to ensure the best possible future for her two daughters Olga (Lena Headey) and Tatyana (Liv Tyler). Olga is warm-hearted but ultimately somewhat insipid; besotted with Lensky, she acts as his poetic muse, and Vladimir reciprocates her affection wholeheartedly. The soulful Tatyana, however, is a very different character: highly intelligent, well-read and independent of mind, she is instantly attracted to the cool, iconoclastic Mr Onegin. Her admiration starts to become apparent when Onegin announces, to the astonishment of his new neighbours, that he intends to rent his uncle's estate to the serfs who farm its land. Madame Larina and Lensky are flabbergasted by Onegin's bold, socially unconventional attitude, whereas Tatyana openly commends it. However, while Tatyana approves of what she perceives to be Onegin's sense of social justice, his actual attitude is, in truth, one of apathy.

Matters become more complicated when Tatyana, increasingly enamoured with Onegin, decides to outline her feelings for him in a heartfelt letter. Delivered to him the following day, Onegin appears nonplussed by Tatyana's impassioned declaration of love, first resolving to burn it before changing his mind and quietly retaining it.

Some time later, Tatyana's family is celebrating her Name Day. Onegin is invited to the party and arrives, albeit late, to Tatyana's unspoken joy. Once the festivities are underway, she breaks off from the crowd and meets with Onegin to discuss her feelings for him. However, he heartlessly rebuffs her advances, advising her to rein in her emotional impulses and voicing his disdain for romance. Marriage, he says, inevitably ends in boredom and is ultimately an unnecessary and pointless diversion. Tatyana is totally crushed by his callousness.

Hardly missing a beat, Onegin then returns to the party and begins to shamelessly flirt with Olga, dancing with her to the increasing discomfort of Lensky. When pressed by the young poet about the impropriety of his behaviour, Onegin merely shrugs off his reprimand, asserting his view that the naïve Olga would be receptive to any man's advances. This bluntness infuriates Lensky, who – desperate to defend the honour of his beloved fiancé – challenges Onegin to a duel.

Although considering the dispute to be something of a waste of time, Onegin answers the challenge and reluctantly takes part in a pistol duel which fatally wounds Lensky. Shocked at the death of the man who had once been his friend, Onegin finds himself wracked with grief for the first time in his life. However, the damage has been done. Witnessing the duel from a distance, a distraught Tatyana races home to inform Olga of the death of Lensky, then later decides to visit Onegin himself to confront him over the issue. However, by the time she arrives, his uncle's mansion is empty. The elderly housekeeper informs Tatyana that Onegin has departed for an unknown destination, and that he appears to have no plans to return.

Some years later, Onegin returns to St Petersburg a changed man. The gambling and trappings of high society which occupied him in times past are now of no interest to him, and he finds himself alienated from old acquaintances. One evening, quite by chance, he is attending a ball hosted by his cousin, Prince Nikitin (Martin Donovan), when he discovers Tatyana once again. However, his elation soon turns to grief when he finds that she is now married to his cousin, and has been for some time.

Vexed by his troubled emotions, Onegin writes to Tatyana in secret to declare his new-found love for her. However, in an ironic reversal of fortune, she burns his letter before Nikitin can uncover his cousin's dishonourable intentions. Faced with no alternative, Onegin decides to face Tatyana in person and pronounce his burning desire for her once and for all. But given the painful history which has passed between them, her response – when it comes – is to have a profound and lasting effect on Onegin.

Tyler's performance as Tatyana is quite unlike any that she had given before; it is almost certainly her strongest on-screen appearance since *Stealing Beauty*. She manages to articulate Tatyana's every emotion with great skill, from the joy of her blossoming love for Onegin to the heartbreak of his thoughtless rejection, and Tyler's trademark subtlety in expressing her character's sensitivity of feeling is honed here to great effect. Through Tyler, Tatyana's still waters run deep, and although she brings great emotional believability to the character in the early part of the film, it is more than matched by her later appearance as the rather more jaded, quietly sorrowful Tatyana – the successful society wife who materially wants for nothing, but yet knows that she can never achieve that which she desired most.

Her performance is aided greatly by the chemistry that exists between Tatyana and Ralph Fiennes' Onegin. By the time of the film's production, the dashing, handsome Fiennes was already a huge star both in his native Britain and in the international arena. He had been twice Oscar-nominated for his appearances in Steven Spielberg's *Schindler's List* (1993) and Anthony Minghella's *The English Patient* (1996), and had also received many nominations ranging from the Golden Globes to the BAFTA Film Awards, where his performance as Amon Goethe in *Schindler's List* won him the Best Supporting Actor Award in 1993. He uses his world-class acting talents in *Onegin* with great distinction, bringing Pushkin's eponymous protagonist to life with all of his world-weary cynicism intact. Furthermore, Fiennes more than looks the part of Pushkin's troubled anti-hero, his saturnine good looks complimented by Onegin's impeccably tailored suits. His black cape and jauntily-angled stovepipe hat mark him out as a distinctive character against the frosty background of wintry St Petersburg.

Onegin's insensitive dismissal of his provincial neighbours, in the face of their accepting and welcoming attitude, effectively foregrounds the character's wider disparagement of the world at large. He is an individual who never truly belongs, and indeed he often seems to make a discernible effort not to fit in. When Tatyana offers him her heart, with all of the vital hope of youth, his uncaring rejection of her – and the devastating pain and embarrassment that this causes Tatyana – is almost painful to watch. Just as Tyler so ably conveys Tatyana's emotional vibrancy, Fiennes provides perfect contrast with Onegin's stark indifference.

However, the tables are turned following Onegin's emotional rebirth following the death of Lensky. Whilst Fiennes perfectly encapsulates the regret and mental anguish which is burgeoning within Onegin, Tyler brings a wonderfully ice-cool equanimity and graceful poise to the older Tatyana. She is faithful to her new husband Nikitin, even in spite of the depth of her feelings for Onegin, and she is adamant that Onegin's folly will not bring shame and scandal upon the new life that she has built for herself. Only in the remarkable final scene between Tatyana and Onegin, in one of the drawing rooms of the Nikitin palace, does she allow her composure to crack. Yet nothing that Onegin can say or do is able to change the fact that his earlier actions have denied him a happiness that is now forever outwith his grasp.

*Onegin*'s visual style is highly accomplished, and Martha Fiennes manages to convey both the beauty of the cold, unforgiving Russian landscape, and the unique individuality of Pushkin's depiction of the Russian people. The contrast is well made between the sympathetic, unpretentious charm of the rural families and the cruel, rather callous edge of St Petersburg's ennui-affected socialites. This comparison between two very different aspects of Nineteenth Century Russian life is also evident in Magnus Fiennes' evocative, haunting soundtrack, which touches on a variety of different musical styles to great effect as it elegantly compliments the transition between the rural and urban way of life.

Toby Stephens is on excellent form as the likeable, gregarious Lensky, whose genuine nature and sincere amity with Onegin is well handled, as is his reaction when his friend's increasingly provocative behaviour forces him into rash and ultimately lethal action. Like Tatyana, Lensky feels betrayed by Onegin, and is similarly confused by his friend's apparently unfounded change of heart. Stephens nicely compliments Ralph Fiennes onscreen, providing a warmth and earnestness which is singularly lacking in Onegin's character.

The film also boasts solid support from some top-notch British character actors, including Alun Armstrong as Zaretsky and Geoffrey McGivern as Audrey Petrovitch, and one of the film's highlights can be found in Simon McBurney's entertaining turn as the pompous, obsequious Monsieur Triquet – the Larin sisters' French tutor – who represents with great panache the film's main source of comic relief. Also worth looking out for is a short appearance from the radiant Francesca Annis, appearing as Katiusha.

Critical reception of *Onegin* was to prove somewhat uneven. Whilst few commentators could deny the film's epic visual appeal and scrupulous faithfulness to Pushkin's original work,[58] many were to judge *Onegin*'s pace to be altogether too deliberate for the taste of modern audiences.[59] One factor which did achieve considerable critical approval was the depth and skill of Tyler's performance, which many considered to denote a high water-mark in her career thus far. Her portrayal of Tatyana Larina was to earn her the Golden Aries Award for Best Foreign Actress at the 1999 Russian Guild of Film Critics Awards – one of Russia's most prestigious film industry ceremonies.

Martha Fiennes was nominated, along with Ileen Maisel and Simon Bosanquet, for the Alexander Korda Award for Best British Film at the 2000 BAFTA Film Awards, and won the ALFS Award for British Newcomer of the Year that same year for her work on *Onegin*. She was to return to motion picture directing in 2005 with her next feature, *Chromophobia*, which was also to feature Ralph

Fiennes.

*Onegin* offered Tyler a role of unparalleled scope and emotional depth, and it was one that she was to engage with fully, bringing intensity and vigour to Tatyana Larina more than any other character that she had portrayed up until this point. Like *Stealing Beauty* and *Inventing the Abbotts* before it, *Onegin* reiterated the fact that Tyler's acting talents were becoming increasingly versatile, and that the adaptability of her performance style was proving to be considerable. Although *Armageddon* had placed her more firmly in the public eye, *Onegin* had confirmed beyond doubt that she had the genuine acting ability to justify her rapidly rising fame, and her performance as Tatyana remains one of her most accomplished and touching to date.

## FURTHER READING

There are a number of different translations of Alexander Pushkin's original verse novel, some more recent than others. One version that is particularly worth reading is Tom Beck's new 2004 translation, which contains a very informative introduction and detailed notes throughout.[60]

Tyler briefly talks about her thoughts on *Onegin*, as well as some of the other films that she was working on at the time, in an interview with Christina Kelly in the August 1998 issue of *Jane* magazine.[61] She also discusses *Onegin*, again only in concise terms, with Cindy Pearlman in the 18 April 1999 edition of the *Chicago Sun-Times*.[62]

An interesting article by Peter Bradshaw, which centres on Ralph and Martha Fiennes' efforts in bringing *Onegin* to the big screen, can be found in the 19 November 1999 issue of *The Guardian*.[63] This theme is also followed in the article 'A Fiennes family affair', which appeared in the 18 November 1999 edition of London's *The Evening Standard*.[64]

Both Martha and Ralph Fiennes are interviewed about the filming on *Onegin* by Richard Mowe in the 14 November 1999 issue of *The Sunday Herald*.[65] A rewarding overview of Ralph Fiennes' career leading up to *Onegin* can be found in Thomas Sutcliffe's profile of the actor, which appeared in the 12 February 2000 edition of *The Independent*.[66]

# 11

# DR T AND THE WOMEN (2000)

*Sandcastle 5 Productions/ Dr T Inc.*

**Director**: Robert Altman
**Producers**: Robert Altman and James McLindon
**Screenwriter**: Anne Rapp

MAIN CAST

| | |
|---|---|
| **Richard Gere** | Dr Sullivan Travis |
| **Helen Hunt** | Bree Davis |
| **Farrah Fawcett** | Kate Travis |
| **Tara Reid** | Connie Travis |
| **Kate Hudson** | Dee Dee Travis |
| **Liv Tyler** | Marilyn |

Robert Altman's first film of the Twenty-First Century was to prove to be a marked change from his most recent, *Cookie's Fortune*. Never one to rest on his laurels, or indeed shy away from exploring new subject matter, Altman was to use his finely-honed observational skills in *Dr T and the Women* to delve into complex subjects such as social class and the nature of femininity, whilst ensuring that the comedy-drama of the film's storyline never remained less than entertaining. Displaying many of Altman's well-known hallmarks, including a very large ensemble cast (the majority of whom were prominent names in the industry) and an ever-playful narrative knowingness, the film was also to provide Tyler with a role that was far removed from her previous collaboration with the director, and which accordingly contained entirely new challenges for her performance skills.

Dr Sullivan Travis (Richard Gere) is a highly successful and respected gynaecologist practicing in an upmarket area of Dallas, Texas. His amiable manner is matched by his professional skill, and his expertise is highly sought after by some of the city's wealthiest and most influential ladies. But Travis is not without influence of his own; he is a valued member of a leading country club, where he plays golf with some of the area's other prominent professionals, and his advice is regularly consulted by lobbyists and other assorted local glitterati.

However, Travis' cushy life is about to become much more complicated. His wife Kate (Farrah Fawcett) is beset by a rare psychological disorder while shopping at an high-class mall in town, which is only discovered when she decides to strip naked and cavort in an indoor fountain. Admitted to a private mental institution, one of the resident psychiatric consultant pronounces that Kate is suffering from Hestia complex – an unusual syndrome which arises in women who, loved by their friends and family and suffering no material want, lose the will to improve themselves due to the fact that their lives are, to all intents and purposes, already perfect. As Kate quickly regresses into a childlike state, the psychiatrists admit that the nature of the complex is so newly defined that they are at a loss as to how to treat it.

Travis is further stressed by the impending wedding of one of his daughters, sometime-cheerleader Dee Dee (Kate Hudson). Intensive preparations are underway to organise an elaborate outdoor wedding, overseen in part by Travis' eccentric sister-in-law Peggy (Laura Dern), who has recently moved into the family home with her three boisterous children.

The ongoing situation with his relatives, while nerve-racking, barely slows Travis down. He thrives in the non-stop environment of his excruciatingly busy clinic. However, even his stalwart head receptionist Carolyn (Shelley Long) is having trouble fitting everyone into the already-packed schedule – particularly with so many unannounced arrivals demanding immediate treatment. Thus he is grateful for his few chances to escape the high-pressure backdrop of work every once and a while, making for the golf course whenever the opportunity avails itself. On one such trip, he meets Bree Davis (Helen Hunt), the club's new female golf pro, who takes a shine to Travis and offers to partner him on the fairway.

Travis and Bree begin to grow close to each other, and slowly she helps him to deal with the difficulties of his wife's inexplicable breakdown. However, Travis' emotions grow increasingly conflicted. His attraction to Bree eventually leads to them sharing the night together, unbeknownst to his family and friends, though Travis has little time to come to terms with his turbulent feelings before receiving an unexpected call from his lawyer at work. Kate, it seems, has decided to divorce him.

Just when things look as though they couldn't get any more convoluted, Travis' other daughter, tour guide and conspiracy theorist Connie (Tara Reid), decides to break some confidential news to him. Dee Dee, whose marriage is now imminent, had a passionate affair a year previously while at college in Houston. This in itself may seem immaterial, but Dee Dee's lover, a cheerful young woman named Marilyn (Liv Tyler), has now been invited to be maid of honour at the wedding. Connie is all but certain that the pair's romantic relationship is being rekindled in secret. Should Travis do as Connie recommends and stop the wedding before the groom uncovers the truth?

*Dr T and the Women* is a strikingly different film from *Cookie's Fortune* both in tone and subject, yet both display Altman's highly distinctive style and dynamism. The opening shot in Travis' waiting room, for instance, is a masterclass in impeccably orchestrated choreography, full of Altman's trademark overlapping dialogue and plenty of well-observed asides from returning screenwriter Anne Rapp. The polished marble of Dallas' upper-class malls and luxurious homes contrasts effectively with Travis' trips to the well-tended golf course and relaxed duck hunting sessions, showcasing the opulence of the locality with some splendid cinematography. There are also some recurring visual motifs, such as the many fountains (both interior and exterior) which crop up throughout the film to good effect, and Lyle Lovett's soundtrack is also notably lively and invigorating, complementing the action well.

Although the film's ambience could not be further removed from the folksy charm of his previous film's Deep South locale, the central target of the satire remains very much the same – the pretensions of the excessively well-groomed chattering classes. From Travis' polymorphously dysfunctional family to the incessant backbiting of his occasionally egregious patients, Altman invariably aims his critical eye unwaveringly at the affected self-importance of the idle rich. Although the film's outcome is not as definitive as the final downfall of Camille Dixon in *Cookie's Fortune*, by the conclusion of *Dr T and the Women* we are left in little doubt of Altman's underlying thematic intentions.

Tyler's role, although rather more brief than her appearance as Emma Duvall in *Cookie's Fortune*, is nonetheless pivotal to the plot. Her appearance as Marilyn was her first attempt at portraying a Sapphic relationship on screen, and she carries it off with both style and confidence. Her scenes with Kate Hudson's

Dee Dee, though sometimes only momentary, do articulate great warmth and genuine affection. It is this convincing chemistry between them which ensures that the resolution of their relationship at the film's conclusion does come across as a logical outcome, rather than an awkwardly forced one. Tyler also works well with Richard Gere in their one short scene together at Travis' clinic, and the subtle comic timing which is shared between them does make it seem rather regrettable that the characters didn't have more mutual screen time.

Richard Gere's lead performance has much to recommend it – particularly his studiously calm, mild-mannered acceptance of his life and family slowly self-destructing around him – and like many of Altman's films, *Dr T and the Women* featured numerous noteworthy supporting performances from top Hollywood acting talent. Among the most notable are Laura Dern as the ditzy Peggy, whose good intentions are inevitably skewed by her secret tippling habit, and Shelley Long's quirky but super-efficient Carolyn. Kate Hudson and Tara Reid complement each other well as the mismatched Travis sisters, though special mention is reserved for Farrah Fawcett's audacious portrayal of Kate's mental breakdown – a performance which is well-observed and never handled flippantly.

The controversial subject matter of *Dr T and the Women* meant that the film almost inevitably divided the critics. Some commentators welcomed Altman's return to the kind of free-wheeling storytelling that he had used to great effect throughout the 1970s,[67] whereas others considered the film's treatment of women and femininity to be too ambiguous, condescending, or even openly misogynistic.[68] This latter charge sparked considerable critical debate which quickly became somewhat entrenched, though it is perhaps germane to note that the film's relatively few male characters – represented largely by Travis' friends at the country club, such as Robert Hays' Harlan – are shown to be at least as directionless and ineffectual as any of the less-sympathetic female characters. Indeed, among the most benevolent of all the female characters is Bree, who is independent and forthright without ever compromising her femininity. Her obvious professional competence at the country club, and her willingness to take the lead in comforting Travis by instigating an informal relationship with him, emphasise that she is in no way depicted detrimentally (or less capably) on account of her gender. Even Carolyn, for all her unrequited desire for Travis, displays unparalleled organisational skills that are obviously key to the smooth running of the clinic. In other words, the characters who are most treated most critically throughout the film – irrespective of gender – are those who most display the most obvious qualities of exaggerated social posturing; those who transcend these limitations are generally treated more compassionately.

*Dr T and the Women* was nominated for a Golden Lion Award at the 2000 Venice Film Festival, and also earned Richard Gere a nomination for a Golden Satellite Award for his performance in the title role. Altman's next film would be *Gosford Park* (2001), which would bring him renewed critical and commercial acclaim and would ultimately excise any concern over the division of commentators on the perceived virtues and vices of *Dr T and the Women.*

*Gosford Park* received near-unanimous critical approval, and earned seven Academy Award nominations (including his fifth nomination of his career for the Best Director Oscar) as well as winning the Alexander Korda Award for Best British Film at the BAFTA Film Awards in 2002. The film received scores of award nominations across the world, and once again underscored Robert Altman's reputation as one of America's most prolific and diversely-gifted directorial talents.

For Tyler, *Dr T and the Women* was to provide another opportunity to demonstrate her ability to convincingly blend dramatic and comedic elements into a role – all the more challenging in this instance, where her screen time was more limited than in her previous appearance in a film directed by Altman. The experience was to serve Tyler well when it came to her next film role, which would call on her to engage comedy skills of a rather less subtle variety.

## FURTHER READING

There are numerous books dealing with Robert Altman's hugely significant contribution to American film over the years. One which is particularly worth looking out for is *Robert Altman's Subliminal Reality* by Robert T. Self,[69] a vastly informative reference work which discusses the many themes underlying Altman's prolific filmography. Most significant to the above discussion is the chapter 'Resisting Women: Madness, Dreams, and Art', which explores elements of both *Cookie's Fortune* and *Dr T and the Women*, amongst some of Altman's many other works.[70]

Tyler talks briefly about working with Robert Altman, on both *Cookie's Fortune* and *Dr T and the Women*, in her interview with Lesley O'Toole in the 19 April 2001 issue of *This Is London*.[71]

A retrospective interview between Tyler and co-star Kate Hudson, conducted by Tyler herself, appeared in the March 2003 edition of *Interview* magazine.[72]

# 12

# ONE NIGHT AT McCOOL'S
## (2001)

*Further Films/ October Films*

**Director**: Harald Zwart
**Producers**: Michael Douglas and Allison Lyon Segan
**Screenwriter**: Stan Seidel

MAIN CAST

| | |
|---|---|
| **Liv Tyler** | Jewel Valentine |
| **Matt Dillon** | Randy |
| **John Goodman** | Detective Dehling |
| **Paul Reiser** | Carl |
| **Michael Douglas** | Mr Burmeister |
| **Andrew Silverstein** | Utah/ Elmo |

With *One Night at McCool's*, Tyler would once again be called upon to exhibit her comic talents – this time in a much darker and more edgy comedy than she had ever appeared in previously. As had been the case in *Stealing Beauty*, she was very much to take the centre stage in *One Night at McCool's*, and like Bertolucci's film before it, she is not only pivotal to the film's action, but is the fundamental activator of the action itself.

*One Night at McCool's* was to be the American feature film debut of Harald Zwart. Already a successful director of music videos and in commercial advertising, Zwart had also previously helmed a number of films in his native Scandinavia including *Parents* (1992), *Act Naturally* (1993) and, most prominently, *Hamilton* (1998). It is difficult to imagine that Zwart could have asked for a more impressive cast to feature in his American motion picture breakthrough; *McCool's* included a solid array of major established talent, from experienced stalwarts of film and television to a bona-fide Hollywood superstar in the form of Michael Douglas, who also served as one of the film's producers.

The film concerns a complicated series of events which begins on one eventful night at a bar named McCool's. The spiralling complexities of the fallout from that night are related from three different points of view, all stemming from one pivotal incident.

Randy (Matt Dillon), the bartender at McCool's, is locking up in the small hours of the morning when he notices a stunning woman (Liv Tyler) being assaulted in a car by the brutish Utah (Andrew Silverstein). Randy manages to save her from her assailant's grasp, and once confronted, Utah speeds away from the scene. The woman introduces herself as Jewel Valentine, and – keen to avoid any further unwanted aggravation from thugs like the one Randy has just fought off – she asks if she can accompany him home to safety. Things go well between them, and to his surprise Randy finds himself spending the night with her.

His high spirits quickly dissipate, however, when he discovers that he has been set up. Jewel is in partnership with Utah, and they have arranged to burgle Randy's house at gunpoint following their impromptu tête-à-tête. However, it is quickly apparent that Randy has nothing of any value worth stealing, so when Utah arrives he decides to return to the bar instead, where he intends to steal the takings from its night-safe. Randy hurriedly tries to gain access to the cash, but as he is doing so Jewel decides to shift her loyalties from Randy to Utah. She takes the initiative and shoots her former partner at point-blank range.

Randy begins to get agitated when the police arrive at the scene of the shooting; from his crouching position next to the safe at the time of the murder, he clearly wouldn't have been able to fire the bullet which killed Utah. However, keen to avoid implicating Jewel in the crime at all, he concocts a none-too-convincing story for the investigating officer, Detective Dehling (John Goodman). Dehling is not for a moment convinced by Randy's story, but in the absence of any extenuating proof he is forced to let him go. However, like Randy before him, Dehling finds himself strangely fascinated with Jewel during a brief passing encounter with her in the bar.

Jewel swiftly moves in with Randy, and slowly but surely begins to transform his drab home into a haven of domestic bliss. Randy, however, is rather uneasy by the rapid pace that Jewel has integrated herself into his life and home – especially as she is quickly racking up purchases on credit in spite of the fact that his source of income has been terminated (he has been sacked from his job at McCool's following the shooting). Randy is further perplexed when he and Jewel are invited for dinner at the home of his cousin, a sleazy attorney named Carl (Paul Reiser), only to find that his relative is also inextricably drawn to Jewel.

Despite Randy's lack of success in finding new employment, Jewel's material ambitions continue to rise. She gets a job at a perfume counter, but the meagre wages are barely covering their existing debt. Deciding that more radical action is necessary, she steals a car (telling Randy that she has borrowed it from an unseen friend), and calculatingly manages to cajole him into burgling the home of his former boss at the bar. The operation goes all too well, and Jewel realises that she has hit on a winning *modus operandi* to perfect her dream home.

Things get complicated when Jewel seduces a squalid, upmarket lawyer by the name of Greg Spradling (Eric Schaeffer), in order to allow Randy time to burgle his opulent house. Randy gains entry easily enough and begins to dismantle Spradling's formidable home entertainment system, only for the lawyer to unexpectedly arrive home with Jewel – against her wishes. Randy hides away while Spradling coaxes Jewel into his bedroom, but finds himself locked in a cupboard as Spradling viciously attempts to rape Jewel. Jewel manages to fight him off, but rather more effectively than she had intended; he is killed when his own DVD player falls on him from a height, crushing his skull.

Jewel is infuriated when Randy refuses to continue his theft of the late Spradling's electronics collection, preferring instead to make a hasty getaway. She berates him for his cowardice, and her disdain comes to a head the following day when the pair are visited by Dehling, who remains highly suspicious of Randy. Jewel reminds the detective of his late wife, and during his questioning he becomes subconsciously protective of her. Discovering that she has suffered injuries during her fight with Spradling, Dehling naturally blames Randy and advises Jewel to take out a restraining order against him. She has no objection to Randy's ejection from his own property, especially when she has the chance of legal advice from his own cousin, Carl.

Carl, however, has other ideas, and instantly abuses his professional relationship with Jewel by talking her into kinky sado-masochistic sex games. Jewel is amenable to this, but on the other hand seems oddly disinterested by Carl's legal expertise. Instead, she begins to toy with the affections of Dehling, who continues to visit her obsessively. The detective has started to take an almost fanatical interest in Jewel, believing a relationship between them to be nothing less than the will of God. However, to complicate things even further, Dehling discovers that Carl was in competition with Spradling for the same promotion in their law firm, which (unknown to Carl himself) provides a motive for murder. When forensic evidence surfaces to implicate both Randy and Jewel in the death of Spradling, Dehling finds himself with a major quandary on his hands.

Randy, now desperate, has been tracking down the services of local assassin Mr Burmeister (Michael Douglas), a mature hitman who has a serious penchant for bingo. After Randy relates his side of the story, Burmeister agrees to take on a job for him: to put an end to Jewel's scheming once and for all.

However, Burmeister later heads for Randy's former home to find not Jewel, but an unexpected (and unintended) assembly of her would-be suitors instead. Before he can take any action of his own, events take a rapid twist due to the unforeseen arrival of a new participant on the scene – someone who will bring permanent finality to events.

*One Night at McCool's* is a nimbly-handled piece of filmmaking, full of surprising turnarounds and inspired developments. It benefits greatly from the fact that the narrative is split between the three male protagonists; while Randy is relating his story (through flashback) to Burmeister, Carl discusses the events from his own point of view to his analyst, Dr Green (Reba McEntire), and an angst-ridden Dehling confesses his emotional torment to his priest, Father Jimmy (Richard Jenkins). Using this method, Zwart keeps the audience guessing all the way through the narrative as to how and why events are transpiring in the manner that they do. Particularly astute is the way that each character pictures themselves as being much more sympathetic than anyone who is competing for Jewel's affections, whilst they personally are being cast as less agreeable in the concurrent accounts of the others. Jewel, on the other hand, is never perceived from an entirely objective view – we see her through everyone else's eyes, but never from her own perspective. This lends the character just the right air of mystery to keep her plans enigmatic enough to engage audience interest; in many ways, Jewel's origins and motivations are just as much a mystery at the end of the film as they were at the beginning, for the nature of her character is projected onto her by the expectation and anticipation of other people.

As Jewel, Tyler seems to delight in sending up her evolving image as a movie sex-symbol. Nowhere is this more evident than in the car-wash sequence, which was to form one of her most memorably iconic scenes to date. Writhing over a soapy automobile in slow-motion soft focus, sponge in hand, as Dehling watches slack-jawed from the distance, Zwart obviously revels in the sheer over-the-top absurdity of the whole scenario, and Tyler plays the scene with a marvellous tongue-in-cheek panache. In short, it can be seen as a modern reflection of Marilyn Monroe's skirts billowing above a subway grating in Billy Wilder's *The Seven Year Itch* (1955), and although the execution between the two films could hardly be more different, the implication of dangerous temptation remains more or less the same.

Stan Seidel's swiftly-moving script is full of pithy dialogue, particularly in the case of the motor-mouthed Carl (a terrifically-observed performance from Paul Reiser), whose dialogue is so rapid that it sometimes seems to be delivered by machine-gun. Reiser's memorably verbose appearance is just one of the film's numerous worthy performances. John Goodman's stoic, self-reproaching detective is nicely handled, but the show is stolen by two-time Academy Award winner Michael Douglas, one of the most sought-after performers in America, who puts in an excellent turn as the cynical, bingo-obsessed assassin Burmeister. Replete with a world-weary growl and a hilariously bouffant wig, Douglas is an admirable foil for Matt Dillon's Carl as the harried bartender relates his increasingly desperate story to the intrigued (but almost totally unmoved) older man.

Dillon had received much praise for his many dramatic roles in films such as *Drugstore Cowboy* (1989) and *Wild Things* (1998), before delighting audiences with his larger-than-life appearance as Pat Healy in Bobby and Peter Farrelly's smash hit comedy *There's Something About Mary* (1998). He reminds audiences of his refined comic talents in *McCool's*, making Randy appear charmingly bewildered from the very moment that he encounters Jewel. He seems lost even in his own home, as Jewel is gradually renovating it into an outlandish habitat where even the familiar can become oddly unfamiliar. (This is achieved via some wonderfully stylised set design – the finely-honed small details of Jewel's offbeat home design master-plan are a joy to uncover in repeated viewings.)

Tyler manages to bring an endearing pseudo-innocence to Jewel's cunningly manipulative scheming, to say nothing of the character's stunningly casual approach towards criminality. Jewel's desire to create the perfect home is, at times, almost touching, even if her obsession with DVD players and other home entertainment technology tends to border on the pathological. It is to Tyler's credit that she manages to craft Jewel into someone who appears rounded and believable even when her character is so indistinct, being (as it is) reflected through the perspective of outsiders and thus never revealing its true nature. Jewel's actions at the film's surprising climax are both startling and oddly logical, and seem entirely in tune with the darkly comic observations of the rest of the film; just like Jewel herself, morality here is entirely a question of individual viewpoint.

The critical reception of *One Night at McCool's* was variable. Many commentators were to equate the film's unconventional narrative structure to Akira Kurosawa's ground-breaking masterpiece *Rashômon* (1950), though some drew this comparison more favourably than others. A number of reviewers praised *McCool's* for its cleverly shifting viewpoint and refusal to take itself too seriously,[73] whereas others were less complimentary, considering some of the film's comedy to be forced and a few of the supporting performances to be a trifle stilted.[74]

Following the high-profile release of *One Night at McCool's*, Harald Zwart would continue in American cinema with another mainstream hit two years later, in the form of *Agent Cody Banks* (2003), as well as providing the story for that film's sequel in 2004.

*One Night at McCool's* had provided Tyler with the perfect chance to show just how far she had developed her comic talents since the time of *Empire Records*. She had taken a relaxed approach to the gentle comedy elements of *Cookie's Fortune* and *Dr T and the Women*, but here she seems to take great care and precision in presenting Jewel as a character with both humorous and dangerous qualities. Jewel is never presented as spitefully malevolent, but her treachery – however persuasively and charismatically it is portrayed – reminds the audience that Miss Valentine is the very embodiment of the modern femme-fatale. This multi-faceted performance, especially given the film's high-status nature, was not only to reassert Tyler's continuing appeal as an attractive lead actress, but also helped to clearly highlight her ever-expanding acting range.

Tyler's well-publicised appearance in *One Night at McCool's* meant that media coverage of her performance was perhaps at its most prominent since *Armageddon*. Consequently, interviews and press articles exploring her portrayal of Jewel Valentine were numerous, and the features listed below are merely the tip of a much larger media iceberg.

Tyler talks about her experiences in filming *One Night at McCool's* in an article by Karen Schoemer in the May 2001 issue of *Elle* magazine,[75] which also contains complimentary quotes from directors who had worked with her previously in her film career. She also discusses *McCool's*, along with her upcoming projects, in William Thomas' interview for the May 2001 edition of *Empire* magazine.[76]

Tyler also discusses her thoughts on acting, both in general and in *One Night at McCool's* specifically, in an interview with Lesley O'Toole for *This Is London*'s 19 April 2001 edition.[77] She gives an informative and personal interview with Stephanie Trong for the April 2001 issue of *Jane* magazine.[78] *One Night at McCool's* is also discussed in detail in Barry Didcock's interview with Tyler, which appears in the 29 April 2001 edition of *The Sunday Herald*.[79]

Tyler talks about the unusual structure of the film in her interview with Joshua Mooney in the 11 May 2001 edition of the *Chicago Sun-Times*.[80] She also discusses her preparation for the role of Jewel, including experiences from her previous films and working with her *McCool's* co-stars, in Pamela Harland's interview for the 27 April 2001 edition of *IF* Magazine.[81]

Tyler gives her experiences on *One Night at McCool's* a more individual angle in her interview with Drew Mackenzie for the 29 April 2001 issue of *The Sunday Mirror*, giving her views on the film's screenplay and discussing her busy life at the time of *McCool's* production.[82] Another quite personal account of her time working on the film can be read in Danny Leigh's article in the 19 April 2001 issue of *The Guardian*.[83] An engaging and informal overview of Tyler's work on *McCool's* can also be found in Emma Forrest's interview with her for the 7 April 2001 edition of *The Daily Telegraph*.[84]

Elif Cercel discusses *One Night at McCool's* with director Harald Zwart, including his thoughts on Tyler's performance, in the 19 April 2001 issue of *Director's World*.[85] A short but rather touching observation of Tyler's feelings at watching herself at cinema screenings of her performances can be found in the article 'Screen Fright' which appears in the 19 April 2001 edition of *The Evening Standard*.[86]

# 13

# THE LORD OF THE RINGS
# TRILOGY (2001-03)

*New Line Cinema/ WingNut Films/ Lord Zweite Productions Deutschland Filmproduktion GmbH/ The Saul Zaentz Company*

**Director**: Peter Jackson

**Producers**: Peter Jackson, Barrie M. Osborne, Fran Walsh, Tim Sanders (*The Fellowship of the Ring* only)

**Screenwriters**: Fran Walsh, Philippa Boyens, Peter Jackson, Stephen Sinclair (*The Two Towers* only), based on the novels by J.R.R. Tolkien

MAIN CAST

| | |
|---|---|
| **Elijah Wood** | Frodo Baggins |
| **Viggo Mortensen** | Aragorn/ Strider |
| **Ian McKellen** | Gandalf |
| **Sean Astin** | Sam Gamgee |

| | |
|---|---|
| **Christopher Lee** | Saruman |
| **Andy Serkis** | Gollum/ Sméagol |
| **Hugo Weaving** | Elrond |
| **Liv Tyler** | Arwen Evenstar |

Although Tyler had by now appeared in a dozen films ranging from character-driven dramas to mainstream comedies, to say nothing of a hugely successful action blockbuster, her appearance as the Elvish princess Arwen Evenstar in Peter Jackson's adaptation of John Ronald Reuel Tolkien's *The Lord of the Rings* remains perhaps her most prominent role in the public eye to date. The unparalleled scope and grandeur of these films, coupled with their mass audience appeal and virtually unanimous international critical approval, were to catapult Tyler and the rest of the trilogy's huge ensemble cast into a period of worldwide fame that would last far beyond the duration of the films' respective cinema releases.

Although fantasy novels had existed before Tolkien's books, it would not be an exaggeration to say that he profoundly re-energised the genre with his Middle-earth novels, creating a highly distinctive prose style and mythic resonance which would generate fertile creative ground for many other authors who would come after him.[87] His books have been firm favourites with readers of all ages, and *The Lord of the Rings* was frequently voted among the favourite novels of the entire Twentieth Century in various public opinion polls. The trilogy has been translated into many languages, and continues to enjoy huge international success more than fifty years after the books' original publication.

However, at the beginning of the Twenty-First Century, only one attempt had been made to adapt Tolkien's mammoth text for the big screen; Ralph Bakshi's *The Lord of the Rings* (1978). A complex fusion of live-action footage and detailed cartoon artwork, Bakshi's film was a cult hit with many fantasy and animation aficionados following its subsequent television broadcasts and release on home video and DVD. However, the film's narrative remained heavily abridged and, ultimately, was frustratingly incomplete: it concluded midway through the storyline of Tolkien's *The Two Towers*, and no sequel was ever to be filmed by Bakshi to conclude the saga on the big screen. There is, however, much to recommend a viewing of the film, not least its distinctive graphical artistry and experienced voice cast (including John Hurt, Anthony Daniels and Christopher Guard), but audiences would have to wait over two decades before the definitive adaptation of *The Lord of the Rings* would reach cinema screens.

There was great anticipation when it was announced that director Peter Jackson would be helming all three films in a new, big-budget adaptation of *The Lord of the Rings* trilogy. Although already a highly-respected director, producer and screenwriter in his native New Zealand, Jackson was less well-known on the international arena, though his reputation was growing rapidly. His directorial career had originally begun with highly memorable, low-budget cult horror films such as *Bad Taste* (1987) and *Braindead* (1992), as well as the technically clever puppet satire *Meet the Feebles* (1989). He had proven, early and beyond doubt, that he had the ability to produce impressive results from budgets which were often slender in the extreme. Soon after, the script which he had co-written for *Heavenly Creatures* (1994) – a film that he had also directed and co-produced – was nominated for the Academy Award for Best Original Screenplay in 1995. His later comic horror-fantasy *The Frighteners* (1996) had also proven to be successful with critics, thanks to its highly imaginative premise and considerable visual verve. Considering Jackson's growing following and his reputation for originality, audience expectation and critical curiosity were piqued by the news that he would now be overseeing such a huge project, with a budget comprising hundreds of millions of dollars. The result would prove to be one of the most extraordinary phenomena in modern cinema.

# THE FELLOWSHIP OF THE RING (2001)

The first film in the trilogy, *The Fellowship of the Ring* (2001), opens with a prologue which outlines the events leading up to the War of the Ring. At the conclusion of the Second Age of Middle-earth, a great army of Elves and Men were locked in battle with the forces of the Dark Lord Sauron (Sala Baker). The brutal campaign against Sauron's army is fought at the gates of Mordor, a sinister fortified land where the Dark Lord has built his stronghold of Barad-dûr (the Dark Tower). Deep within Mordor, Sauron has secretly forged the One Ring, a virtually indestructible weapon of near-limitless power which has granted him control over the lesser Ring-bearing peoples of Middle-earth – Elves, Men and Dwarves. Although it appears at first glance to be nothing more than a simple piece of costume jewellery, the One Ring is Sauron's ultimate source of power, and the massed Free Peoples of Middle-earth appear to have little chance of stopping his ruthless march to conquer the many different races who inhabit the land.

All of this is to change, however, when Sauron's plans unexpectedly go awry. Appearing on the battlefield of Dagorlad in a massive armoured suit, Sauron slays the Gondorian High-King Elendil (Peter McKenzie). The King's son, Prince Isildur (Harry Sinclair), appears destined to be the next to fall, but in a desperate fight for his life he manages to hack off one of Sauron's gloved fingers, taking the One Ring with it. Bereft of his power, Sauron's body is instantly destroyed, and his evil army of Orcs (base, corrupt creatures who serve the Dark Lord's will) is defeated soon after.

Recovering Sauron's prize, Isildur refuses to cast the One Ring into the fires of Orodruin, otherwise known as Mount Doom. This is the place of the Ring's creation, deep within Mordor, and its molten lava furnace is the only known way to destroy the weapon once and for all. The Ring is imbued with the same qualities of malice and deception as its creator, and has the ability to greatly influence the mind of its bearer. Therefore Isildur craves the power that he senses within the Ring, and will not allow himself to be parted from it. This is soon proven to be largely irrelevant, as Isildur's royal vanguard is later ambushed by a vicious party of Orcs and he is cast into the tides of the mighty River Anduin. The One Ring appears lost forever.

This opening sequence is a quite remarkable feat of cinema in itself, compressing a highly significant part of Tolkien's *Silmarillion* into a sequence which is both erudite and exciting. Jackson, and his co-writers, make plain their knowledge of (and respect for) the source text even from this early point, and the raw power of Sauron's will – as well as the dangerous persuasiveness of the One Ring – foreshadows much of the action that is to come.

Millennia later, in the Third Age of Middle-earth, Sméagol (Andy Serkis) – a Hobbit fisherman – accidentally discovers the long-forgotten One Ring on the riverbed and claims it for his own. Hobbits are diminutive, civilised bipeds, and are generally placid and social creatures. However, once Sméagol comes into the possession of the One Ring it quickly takes control of him, influencing his actions to ensure its continued survival. Turning to theft and murder, the One Ring warps Sméagol's mind and, eventually, his physical form as well. His former acquaintances brand him with the name Gollum, due to an adverse vocal tic that has afflicted him. Gollum exploits the Ring's power to grant its bearer invisibility in order to prey on others, though eventually his community works together to cast him out, exiling him to a life in the faraway Misty Mountains.

The One Ring also has the ability to greatly extend the life of its owner, however, and Gollum ekes out an existence in the caverns beneath the Misty Mountains for many centuries. Eventually, his hermit-like existence is disturbed by the arrival of another Hobbit, Bilbo Baggins (Ian Holm), who is on a journey and has lost his way. Bilbo stumbles across the One Ring, which has escaped Gollum's grasp, and resumes his adventure with little suspicion of Gollum's fury at losing his prized possession.

Bilbo returns to his home at Bag End in the Shire where he lives in peace for several decades, never imagining the power of the Ring that he has in his possession. A kind-hearted soul, Bilbo rarely uses the One Ring's power of invisibility – and even then, never for malice. However, it has extended his life to a degree which has started to raise suspicion with others in the area, and his friend and occasional adviser Gandalf the Grey (Ian McKellen) – a mysterious travelling wizard – counsels Bilbo to surrender the One Ring to his nephew, Frodo (Elijah Wood). Unbeknownst to Bilbo, Gandalf and others of his order have come to realise that Sauron is beginning to exert his influence in Middle-earth once more. Although his body had been destroyed many centuries previously, his consciousness will continue to exist as long as the One Ring remains at large. Gandalf supports Bilbo's plan to leave Hobbiton and retire to the Elvish community of Imladris Rivendell. For Frodo, however, Gandalf has other plans.

Ian McKellen and Ian Holm both make the most of these charming early sequences in Hobbiton, an idyllic community in the Shire which reflects the Hobbits' restrained, sociable approach to life. The relationship between Gandalf and Bilbo refers to *The Hobbit*, an earlier text of Tolkien's, and the adventure that the two characters shared is alluded to throughout Jackson's film. McKellen in particular is impressive in balancing Gandalf's concern for his old friend with rising alarm, as he begins to realise the true nature of the Ring that Bilbo has been harbouring over the years. Holm, on the other hand, perfectly encapsulates the whimsy and eccentricity of one of Tolkien's best-loved characters, lending him a warmth and childlike fervour for adventure that quickly endears him to the audience.

Gandalf learns that Sauron's forces are beginning to gather in Mordor once again, and that the fortifications of the Dark Lord's ancient bastion are rapidly being rebuilt. Knowing that Sauron's deadly servants, the virtually unstoppable Nazgûl (or Ring-wraiths), will be seeking the One Ring, Gandalf returns to the Shire and advises Frodo to take flight for the village of Bree. The wizard himself has other tasks to attend to, so Frodo must team up with his gardener Sam Gamgee (Sean Astin) and friends Pippin Took (Billy Boyd) and Merry Brandybuck (Dominic Monaghan), in order to spirit the One Ring away on a tortuous journey to the Elvish enclave. They face many perils along the way, but manage to evade the deadly Nazgûl thanks to the timely intervention of an enigmatic stranger named Aragorn (Viggo Mortensen) – a Ranger who claims to be an old acquaintance of Gandalf's.

Gandalf's return to the Shire, and Frodo's flight from Hobbiton, marks one instance where Jackson's film deviates quite significantly from Tolkien's original text. The time-scale is quite dramatically compressed for the benefit of the film's narrative; in the book, some seventeen years pass between Bilbo leaving for Rivendell and Gandalf reappearing at Bag End to encourage Frodo to flee. Likewise, the journey from the Shire to Bree is much shorter than Tolkien's book had suggested, and eliminates entire characters and incidents such as Tom Bombadil and the Barrow-wights in order to retain the film's swift momentum.

Viggo Mortensen makes an instant impression as Aragorn, who – along with Frodo – holds co-equal status as the hero of the trilogy. His ingenuity and dry wit are immediately apparent from his first appearance at the Inn of the Prancing Pony, and Mortensen's brooding, ominous performance perfectly encapsulates the enigmatic nature of the mysterious Ranger of the

North.

Gandalf, meanwhile, has journeyed to the tower of Orthanc in the fortress of Isengard, where he hopes to confer with the head of his Order, Saruman the White (Christopher Lee). To his dismay, it quickly becomes apparent that Saruman's mind is in thrall to the newly-arisen Sauron, and Gandalf finds himself trapped by his former friend. He witnesses Saruman's transformation of Isengard's lush grounds into a grim industrial nightmare, and realises that the White Wizard is planning to raise an army in support of the Dark Lord. Thanks to some unexpected assistance, Gandalf makes good his escape.

British acting legend Christopher Lee brings all of his weighty screen presence to bear on the character of Saruman, injecting the White Wizard with a malign intelligence and corrupt wisdom which is tinged with just the subtlest hint of underlying insanity. A veteran of many fantasy films and literary adaptations, Lee showcases his more-than-substantial experience to great effect, and finds an excellent foil in McKellen, whose own performance brilliantly reflects Gandalf's growing desperation at his friend's unfathomable betrayal.

Aragorn suggests that Frodo and his party head for Rivendell, where they will meet Gandalf. However, things begin to look grim following another attack by Sauron's minions. During a bitter struggle with the Nazgûl, Frodo is stabbed by one of the Ring-wraiths' Mordor blades and becomes seriously ill. His life is saved by the appearance of the beautiful Elvish princess Arwen Evenstar (Liv Tyler), Aragorn's lover, who uses her peerless horse-riding skills and mystical powers over the elements to speed Frodo and the One Ring safely away from their pursuers. Once at Rivendell, Arwen's father Elrond (Hugo Weaving) – the leader of the community – has Frodo's health restored, though a shard of the Mordor sword embedded in his body continues to affect him adversely.

Tyler's unexpected appearance as Arwen is inspired, and indeed her early understated playfulness with Mortensen's

Aragorn presages later explanations of the depth of love that has been shared between these two characters for many years. Likewise, Arwen's victorious escape with Frodo on horseback underscores the character's many obvious capabilities and qualities of resourcefulness, demonstrating that she is indeed a worthy match for Aragorn in a number of ways. Tyler manages to portray both urgency and serene proficiency in Arwen's manner, but most importantly of all, she makes the character's affection for Aragorn obvious and affecting from the moment that she encounters Frodo's party.

The prominent inclusion of the character of Arwen in *The Fellowship of the Ring* was to prove contentious with some Tolkien admirers and literary purists. Arwen appears only very briefly in Tolkien's original text, and the bulk of the story detailing her relationship with Aragorn is told only in the book's appendices. Her expanded role in Jackson's film led to fears that the character would be depicted as a Boadicea-style warrior queen, though of course these anxieties were ultimately to be allayed. Nonetheless, there was antagonism in some corners over the fact that the character of Glorfindel – a powerful Elf-lord of Rivendell in Tolkien's novel – had been removed in order to enlarge Arwen's role. In hindsight, this can be seen as a necessary amendment on Jackson's part in order to more convincingly develop the love story between Arwen and Aragorn, which is crucial to both characters. There is also the fact that, as Tolkien's original narrative featured very few female characters in comparison with the majority of modern films, the significance of the three foremost female players would need to be advanced as much as possible in order to promote the most effective gender balance achievable, whilst remaining true to Tolkien's initial storyline.

Lord Elrond has called together a council of war to decide how to proceed in the brewing war against Sauron. Representatives have arrived from every corner of Middle-earth, and most have widely differing opinions over how best to proceed. After much heated debate, Gandalf and the others broker a plan whereby a small group comprising a variety of different Middle-earth races will attempt to sneak the One Ring into Mordor by stealth. Together, they will destroy the Ring in Sauron's forge at Mount Doom before the Dark Lord becomes aware of the plan. Frodo volunteers to bear the Ring to its destination, and his friends Sam, Pippin and Merry agree to accompany him. Gandalf and Aragorn also join the party, and the Fellowship of the Ring is completed by talented Elvish archer Legolas Greenleaf (Orlando Bloom), Dwarf warrior Gimli (John Rhys-Davies), and Boromir (Sean Bean), a human nobleman from the Gondorian capital of Minas Tirith.

The Fellowship's task commences with difficulty and becomes gradually more arduous as they progress. Following an abortive attempt to cross the treacherously icy mountain pass of Caradhas, Gandalf reluctantly leads the group into the abandoned underground Dwarf kingdom of Moria. There, they are besieged by a huge host of Goblins and a deadly Balrog – a gigantic fire demon which had been trapped for millennia beneath the Dwarves' mithril mines. The Balrog is driven back by Gandalf, but only at the cost of his own life – he is dragged by the falling demon into the depths of the Moria cave system. Although devastated at the loss of their wise friend, the rest of the Fellowship barely manage to escape from the underground city with their lives.

The atmospheric journey through Moria is one of the most memorable sequences of *The Fellowship of the Ring*, and brings to the forefront many aspects of the Fellowship which would be developed in later films. The shared antagonism between Legolas and Gimli, for instance, shows the very first signs of transforming into a friendship forged through mutual adversity. The bungling of the good-natured Pippin and Merry provides some much-needed light relief, whereas Gollum makes an early appearance on the scene – albeit sparingly, and only from the shadows.

The Fellowship, though reduced in number, make their way to the hidden Elvish realm of Lothlórien, which is ruled by Celeborn

(Marton Csokas) and Galadriel (Cate Blanchett). Galadriel wields one of the original Rings of Power which were made subordinate to the One Ring during Sauron's previous reign of terror, and she uses her mystical strength to keep Lothlórien safe from the dark forces that are once again encroaching on Middle-earth. Before the Fellowship is re-equipped to resume its quest, Galadriel grants Frodo a look at possible futures in her mirror, emphasising the importance of his quest.

Keen to avoid further entanglements with Sauron's agents, the Fellowship take to the water, sailing down the River Anduin on the next leg of their journey. However, they are besieged by a vicious brigade of specially-bred Uruk-hai Orcs which have been developed by Saruman at Isengard. The Uruk-hai are a hybrid of Orc and Goblin, and are stronger and more intelligent than either. They battle ferociously with the Fellowship, and in great numbers. Boromir, who had begun to fall under the influence of the One Ring and desired to seize it from Frodo, redeems himself by facing off against the Uruk-hai attack force, but only at the cost of his own life. Frodo, disillusioned after Boromir's attempt to steal the One Ring from him, decides to leave for Mordor alone, although he acquiesces to Sam's demands to accompany him. Merry and Pippin are kidnapped by the remains of the Uruk-hai brigade, and Aragorn – reluctantly honouring Frodo's wish to continue his quest without the Fellowship – leads Gimli and Legolas in pursuit of the retreating Orcs.

What is perhaps most surprising of all about *The Fellowship of the Ring* is that, despite being so massively epic in scope, much of its beauty lies in its fine detail and elaborately-observed characterisation. The melancholy wisdom of Hugo Weaving's Elrond, for instance, brilliantly articulates the concerns of an ancient warrior and intellectual, whose youthful appearance disguises his advanced age. Sean Bean is also to be commended for his approach to the character of Boromir – a brave but flawed champion of Gondor, his apparent arrogance is subsequently (and believably) revealed to be structured by great pride in his homeland and concern for the future of Middle-earth. John-Rhys Davies and Orlando Bloom both set up the foundation for one of the most remarkable (and unlikely) double-acts in the trilogy, the dynamism of Legolas contrasting nicely with Gimli's overstated bravado. Yet perhaps the most notable of all the film's appearances can be found in Elijah Wood and Sean Astin as Frodo and Sam, two firm friends caught up in a conflict that neither of them fully understands, yet one which both are determined to see through to the end. Just as Astin so finely depicts Sam's down-to-earth attitude and dedication to his friend, Wood is superb as the conflicted, slightly mercurial Frodo.

There are many fine performances throughout *The Fellowship of the Ring*, and despite the film's expansive ensemble cast there is no readily apparent weak link in the entire roll-call of international actors. Due to her rising fame, Tyler was perhaps one of the most immediately recognisable names amongst many hugely admired screen luminaries, and she more than manages to hold her own against some of the most impressive talents in the acting profession. Although Arwen cannot boast as much screen-time as some of the other characters, Tyler makes the most of every moment that features the Elvish princess, imbuing her with seemingly boundless compassion and empathy. In spite of the fact that Arwen is an old soul, being born immortal many centuries ago, Tyler permeates her with a timeless joy for life. Her love for Aragorn outshines even her concern for the future of Middle-earth, though as she will later find, the two are to be fundamentally interlinked. Arwen's great wisdom, coupled with her mastery of horsemanship and magic, further delineates her as a character with dimensions not immediately suggested by Tolkien's novel – and an embellishment much admired by fans of Jackson's films.

*The Fellowship of the Ring* was an immediate success with audiences worldwide, and was embraced by the overwhelming majority of critics.[88] The most noteworthy observation amongst commentators was that the film had remained very true to the spirit of Tolkien's original text, and the alterations (and omissions) made in translating the complex narrative to the big screen were accepted by the greater part of the critical community as being necessary to the success of the film. Jackson was also praised for the stunning achievement of melding New Zealand's beautiful scenery with digitally-created surroundings in order to create some of Tolkien's most distinctive environments. From the homeliness of the Shire to the wintry cold of Caradhras, from the Balrog's fiery attack to the serene waterfalls of Rivendell, the film is immediately evocative of Tolkien's highly distinguished writings, and perfectly encapsulates the book's often-admired sense of the majestic and otherworldly. Composer Howard Shore was also much praised for his masterful score, which deservedly went on to sell very strongly on audio CD.

Following the success of *The Fellowship of the Ring* in cinemas, New Line Cinema announced that a special extended edition would be released on DVD. Much more than a straightforward director's cut, the extended version of the film included around thirty minutes of extra footage; some scenes were lengthened, others were rearranged, and a number of brand new sequences were added. Although Tyler enjoys some much-deserved additional screen-time as Arwen during her appearances in Rivendell, the extended version has a much more pivotal effect on the character of Aragorn, who is fleshed out even more fully than he had been in the theatrical edition. The viewer learns more of his past, his character, and even a little of his feelings for Arwen. There are many more subtle additions which will delight Tolkien fans, including the appearance of the Trolls which had appeared prominently in *The Hobbit*, and there are some significant extra scenes in Moria and Lothlórien, as well as a number of other embellishments. Without the time constraints necessary for a commercial cinematic release, the extended edition of the film is a quite different experience – and one which, for readers of Tolkien's novel in particular, is even more satisfying than the theatrical version had been.

*The Fellowship of the Ring* went on to perform very impressively at awards ceremonies across the world, winning four Academy Awards for Best Cinematography, Best Visual Effects, Best Makeup and Best Original Score, and being nominated for no less than nine other Oscars, including Best Picture, Best Director, Best Supporting Actor for Ian McKellen, and Best Original Song for Enya's haunting 'May It Be'. The film also won four BAFTA film awards, including the David Lean Award for Direction for Peter Jackson, and was nominated for a further nine categories. It was also nominated for Golden Globes and the Satellite Awards, and had wins at the Grammies and the Screen Actors Guild Awards amongst a great many other ceremonies. Tyler's performance as Arwen was nominated for the 2002 Teen Choice Award for Choice Actress in a Drama/ Action Adventure, as well as being part of the winning group who received the Phoenix Film Critics Society Award for Best Acting Ensemble. She was likewise nominated (again, together with the film's ensemble cast) for the Screen Actors Guild Award for Outstanding Performance by the Cast of a Theatrical Motion Picture.

Peter Jackson had succeeded in capturing the imagination of filmgoers the world over, and with more success than anyone could have predicted. With sales of Tolkien's already-popular novels soaring, and public interest in *The Lord of the Rings* at an all time high, the critical community waited patiently to see if Jackson could sustain the success and momentum of his adaptation whilst retaining the immense appeal of Tolkien's texts.

# THE TWO TOWERS (2002)

Beginning at the same point that *The Fellowship of the Ring* had concluded, Frodo and Sam are heading for Mordor in spite of grave misgivings as to how they intend to gain entry to the Dark Land. During a rest stop, they are besieged by Gollum, who is desperate to regain ownership of the One Ring. Together, Frodo and Sam are able to restrain him, and with some persuasion manage to convince the corrupt former Hobbit to lead them to the Black Gate of Mordor. Sam greatly distrusts Gollum, but like Frodo he sees no option other than to follow his directions.

The implementation of Gollum is one of the most successful features of the whole trilogy. A fully computer-generated character who is voiced by actor Andy Serkis, Gollum was integrated seamlessly into the film's action in a very satisfying way, which is particularly crucial given his character's pivotal importance to the narrative. Gollum's presence seems entirely natural, and is no more guilty of rousing the audience's disbelief than are the various techniques which were used to render the films more diminutive characters (Hobbits and Dwarves alike) as appearing realistically much smaller than the actors who were playing them.

Pippin and Merry remain in the grasp of Saruman's Uruk-hai troops, though Aragorn, Legolas and Gimli maintain an unceasing pursuit. They are unaware that in the meantime, Saruman has been inciting an uprising of Dunlander Wild Men, who are now in revolt against the kingdom of Rohan. While a number of vicious assaults on Rohan's outlying villages are breaking out, Prince Théodred (Paris Howe Strewe) is mortally wounded in an Orc attack, and is returned to the Rohirrim capital of Edoras by his cousin Éomer (Karl Urban). Éomer explains the desperate situation to Rohan's king, Théoden (Bernard Hill), but the monarch's mind is being influenced by Saruman's sorcery and the manipulations of his royal advisor, Gríma Wormtongue (Brad Dourif). Éomer is unable to rouse his uncle Théoden into launching reprisals against the enemies of the kingdom, much to the dismay of his sister Éowyn (Miranda Otto), who has witnessed the king's decline first-hand. Wormtongue, realising that Éomer suspects a link between himself and Saruman, has the king's nephew exiled from the realm.

The introduction of the kingdom of Rohan into the narrative adds a number of memorable characters into the mix. The hugely versatile Bernard Hill makes a striking first appearance as the addled King of Rohan, grown old far beyond his time due to Saruman's dark conjuring, and this somewhat dazed manifestation of the character contrasts well with the more determined, resolute Théoden who is introduced later in the story. Brad Dourif, one of the hardest-working and most recognisable character actors in America, makes for an unforgettable Gríma Wormtongue, effectively conveying all of the character's scheming venom and thinly-veiled spitefulness. Also, Miranda Otto – one of Australia's most talented young actresses – brings both grace and fortitude to Rohirrim noblewoman Éowyn. Known to audiences for noteworthy appearances in films as varied as Clytie Jessop's *Emma's War* (1985), Gillian Armstrong's *The Last Days of Chez Nous* (1992) and Robert Zemeckis' *What Lies Beneath* (2000), she fully demonstrates her outstanding acting experience and fine command of emotional intensity all the way throughout her part in *The Lord of the Rings* trilogy.

During a short break from their seemingly-endless race back to Isengard, the Orcs guarding Pippin and Merry are ambushed by Éomer and a band of his fellow exiles. In the chaos which ensues, the two Hobbits manage to escape into Fangorn forest, a dense woodland territory. There, they encounter an Ent named Treebeard (voice of John-Rhys Davies) – a huge wooden creature who herds the forest's many living trees. Although the Hobbits' ways are strange to the ancient Ent, he escorts them both to sanctuary further into woods.

Aragorn and his company meet up with Éomer and his horsemen on their entry into Rohan. Éomer explains the kingdom's current situation to Aragorn, and also puts them on the trail of the band of Orcs which his party had slaughtered previously. Aragorn examines the scene of the battle and deduces that Pippin and Merry had fled to comparative safety in the nearby forest. Following their tracks, they are astonished to encounter none other than Gandalf – rejuvenated and seemingly uninjured after his apparent death in the mines of Moria. Gandalf explains that he had fought the Balrog to the death, but only at the cost of his life. However, his work in Middle-earth not yet done, he had been returned from the abyss in a revitalized form. He is also now dressed in white – usurping the role of the other White Wizard, Saruman. Gandalf urges Aragorn, Legolas and Gimli to journey with him to Edoras, where he intends to resolve the political deadlock at the heart of Rohan.

The moody ambience of Fangorn forest is wonderfully realised, and even the intricate Treebeard – who, in lesser hands, could have been a potential disaster – is rendered most proficiently, both in scale and aspect. The unexpected return of Gandalf also galvanises the resolve of Aragorn and his company, the presence of the incomparable Ian McKellen signifying a renewed bulwark against the tide of darkness in Middle-earth.

Gollum continues to lead Frodo and Sam ever closer to Mordor. They manage to survive a passage through the perilous Dead Marshes and narrowly evade a reconnaissance flight of Nazgûl before arriving at the Black Gate – the heavily-fortified entrance to Sauron's domain. However, it quickly becomes apparent that their chances of entering undetected are close to nil. Rather than risk Frodo's capture, which will almost certainly mean losing the One Ring to Sauron, Gollum suggests that they try a precarious back-route into Mordor instead – one which will elude the detection of the Dark Lord's sentries. Reluctantly, Frodo and Sam agree to his plan.

At Edoras, Gandalf successfully manages to break Saruman's hold over Théoden. The newly reawakened king attempts to kill Wormtongue in vengeance, but Aragorn stays Théoden's hand, allowing the traitor to rush back to Isengard in defeat. However, even when the king is freed of Saruman's grip, Gandalf is unable to persuade him to retaliate against the Orc and Wild Men attacks; Théoden fears a near-total rout of his remaining forces. Instead, the beleaguered monarch orders an evacuation of the city, and commands the Rohirrim to regroup at the ancient fortress of Helm's Deep. Although a seemingly impenetrable stronghold, Gandalf fears that the Rohirrim army will be unable to resist a full-strength onslaught by Saruman's Orc army. Aragorn, Legolas and Gimli agree to accompany the king and his people to Helm's Deep, while Gandalf departs on unexplained business of his own.

On the road around the mountainous boundaries of Mordor, tempers are beginning to strain within Frodo's company. Sam disapproves of Frodo's growing sympathy for Gollum, whose behaviour is becoming increasingly schizophrenic in nature. Frodo, however, realises only too well that Gollum's personality has been warped by the One Ring, as the early effects of the Ring-bearer's bane are also being felt by him. However, their emerging conflict is held at bay when the party stumbles across a Haradrim taskforce heading for Mordor with several massive Oliphaunts – huge mammoth-like creatures armed for battle. As Sam and Frodo watch, the Haradrim are subjected to a surprise attack by a host of Gondorian soldiers. They attempt to sneak away in the ensuing mayhem, but are detained by the Gondorian militia leader, Faramir (David Wenham).

This sequence develops the theme of the Ring's detrimental effects on Frodo as he draws nearer to Mordor, and of the wedge that it is driving between Sam and himself. In Gollum, Frodo believes that he has discovered the only other living being who is fully capable of understanding quite how devastating the One Ring's influence can be. However, as Sam knows, Frodo has underestimated the sheer depth of deception and borderline insanity that lurks beneath Gollum's façade of jovial compliance. The scene is well played by all, with Wood's effective deepening of Frodo's trauma contrasting productively with Serkis' silkily-delivered articulation of Gollum's deceptiveness. Astin, meanwhile, remains steadfastly likeable and grounded as Sam, who never allows his concerns over the task in hand overshadow the loyalty that he feels to his friend. His wonderment at seeing the Oliphaunts on the march, only to reflect sadly that nobody will ever believe that he witnessed such a sight, is a joy to behold.

The citizens of Rohan have packed up their belongings and are on the road to Helm's Deep. Aragorn and his company attempt to keep their new acquaintances in good spirits, and the Ranger begins to suspect that Éowyn has feelings for him. This prompts him to remember a conversation with his cherished Arwen in Rivendell, when she had assured him of the depth of love that she feels for Aragorn. Her affection was symbolised by her Evenstar jewel, which she gave to Aragorn as a lasting emblem of the bond between them. However, Aragorn also remembers a subsequent exchange with Elrond, where the Elf lord had berated him for his selfishness in returning Arwen's love. Elrond feels that Arwen's place is with others of her kind, who are in the process of departing over the seas to the mythical land of Valinor. Once they have sailed from the Grey Havens, Elves may not return to Middle-earth, and Elrond knows that Arwen's partnership with Aragorn will condemn his daughter to mortality, denying her an eternal life in the Undying Lands. Much as it grieves him, Aragorn respects Elrond's wishes and tells Arwen that he will not exchange her immortality for his own happiness. Arwen, however, will not accept Aragorn's attempt to return her Evenstar, and entreats him to keep it for his own.

Aragorn's flashback builds greatly on the foundation of his insurmountable love for Arwen that had been established in *The Fellowship of the Ring*, and also fleshes out the issue of Arwen's choice in facing her future – either to live one natural lifespan with her beloved, or exist eternally in Valinor with only a mere reminiscence of the tenderness they shared. Tyler continues to deepen her portrayal of Arwen's profound emotional reserves, depicting most effectively the character's devoted romantic bond with Aragorn. This is reflected in the potent chemistry between the two seen in the flashback, with Mortensen impressively rendering Aragorn's stoical, noble desire to act in Arwen's best interests, even when making that decision is clearly breaking his heart. It is also significant to note that, as had been the case in *The Fellowship of the Ring*, Tyler gives a faultless delivery of her Sindarin dialogue – lines written in the Elvish language that had been uniquely devised by Tolkien. It is particularly touching for readers of Tolkien's original texts to hear this fictional language being brought to life on the big screen with such detail and accuracy, much to the credit of Jackson and his co-writers.

As Théoden's party continue on their march from Edoras, they are ambushed by an attack force of Orcs mounted on Wargs – vicious quadrupedal animals with a taste for human blood. The Rohirrim and the remaining Fellowship manage to fight off their assailants, but only at a terrible price – many soldiers die in the defence of Rohan's civilians. Then, in the thick of battle, Aragorn is pulled over a nearby precipice. Although his comrades are reluctant to presume their friend dead, there is no sign of him anywhere.

Somewhat chastened at the loss of Aragorn and so many militiamen, Théoden's party arrive at Helm's Deep and begin to fortify their position. They are unaware that, simultaneously, Saruman is ordering a massive host of Uruk-hai to march from

Isengard and attack Helm's Deep ceaselessly, until no man, woman or child is left alive.

At Rivendell, Elrond is still encouraging Arwen to depart Middle-earth for Valinor before Sauron's forces are unleashed from Mordor. Arwen, however, remains reluctant to leave while there remains a chance that Aragorn will be triumphant against the Dark Lord. Elrond continues to press her, however, imploring her not to throw away everything in exchange for the love of one man – even although that man is the direct descendant of Isildur himself, and rightful holder of the throne of Gondor. Arwen is distraught, her loyalties divided between her devotion to Aragorn and her affection for her father.

Although the Rivendell sequences in *The Two Towers* do not occur anywhere in Tolkien's novel, they greatly enhance Jackson's film and assist in keeping Arwen – and her relationship with Aragorn – in the mind of the audience. The love of Arwen is, of course, just as important to Aragorn as the freedom of Middle-earth, and these motivations greatly influence his actions throughout the trilogy. Although Aragorn's bloodline inextricably links him to the One Ring and its malign effects, it is Arwen who continually comes to his mind when he considers what will be lost if Sauron should conquer the land. Additionally, Tyler's highly distinctive performance as the ethereally beautiful Elvish princess helps to balance Arwen's prominence against the other significant female character in *The Two Towers*, Éowyn, who has unique qualities all of her own.

At Lothlórien, Galadriel contemplates the developments of the war thus far, considering the inherent dangers of Sauron's control over Saruman, and the encroachment of Mordor forces on Gondorian territory. She communicates with Elrond and suggests that the Elves send forces to bolster the fight against the Dark Lord's armies. Meanwhile, Arwen appears to use mystic Elvish clairvoyance to revive Aragorn, saving him from a watery grave. Still weakened, he mounts a Rohirrim horse that comes to his aid and makes his way to Helm's Deep.

Frodo and Sam are being interrogated by Captain Faramir, who reveals himself to be the brother of the late Boromir and the son of Gondor's Steward. Frodo is reluctant to reveal the true nature of their mission, but when some Gondorian scouts discover Gollum the truth is soon deduced. Sam begs Faramir to let them go on their way before the One Ring can be discovered by Sauron, but the Captain is instead resolved to use it in the defence of the Gondorian capital, Minas Tirith. Before he can seize it from Frodo, however, his party are called away to the lightly-defended outpost city of Osgiliath, which is under siege by Mordor Orcs.

Aragorn arrives at Helm's Deep and breaks disturbing news to Théoden – during his journey, he has seen Saruman's Uruk-hai army on the march, and they number ten thousand at the very least. Although Théoden has mustered every man and boy to fight in the defence of the fortress, he knows that it will almost certainly be a fight to the death. The spirits of the Rohirrim are buoyed by the unexpected appearance of a band of Elvish archers led by Haldir of Lothlórien (Craig Parker), who offer to fight alongside them against the coming attack.

Saruman's forces arrive on schedule, and wage a ferocious assault on Helm's Deep. The Elves and Rohirrim, assisted by Aragorn and his company, put up a valiant fight, but their efforts are stretched to breaking point by the sheer magnitude of their enemy's army. Things turn increasingly desperate when one of the Uruk-hai troops delivers an explosive device to a weak spot in the fortress's outer wall, breaching the perimeter and allowing Saruman's hordes to swarm into the inner compound.

The Battle of Helm's Deep is one of the most distinguished pieces of film-making in all of the trilogy, and is a spectacular combination of computer-generated effects, mounting tension, and well-observed acting. The early brinkmanship between the barricaded Rohirrim forces and the brutish Uruk-hai hordes is particularly memorable, as is Bernard Hill's astonishing performance as the gallant Théoden – a king determined to turn near-certain defeat against overwhelming odds into a dignified end worthy of legend.

Deep in Fangorn forest, Treebeard has called a conference of other Ents to decide on a course of action concerning their part in the war. After much deliberation, it is decided that they will not involve themselves in outside affairs, much to the disdain of Pippin and Merry. However, on returning the two Hobbits to the outer limits of the woodland, Treebeard becomes aware of the sheer scale of the deforestation caused by Saruman's industrial-isation of Isengard. Enraged at the wanton destruction of so many trees, several of whom were sentient and personally known to Treebeard, the Ent vows revenge against Saruman.

Osgiliath is being over-run, and Faramir's party are unable to hold back the tide of Sauron's Orc force. Faramir still intends to send Frodo and the One Ring to his father at Minas Tirith, but a very close encounter with a Nazgûl mounted on a massive winged beast ultimately persuades him that Frodo may just be the last hope for Middle-earth after all. Resigned to face the penalty for letting the One Ring slip through his grasp, Faramir frees Frodo, Sam and Gollum to continue their journey even as much of Osgiliath falls around them.

Treebeard and a host of Ents lay waste to the largely depopulated Isengard, breaking open a dam and flooding the area which surrounds the tower of Orthanc. His manufacturing facilities ruined, Saruman watches in bewilderment as the Ents devastate everything that he has worked towards. As the forces of nature once again take possession of Isengard, the trapped Saruman retreats back into his tower to consider his next move.

The end appears to be nearing for Théoden and the others at Helm's Deep. The Uruk-hai are overtaking the inner sanctum of the stronghold, and as dawn breaks the king begins to reflect that the Rohirrim cannot survive much longer. He and Aragorn agree to lead a suicidal charge on horseback against the invading hordes. But just as things appear to be at their most hopeless, Gandalf arrives with Éomer and hundreds of mounted Rohirrim horsemen. They engage the startled enemy at full strength, decimating Saruman's remaining army. Soon after, Théoden is able to declare victory, but Gandalf is less elated. The triumph at Helm's Deep will doubtlessly have enraged Sauron, who even now will be readying the final phase of his plan to dominate all of Middle-earth.

With *The Two Towers*, Peter Jackson managed to achieve something that many had thought impossible; he had not only matched the exceptional quality of *The Fellowship of the Ring*, but had actually exceeded it in terms of epic scope and grandeur. Performances which had already been note-perfect in the previous film were honed still further, and a new group of characters were added to the central cast to great effect. The ominous air of foreboding which had been so expertly established in *The Fellowship of the Ring* was to pay dividends in *The Two Towers*, with battles such as Helm's Deep and the Ent assault on Isengard providing abundant evidence that the War of the Ring was indeed at hand. Yet as Gandalf speculates at the film's conclusion, with the Eye of Sauron still safely ensconced atop Barad-dûr, Middle-earth's grandest battle was still to arrive.

Like its predecessor, *The Two Towers* contains many departures from Tolkien's book, all of which greatly enhance the film's structure and narrative for the benefit of the wider audience. Most noticeable of all is the fact that whereas Tolkien split his narrative cleanly in two – firstly describing the travels of Aragorn's party and the build-up to Helm's Deep, and secondly following Frodo and Sam's journey to Mordor exclusively – Jackson interweaves the two storylines into a combined, concurrent narrative. Additionally, the disposition and actions of some of the characters were altered for the film, with Théoden initially appearing rather less sure of himself than his literary counterpart had been, and Faramir being much more conflicted over his decision to release Frodo and let him continue his quest into Mordor. There are also a number of embellishments to the story, such as the inclusion of Elrond, Galadriel and Arwen, which did not occur in Tolkien's original text. As had been the case with *The Fellowship of the Ring*, however, Jackson and his co-writers stay entirely faithful to the spirit of Tolkien's writings, even although they do not always echo his every word.

Tyler's task in developing Arwen Evenstar into such an engaging character is made all the more challenging due to the fact that her character was used so sparingly by Tolkien – and even then, in the books she tended to be referred to mostly by allusion rather than personal appearance. Yet by *The Two Towers*, it is clear that Tyler had well and truly made Arwen's role her own, consolidating the character's compassionate nature and meaningfully articulating the emotional variance that she feels due to the clash caused by her competing affections for Aragorn and her respect for her father's wishes. Tyler again capitalises on every moment that she is present on-screen, bringing vibrant life and emotional resonance to a character who had largely been an enigmatic mystery to readers of the original novels.

Just as *The Fellowship of the Ring* before it, *The Two Towers* was subsequently to be released for home entertainment systems in a special extended edition, which added over forty minutes of further footage to the narrative of the film. These additions were even more substantial than had been the case with the first film, and very elegantly augment the existing characterisation and events of *The Two Towers*. Extra scenes are added to flesh out Merry and Pippin's alliance with Treebeard in Fangorn forest, and the siege of Osgiliath is further developed (particularly noteworthy is Faramir's shocked realisation of Gollum's intended path into Mordor, the dangers of which would be explained more fully in the next film). Other events from the theatrical edition of the film, such as Aragorn's apparently coincidental encounter with a Rohirrim steed after his presumed death on the road to Helm's Deep, are clarified much more satisfyingly, and numerous significant sequences from the film are embellished further, such as the aftermath of the Ent decimation of Isengard, and Aragorn's heart-rending flashback to his time with Arwen at Rivendell.

Critics were greatly impressed by *The Two Towers*, perhaps even more so than they had been with its predecessor,[89] and there were very few dissenting voices in the near-unanimous chorus of approval.[90] The film was to perform exceptionally well at awards ceremonies, picking up Academy Awards for Best Sound Editing and Best Visual Effects along with nominations for four other Oscars, including Best Picture. *The Two Towers* also won three BAFTA Awards (including the much sought-after Audience Award), and received dozens of other nominations at prestigious ceremonies including the Broadcast Film Critics Association Awards, Golden Globes, Directors Guild of America Awards, Australian Film Institute Awards, Art Directors Guild and People's Choice Awards, amongst a great many others. Many of these nominations were to be won outright. Tyler, along with the rest of the main cast, was awarded the 2003 Online Film Critics Society award for Best Ensemble, and for the second year running the central players also won the Phoenix Film Critics Society Award for Best Acting Ensemble. The film's key players, including Tyler, were also nominated for the Screen Actors Guild Award for Outstanding Performance by a Cast in a Motion Picture, as had also been the case the previous year.

The overwhelming (and continuing) critical and public success of *The Lord of the Rings* trilogy had proven beyond doubt that with *The Two Towers*, Peter Jackson and his cast had continued to build effectively on the spectacular success of *The Fellowship of the Ring*. The films were now deeply permeating the international cultural psyche, with clever marketing techniques and huge sales of the film on DVD and video further enhancing the world's perennial interest in Tolkien's stories. The audience's appetite now well and truly piqued, spectators across the world waited in anticipation for the final chapter of Jackson's epic masterpiece to arrive on cinema screens.

# THE RETURN OF THE KING
## (2003)

Growing ever closer to Mordor, Gollum is finding it increasingly difficult to keep his treachery in check. He greatly desires to steal the One Ring from Frodo and once again claim it as his own, but is horrified at the thought of Sauron seizing it before he has the chance. Sam, meanwhile, is becoming concerned at their party's dwindling resources, particularly as Gollum has given them little real idea of how much further they will have to travel.

Gandalf, Aragorn and company arrive at the ruins of Isengard, where they are reunited with Merry and Pippin. The two young Hobbits are hale and hearty, feasting on bounty from Saruman's fallen stronghold. Treebeard explains that he will maintain custodianship of Orthanc tower, which still contains the trapped Saruman. Gandalf adds that the former White Wizard no longer has any power at his disposal, mystic or otherwise; his machinery of war has been devastated forever. However, before they depart, Pippin discovers a palantír – a mystical seeing-stone used by Saruman to commune with Sauron – amongst the wreckage of Isengard. Alarmed, Gandalf takes possession of the palantír and covers its surface before Sauron can exploit the stone's magical properties for his own ends.

The reunited party return to Edoras, where Théoden and his

royal house celebrate their recent victory at Helm's Deep. The revelry comes to an abrupt halt, however, when Pippin's curiosity overcomes him and the young Hobbit decides to gaze into the palantír. Sauron is instantly aware that Pippin has accessed the stone, and attempts to interrogate him as to the location of the One Ring. Pippin does not respond to the Dark Lord's questioning, but inadvertently catches partial sight of Sauron's own battle strategy. It seems that, having deduced that Aragorn is the rightful heir of Isildur, Sauron fears that the hitherto-scattered peoples of Middle-earth may yet come together under the command of one strong leader. Therefore, as his next planned stratagem, the Dark Lord has decided to launch an all-out assault on the Gondorian capital city of Minas Tirith, which to all intents and purposes would terminate any possibility of effective reprisals from this primary threat to Mordor's frontier. Deciding that there is no time to lose, Gandalf rides to Minas Tirith with all due haste to warn the Gondorians of the imminent threat. His travelling companion is Pippin, who Sauron now suspects to be the bearer of the One Ring.

Arwen is also currently on a journey – in her case, to a ship which will bear her away to the Undying Lands, saving her from the coming storm that is about to engulf Middle-earth. However, before she can reach the harbour of the Grey Havens she witnesses a vision of her possible future, where she and Aragorn raise a child together at Minas Tirith. She races back to Rivendell and confronts Elrond about this revelation. Pained, he admits that the outcome she has witnessed was indeed a potential future, though only one of many. Seeking to spare Arwen from other less favourable futures, he had hidden the full truth from her, but now she has decided on her own course of action. Elrond discovers that her immortality is fading, and that soon her Elvish heritage will have given way to a fully human physiology. Left with no recourse but to support Arwen in her newly-chosen direction, Elrond accedes to her request to re-forge Isildur's ancient, shattered sword in the furnaces of Rivendell. The blade that slew

Sauron at Dagorlad is made whole once again.

Tyler and Hugo Weaving build upon the solid emotional foundation which they established in *The Two Towers*, bringing a poignant conclusion to Arwen's agonising choice regarding her future. Tyler effectively and movingly articulates Arwen's sense of betrayal at Elrond's protective equivocation from the truth, just as she likewise conveys the underlying love and understanding that so clearly exists between this long-lived father and daughter. Weaving is also to be commended for his continuing exceptional portrayal of the hugely complex Elrond; he so ably expresses the sadness and despondency of the intense Elvish patriarch not only at the loss of his daughter's immortality, but also the heartbreaking notion that – with Middle-earth nearing its final stand against Sauron – her sacrifice may still prove to have been for naught.

Gandalf arrives at the throne room of Minas Tirith, but finds little welcome from Gondor's Steward, Denethor (John Noble). Embittered by the death of his son Boromir and overcome by the prospect of Mordor's seemingly limitless resources, Denethor is unreceptive to Gandalf's call to arms – particularly as he knows that the White Wizard seeks to restore Aragorn to his rightful place as King of Gondor. Pippin pledges his service to Denethor in acknowledgement of Boromir's noble death, which the Steward accepts. However, the Hobbit's gesture does nothing to soften Denethor's resolve – he will not call on assistance in the fight against Mordor, even although the time of Sauron's strike is at hand.

John Noble makes for a memorable Denethor, subtly underplaying the character's irrationality – particularly given the fact that Denethor's antipathy for Gandalf has such a believable basis. The Steward is unable to see the benefits of the restoration of Gondor's throne, partly due to the deleterious effect it would have on his own position, and also because he perceives Gandalf's machinations to be essentially manipulative at Denethor's own expense. Despite the fact that the Steward's decision-making is innately unsound for Gondor in the long term, Noble's intricate performance reminds us that Denethor has been a sharp and capable leader in his own right; a fact which complicates Gandalf's task still further.

Sam and Frodo have now reached the dead city of Minas Morgul, once a prominent Gondorian metropolis but now an outpost of the Nazgûl. Gollum conceals the pair in the mouth of a hidden passageway which, he says, will lead them to Mordor without raising enemy suspicion. As they continue on their way, the gates of Minas Morgul open to reveal an enormous Orc army, set to march on Gondor under the banner of Sauron. Leading the attack is the much-feared Witch King of Angmar (Lawrence Makoare), the lord of the Nazgûl.

Gandalf has witnessed the Dark Lord's unleashing of his armed hordes, and realises that the time for action has come. He enlists Pippin to light the beacon of Minas Tirith, outwith the knowledge of Denethor. The lit beacon begins a chain reaction across other such outposts leading from Gondor to Rohan, and soon the signal is spotted by Aragorn at Edoras. Théoden is reluctant to assist Gondor when Minas Tirith had not assisted the Rohirrim in their fight at Helm's Deep, but ultimately his trust for Aragorn makes the decision for him. Rohan will commit as many forces as can be mustered in order to come to the aid of Gondor.

Meanwhile, the last of Osgiliath has finally fallen to Mordor after a substantial reinforcement of Orcs. Faramir, who is still leading a Gondorian detachment in the city, is disinclined to back down, but is forced into full retreat following the arrival of the Nazgûl. Few soldiers make it back to Minas Tirith, and even then only with the assistance of Gandalf, who succeeds in driving off the pursuing Nazgûl. Denethor, however, is displeased that his son has abandoned Osgiliath even in the face of overwhelming odds, and sends him back on a virtual suicide mission to retake it from the now-entrenched Orc army. Faramir dutifully complies, but his taskforce is grossly outnumbered by the forces of Mordor, and the Gondorian counterattack is overwhelmed before it can even reach Osgiliath.

The theme of Denethor's dissatisfaction with Faramir, especially following the demise of Boromir, had previously been hinted at in *The Two Towers*, but here it underscores the starkness of the Steward's increasingly tenuous hold on reality. David Wenham displays a laudably moving resignation in his portrayal of Faramir, heading for near-certain defeat and death due to a hope – however slim – that he may still win his father's approval. Wenham's efforts are matched by John Noble's own skilful depiction of Denethor's mounting irrationality, which was now beginning the build-up to its apex.

Théoden has assembled some six thousand Rohirrim troops to his cause, and readies his host for combat. On the eve before riding to war, Aragorn is visited by Elrond, who informs him that Arwen – now fully human – is ailing badly; the light of the Evenstar will weaken so long as Sauron's power is on the rise. If Aragorn desires to save his beloved, he must ensure that the Dark Lord – and the One Ring – are destroyed utterly. Elrond also gives Aragorn the re-forged sword of Isildur, rechristened Anduril, the original role of which will not have been forgotten by Sauron. However, Elrond brings even graver news; Mordor has at its disposal a fleet of corsair ships bearing reinforcements from the south. When the attack against Minas Tirith commences, Sauron will attempt to catch the Gondorian defenders in a pincer movement.

Elrond suggests a possible course of action to intercept the reinforcement fleet, but one which Aragorn is extremely disinclined to follow. Taking leave of Théoden, Éowyn and Éomer, Aragorn rides to the Dark Door of Dunharrow accompanied by Gimli and Legolas. There, deep underground, he encounters a huge army of the dead – traitors who had sworn allegiance to Gondor many centuries previously, but who had been cursed when they reneged on their pledge. As Isildur's heir, Aragorn promises amnesty to the ghostly multitude if they will assist him in waging war against Mordor.

At Minas Tirith, an unconscious Faramir returns on his injured horse – the sole survivor of the battle to retake Osgiliath. Denethor is overcome with grief at the gravity of his son's condition, but it is too late for recrimination; tens of thousands of Mordor Orcs are assembling on the Pelennor Fields surrounding the city. When Denethor, despairing, orders that the citadel guard abandon their posts, Gandalf knocks him out cold and commands the defence of Minas Tirith himself. The city puts up a spirited defence, its catapults making short work of the enemy front divisions, but the battle rapidly becomes more complicated with the arrival of armoured Nazgûl mounted on foul winged beasts.

The Battle of the Pelennor Fields is among the most staggering filmic achievements in the entire *Lord of the Rings* trilogy, and one which was unrivalled by other films of the time for its sheer spectacle and epic scope. The ancient city of Minas Tirith, simultaneously resilient and crumbling, makes for an exciting and engaging locale as its frantic denizens defend against an ever-widening array of outlandish creatures spawned from Mordor's hellish realm. Ian McKellen, whose performance had already been exemplary, adds yet another dimension to Gandalf, developing the White Wizard full-circle from a secretive, introverted mystic into a tactically-gifted battlefield commander. The incisive power of his portrayal is quite stunning to behold.

Gollum has finally succeeded in alienating Frodo from his companion, having framed Sam for devouring the last of their food supplies. Frodo sends Sam away, then continues alone with Gollum along the perilous passage of Cirith Ungol. There, Gollum abandons him into the clutches of Shelob, an enormous spider who has built her lair on the pathway to Mordor. Frodo initially manages to escape her web and angrily confronts Gollum, but the traitor pitches over a rocky precipice following their altercation. Shelob mounts another attack, rendering Frodo unconscious with her venomous stinger, but is fought off and fatally injured by Sam, who has secretly been following Frodo. Unfortunately, the comatose Frodo is captured by an Orc patrol and taken to a nearby guard-post before Sam is able to carry him away from the area.

Sauron's army is attempting to destroy the main gates of Minas Tirith with an immense battering ram. However, their assault is interrupted by the sudden arrival of Théoden and his mounted troops, the sight of which momentarily daunts the attacking Orcs. Riding with Théoden, though unbeknownst to him, are Éowyn and Merry, who he had ordered to stay behind in Rohan. Théoden rallies his troops, who charge into Sauron's assembled army like wild animals, decimating all in their path. The Rohirrim inflict considerable damage to the Orc hordes until the Haradrim enter the battle with massive armoured Oliphaunts, which begin to turn the tide against Théoden's mounted warriors. Then, the cruellest blow of all is struck – Théoden is toppled from his horse and mortally wounded by the Witch King of Angmar. Éowyn, overcome by grief, confronts the Nazgûl lord in single-combat, decapitating his winged fell beast and then accomplishing what had been thought impossible – killing the Witch King outright.

Bernard Hill and Miranda Otto both give thoroughly show-stealing performances at the Battle of Pelennor Fields, and it is perhaps this sequence more than any other in the trilogy which defines their characters. Hill's rendering of Théoden is staggering, eclipsing his Helm's Deep appearance, and this is no more true than during his pre-battle speech; rallying his six thousand mounted troops, he is every inch the noble hero of old, riding to war in spite of overwhelming odds. Likewise, Otto brings Éowyn's bravery to a logical conclusion by fully embracing the opportunity to become the skilled heroine that the character was always capable of being. Given that Éowyn's courage and insight had been on display from her appearance in *The Two Towers* – in particular, as she contemplated the possibility of battle as Helm's Deep drew to its bloody conclusion – Otto delivers a masterful interpretation of the character as she comes fully into her own. Théoden's death scene, where Éowyn bids a tearful farewell to the man who was both her surrogate father and king, is a truly affecting piece of cinema in its own right.

At the pinnacle of Minas Tirith, Denethor – now completely unhinged – is building a funeral pyre for himself and the still-unconscious Faramir. At Pippin's urging, Gandalf storms into Denethor's chambers and attempts to interrupt the insane ceremony. Pippin drags Faramir from the flames, which outrages Denethor, but the Steward himself catches fire as he struggles with the young Hobbit. Delirious, Denethor races out of the palace and plummets over the edge of the city's uppermost level, falling hundreds of feet to his death.

Just as the Orc army attempts to regain the upper hand in the battle raging around Minas Tirith, the black corsair ships spoken of by Elrond appear from the south. The Mordor forces rejoice, believing their reinforcements to have arrived, but they are stunned to find Aragorn instead – along with the army of the dead, several thousand strong. Sauron's remaining hordes have no defence against the ghostly spectres, as they cannot strike a blow against their incorporeal forms, and thus the Mordor army are soon scattered in disarray. With Gondor's enemies retreating in confusion, Aragorn holds to his agreement and releases the dead from their curse, allowing them to disperse into the abyss.

At the tower of Cirith Ungol, Sam takes full advantage of a brutal argument between the Orc guards to come to Frodo's rescue. Reconciled after Gollum's earlier attempts to drive them apart, the two friends have finally made their way into the dark land of Mordor. However, it becomes clear that the final leg of their journey will not be easy; the Plain of Gorgoroth, which leads to Sauron's furnace at Mount Doom, is a bleak and desolate place full of many hundreds of Orc encampments.

Back at Minas Tirith, Gandalf's foresight tells him that if Frodo and Sam have passed into Mordor then a distraction will be required to aid the last stage of their quest. Aragorn boldly suggests that the remaining combined army of Gondor and Rohan, though now depleted to only a few hundred in number, should march on the Black Gate of Mordor in an attempt to divert both Sauron and his extensive armies. The plan is desperate, but there is no readily apparent alternative.

On the approach of Aragorn's army, the Black Gate opens to expel thousands upon thousands of Orcs – an army whose numbers far exceed even the multitude that had besieged Minas Tirith. Aragorn valiantly encourages his troops, who remain true to his leadership even in the face of truly awe-inspiring adversity, but as Sauron's undisciplined hordes continue to spill out of Mordor it becomes increasingly clear that their fight will be over more or less before it has a chance to begin.

Viggo Mortensen turns in a hugely dignified performance as Aragorn, a hero who is willing to put his life and his kingdom on the line in order simply to save a friend (the One Ring, for all its deadly significance, seems almost secondary to Aragorn's genuine concern for his young Hobbit compatriot). Mortensen radiates courage and quiet stateliness as Aragorn, proving that the no-nonsense practicality of the wild Ranger encountered by audiences in *The Fellowship of the Ring* continues to live on in the fledgling King of Gondor. His rallying speech to Aragorn's dwindling troops is every bit as powerful and stirring as Bernard Hill's had been to the Rohirrim, without ever allowing an overlap between the content and style of delivery.

Thanks to the diversion caused by Aragorn's desperate last stand, Frodo and Sam have finally made their way to the raging inferno of Mount Doom. There, they are assailed by Gollum, who steals the One Ring from Frodo at the last moment by biting off one of his fingers. Frodo, however, reciprocates by toppling Gollum himself into the seething river of molten lava below, destroying both the One Ring and the treacherous former Hobbit. The effect of the Ring's destruction is virtually instantaneous; the Eye of Sauron explodes, followed shortly after by the tower of Barad-dûr, which shatters to its very foundations. Aragorn and his compatriots watch in slack-jawed amazement as the Black Gate collapses and Sauron's hordes disperse in a frantic state of panic.

Although the party mourn for Frodo and Sam, whose situation at the heart of the disintegrating Mordor appears bleak at best, Gandalf has one last surprise up his sleeve which will reunite the surviving Fellowship of the Ring one last time.

The new Fourth Age of Middle-earth is dawning as Gandalf formally crowns Aragorn the new King of Gondor at a coronation ceremony in Minas Tirith. Buoyed by the total victory against Sauron, Aragorn pledges to mend the damage of the War of the Ring and ushers in a new era of peace for all the peoples of Middle-earth. Yet the crown of Gondor is not the only prize that Aragorn accepts on his coronation. A party of Elves arrives, escorting none other than Arwen, who is to be his new queen. Even Elrond cannot contain his joy as the two lovers are reunited against all odds. The four Hobbit friends have also been invited to the coronation, returning to the Shire soon after. Yet as the story draws to a close, we find that for some of their number, the final journey is yet to come.

*The Return of the King* is a truly breathtaking piece of cinema, and it draws to a close a trilogy which is unrivalled in modern film-making for its scope and mythic grandeur. What is perhaps most remarkable about the film, and indeed the trilogy by extension, is the way in which Jackson never allows the many state-of-the-art special effects and the films' prodigious scope overwhelm the rich variety of performances and finely-honed character moments which run all the way throughout the cycle. There are many beautifully observed moments of character interplay – between Sam and Frodo, Aragorn and Arwen, Pippin and Merry, Merry and Éowyn, and Legolas and Gimli, to name but a few – which greatly encourage the audience's emotional investment in the characters and lend the films' ultimate consequence much more weight than is usually the case in blockbusters of this magnitude. In spite of the huge ensemble cast running throughout all three films, it is impossible to find one poor performance amongst them; from accomplished masters of the acting profession to international film stars and even some new, rising talent, the trilogy was well served by its entire company of performers. Indeed, the nature of the well constructed, multi-faceted characters, their rarefied environment and the tense situations confronting them all combined to lend great immediacy and profundity to the high-quality portrayals given by the lead cast. This was not only true of the human actors, either: computer-generated characters, such as Gollum, Treebeard, and the ferocious airborne Nazgûl were all brought to life with accuracy and realism, their sometimes outlandish aspects rendered both believably and earnestly. This was not only due to the remarkable technical wizardry of Jackson's effects department, but also the gifted voice cast which would bring Tolkien's highly distinctive creations to life. Special mention must also be reserved for all of the stunning New Zealand location shooting throughout the trilogy. The much-praised cinematography made full use of the country's widely varied topography, and – coupled with even more peerless effects work – created a unique and genuinely unforgettable evocation of Tolkien's Middle-earth.

With *The Return of the King*, Tyler brought Arwen to the end of her journey; this was true both emotionally, in terms of her love for Aragorn, and spiritually, with regard to her final choice to abrogate her eternal life. Although Arwen's screen time was not as abundant as that of the Fellowship, Tyler's distinctive portrayal of the character and the importance of Arwen within the main narrative (particularly due to her all-important connection to Aragorn) means that she was arguably the most prominent of the trilogy's three main female characters. Whether gliding airily through the ancient halls of Rivendell or riding atop her elegant horse Asfaloth (originally Glorfindel's steed in Tolkien's books), Tyler made for a truly distinguished Arwen Evenstar, bringing to the character all of the noble refinement and wisdom that Tolkien's books had suggested whilst also developing her into someone who seemed, for all her ancient years, both vibrant and emotionally energised.

As had been the case with the previous two films in the trilogy, the narrative of *The Return of the King* contained a number of deviations from Tolkien's book. Most notable amongst them was the fact that the eerie confrontation with Shelob had, in the novels, occurred in *The Two Towers*, but was shifted into the third film by Jackson and his co-writers in order to heighten the dramatic effect (as others have noted, Frodo and Sam's journey would have seemed comparatively uneventful throughout *The Return of the King* otherwise). There were a number of lesser changes, including the heightening of distrust between Frodo and Sam (which was greatly embellished in comparison to the book), while Denethor's actions appear slightly different in Tolkien's novel when weighed against the film; the section which involves Gandalf and Pippin lighting the beacon of Minas Tirith against the Steward's will does not occur in the book, for instance, where Denethor is already preparing for the coming battle and has set the beacon alight before Gandalf has even arrived in the city.

More controversially, the 'Scouring of the Shire' section of Tolkien's book, which occurs near the novel's conclusion and concerns the final fate of Saruman, has been removed from the film's narrative altogether. Instead, Saruman's destiny is discovered not in the theatrical version of the film (where he remains an unseen captive in Orthanc Tower), but in its extended edition. This sequence, which also reveals the fate of Gríma Wormtongue, contains first-rate performances from both Christopher Lee and Brad Dourif, and the film benefits greatly by its inclusion. The extended edition contains many other such welcome additions, including an interesting exchange between Aragorn and Sauron via a palantír in the Gondorian throne room, and the much-anticipated appearance of the Mouth of Sauron (Bruce Spence) at the Black Gate of Mordor. There is also a point of special interest with regard to Tyler's performance; the extended edition showcases her recital of 'Arwen's Song' near the end of the film. Tyler demonstrates her beautiful soprano singing voice to breathtaking effect, and the song's poignant lyrics seem perfectly matched to Arwen's warmly affectionate character.

As had been widely anticipated, *The Return of the King* performed exceptionally well with critics internationally, many of whom praised not only the film itself but also the achievement of the trilogy as a whole.[91] The film's remarkable success continued with its accomplishment at awards ceremonies. It performed astonishingly well at the Academy Awards in 2004, winning Oscars in each of the eleven categories in which it had been nominated. These included crucial awards such as Best Picture, Best Adapted Screenplay and Best Director for Peter Jackson, yet the film was just as successful with technical awards such as Best Set Decoration, Best Costume Design, Best Editing, Best Makeup, Best Sound and Best Visual Effects. Howard Shore deservedly picked up the Best Original Score Award for his magisterial soundtrack, and Annie Lennox's evocative performance of 'Into the West' won Best Original Song. Yet this clean sweep of the Academy Awards was not the end of Jackson's achievement; with *Return of the King, The Lord of the Rings* became the first film trilogy since Francis Ford Coppola's *Godfather* series to have all three entries in its cycle be nominated for Best Picture Oscars.

The film performed similarly well at other ceremonies, winning four BAFTA Film Awards (with nominations for eight others), four Golden Globe Awards, nine awards from the Online Film Critics Society (as well as two other nominations), two Grammy Awards, and seven nominations for the Satellite Awards, winning a Golden Satellite for Best Art Direction. This pattern of success continued across literally dozens of other awards ceremonies, and the path of honour certainly did not exclude Tyler's performance. Along with the rest of the film's central cast, she was the joint winner of Best Ensemble Acting Awards issued by the National Board of Review, the Broadcast Film Critics Association and the Screen Actors Guild, and was also nominated for the Phoenix Film Critics Society Award for Best Acting by an Ensemble. Additionally, she was to be nominated for the Teen Choice Award for Choice Movie Actress in a Drama/ Action Adventure.

Peter Jackson had achieved nothing less than global acclamation for his outstanding cinematic achievement, and had accomplished what many had believed hopelessly unattainable. Not only had he translated Tolkien's enormously complicated texts into a faithfully realised modern classic, but he had created a series of massively successful blockbusters in the process. The appeal of *The Lord of the Rings* film trilogy transcended both age and nationality, like Tolkien's books before it, charming and enthralling audiences across the world. Jackson had been a respected but relatively little-known figure before helming *The Lord of the Rings*; at the end of the trilogy, he was one of the best-known directors on the planet. His massive success was to continue with his next film, *King Kong* (2005), a stylish remake of the 1930s cinema classic which would again capture the imagination of audiences and critics alike.

*The Lord of the Rings* was enormously significant to Tyler's career, and indeed the films' cultural prominence was such that her performance as Arwen Evenstar is almost certain to be one of the best-remembered roles of her entire career. Although her worldwide fame had steadily been mounting since her appearance in *Armageddon*, the success of Jackson's trilogy was to push her recognition – both with commentators and the general public – onto an entirely new level altogether.

## FURTHER READING

On a subject such as *The Lord of the Rings*, it is difficult to know where to begin in terms of recommended writings. Analyses of Tolkien and his works had been incredibly extensive and diverse for decades before the success of Jackson's films, but the cinematic significance of the latter has undoubtedly generated more interest in the late professor's texts than had been the case in recent years. Therefore, any recommendations given here are merely scratching the surface of an immense corpus of study, as a comprehensive breakdown of articles, textbooks and other writings on Tolkien would fill many volumes of equivalent size to this one. A visit to the Internet websites of respected Tolkien organisations, such as the Tolkien Society, will give some indication of the huge wealth of information currently available on the subject.

First and foremost, it is all but essential to refer to Tolkien's original work itself, *The Lord of the Rings*,[92] which remains readily available in many different variations including one- and three-volume editions. Of particular interest are the trilogy's famously exhaustive appendices, found at the end of *The Return of the King*, which describe in greater detail (amongst many things) the relationship between Arwen and Aragorn both before and after the conclusion of the book's main narrative.

For those seeking further insight into Tolkien's development of Arwen, his twelve-volume *History of Middle-earth* cycle – edited by his son Christopher Tolkien – is an invaluable resource for anyone wishing to find out what manner of alternative directions Tolkien considered taking when writing *The Lord of the Rings*. Of specific interest is Volume IX of the series, *Sauron Defeated: The End of the Third Age*,[93] which is the entry most concerned with Arwen and her depiction.

Among the many reference books on Tolkien's texts are classics such as Robert Foster's *The Complete Guide to Middle-earth*[94] and J.E.A. Tyler's *The Complete Tolkien Companion*,[95] both of which are encyclopaedic guides not only to *The Lord of the Rings*, but also Tolkien's other Middle-earth works such as *The Hobbit* and *The Silmarillion*. Numerous other such reference guides are readily available.

For in-depth textual analysis, Paul Kocher's *Master of Middle-earth* is well worth checking out due to its detailed study of the relationship between and Arwen and Aragorn.[96] The newly revised and expanded edition of Tom Shippey's celebrated *The Road to Middle-earth* is also crucial reading, as it now includes an exploration of the filmic *Lord of the Rings* in addition to its detailed examination of the style and content of Tolkien's textual work.[97] Again, it must be noted that a great many scholarly works on Tolkien's compositions are available, both in and out of print, originating from writers of various different nationalities across the globe.

A concise yet comprehensive look through *The Lord of the Rings'* impact on popular culture – both the novels and the film trilogy – can be found in *The Rough Guide to the Lord of the Rings*, edited by Paul Simpson, Helen Rodiss and Michaela Bushell.[98] An illustrated guide, containing many striking images from Jackson's films, can be found in Jude Fisher's *The Lord of the Rings Complete Visual Companion*,[99] which demonstrates the trilogy's unique stylistic flair in all its glory.

Peter Jackson's impressive rise to global fame has also been the subject of a number of books recently. One which is particularly worth referring to is *Peter Jackson: From Gore to Mordor*,[100] edited by Paul A. Woods, which collects together a number of articles about Jackson over the course of his entire directorial career thus far. Peter Jackson also talks about his artistic goals on the year of *The Fellowship of the Ring*'s theatrical launch in an article written by Christopher Howse and Tim Robey, which appeared in the 11 December 2001 issue of *The Daily Telegraph*.[101] A more retrospective appraisal of the trilogy's cinematic fortunes, including quotes from Jackson and some of the cast, can be found in Susan Wloszcznya's article of 21 August 2003 for *USA Today*.[102] A thematic overview of *The Lord of the Rings* trilogy, drawing ideological parallels between Tolkien's story of good versus evil and the horrors of modern terrorism, appears in an article by Duane Dudek which appears in the 16 December 2001 issue of *The Milwaukee Journal Sentinel*.[103] This was only one of many articles written during the period which identified relevant modern-day allegories in Tolkien's stories, and also throughout Jackson's adaptations.

For a wonderfully in-depth look behind the scenes of *The Lord of the Rings* trilogy, one need search no further than Sean Astin's much-praised biographical work *There and Back Again: An Actor's Tale*, which discusses his time working on the films in the role of Sam Gamgee, and his views on the enormous public interest which was later to surround the trilogy's rise to cultural prominence.[104]

Like Peter Jackson and most of the main cast, Tyler was to field a staggering number of interviews over the entire course of *The Lord of the Rings* films' cinematic run, and it would be next to impossible even to attempt to list them all here. In addition to press coverage, she also regularly appeared on television interviews and on radio broadcasts all across the world. Therefore, what follows is merely the briefest of overviews outlining some of the discussions that she held with the printed media concerning her portrayal of Arwen Evenstar.

Tyler talks about her approach to the role of Arwen, including the casting process, in an in-depth interview with Dan Madsen for the November 2002 issue of *The Lord of the Rings Fan Club Official Movie Magazine*.[105] She discusses the challenge of learning dialogue written in Tolkien's fictional Elvish language in an article by Bruce Kirkland which appeared in the 18 December 2001 issue of the *Toronto Sun*.[106]

Ian Spelling conducts an interesting interview with Tyler in November 2001's *Starlog* magazine, where she talks about Arwen's appearance in *The Fellowship of the Ring*.[107] In the November 2001 issue of *W* magazine, she gives voice to her thoughts on the controversy surrounding the significant expansion of Arwen's role in comparison to Tolkien's original text.[108]

In Simon Dumenco's detailed interview for January 2002's *Allure* magazine, Tyler talks about her career at the time of *The Fellowship of the Ring*, and her views on the success of the film.[109] She converses about the filming process, and speaks approvingly of Peter Jackson's directorial skills, in Kathleen Mantel's interview for January 2002's *Pavement* magazine.[110] The development of Arwen's character from novel to screen is the subject of Tyler's interview with Jenny Cooney Carillo in the March 2002 issue of *Dreamwatch*.[111]

Tyler discusses her experiences on the first two films in the trilogy with Pam Baker in a very comprehensive interview for the 30 November 2002 issue of *The Scotsman*.[112] She also talks about the relationship between Arwen and Aragorn, as well as filming in New Zealand, in an interview with Simon Schwartz for *WideScreen* magazine's December 2002 issue.[113] The stress of filming so far away from her home in New York is also discussed in an interview which appears in the 4 December 2002 edition of *Now* magazine.[114]

Arwen and *The Two Towers* are discussed by Tyler in an interview with Joanna Weinberg, which appeared in the 6 December 2002 issue of *The Evening Standard*.[115] She talks about Arwen's elaborate costumes and prosthetic make-up in a light-hearted interview in the December 2002 edition of *Cool* magazine.[116] Tyler discusses the complex CGI character of Gollum, along with the film in general, with Ian Nathan for the January 2003 issue of *Empire* magazine.[117]

Tyler contemplates the impending conclusion of the trilogy, as well as her life at the time, in an interview with Donna Walker Mitchell for the May 2003 issue of *B* magazine.[118] The same theme is discussed in her interview with *OK* magazine for their December 2003 edition.[119] Tyler reflects on the changes in her life since the small-scale independent features of her early career in an in-depth article by Clare Goldwin for the 22 November 2003 issue of *The Daily Mirror*.[120]

The spectacular box-office success of *The Lord of the Rings* series is discussed with reference to Tyler's career in Lisa Arcella's interview for *the New York Daily News'* 3 December 2003 issue.[121] Tyler and co-star Orlando Bloom discuss *The Return of the King*, and their feelings on the conclusion of Jackson's epic project, in an interview with Lynn Barker which appeared in *Teen Hollywood*'s 10 December 2003 edition.[122] Tyler and Bloom pick up on the same theme, as well as retrospectively discussing their characters, in a later interview which was to appear in the June 2004 issue of *One* magazine.[123]

Tyler discusses her post-Arwen career in an interview with Josh Rottenberg in February 2004's *InStyle* magazine.[124] She offers some closing thoughts about playing Arwen in an interview with Ian Spelling for March 2004's *Starlog* magazine.[125]

On a final note, the central cast of the trilogy discuss their feelings on the entire *Lord of the Rings* project, as well as where their careers would be taking them next, in an article by Susan Wloszcznya for *USA Today*'s 13 January 2004 issue.[126] Cindy Pearlman also talks about the upcoming roles of the trilogy's main stars in her article of 22 December 2003 for the *Chicago Sun-Times*.[127]

# 14

# JERSEY GIRL (2004)

*Miramax Films/ Beverly Detroit/ Close Call Films/ View Askew Productions*

**Director**: Kevin Smith
**Producer**: Scott Mosier
**Screenwriter**: Kevin Smith

MAIN CAST

| | |
|---|---|
| **Ben Affleck** | Ollie Trinké |
| **Liv Tyler** | Maya Harding |
| **George Carlin** | Bart Trinké |
| **Raquel Castro** | Gertie Trinké |
| **Jennifer Lopez** | Gertrude Steiney |
| **Jason Biggs** | Arthur Brickman |

After the majesty and grandeur of *The Lord of the Rings* trilogy, almost any subsequent project would have been a significant change of pace for Tyler, and this was certainly true of her next project – an offbeat romantic comedy-drama that seemed a world away from the timeless saga of Arwen and Aragorn. *Jersey Girl* was not only to see her working with Kevin Smith – one of the most celebrated figures in American cult film-making – but would also reunite her on-screen with Ben Affleck for the first time since their cinematic pairing in *Armageddon*. Yet, as we will see, *Jersey Girl* would prove to be just about as different in style, tone and content from Michael Bay's film as was humanly possible.

By the time of *Jersey Girl*'s release, Kevin Smith enjoyed great acclaim not only as a talented director, but also as an actor, screenwriter and producer. He had shot to prominence with *Clerks* (1994), a sophisticated and hugely successful low-budget comedy which had fruitfully tapped into the Generation X zeitgeist of the early 90s, and even now remains a perennial cult favourite amongst audiences. This was followed by teen comedy-drama *Mallrats* (1995); *Chasing Amy* (1997), which explored themes of friendship and the complexities of sexuality; the religiously contentious *Dogma* (1999), and the madcap *Jay and Silent Bob Strike Back* (2001). All but one of these directorial outings had featured Ben Affleck, whose many appearances in Smith's films had showcased his versatile acting range and considerable charm as a comic actor. *Jersey Girl* was to mark a subtle shift in gear for Smith, with many commentators noting a new maturity and refinement in the presentation of his subject matter.

Things are going well in the life of successful New York music publicist Ollie Trinké (Ben Affleck). He is respected by his staff and clients, enjoys a high profile amongst his peers, and has a beautiful soul-mate in book editor Gertrude Steiney (Jennifer Lopez). When they discover that Gertrude is pregnant with their first child, it seems that things just can't get any better.

However, fate deals a cruel hand for the star-crossed couple when Gertrude dies in childbirth, leaving Ollie to raise their new daughter on his own. He soon finds his high-pressure lifestyle to be in conflict with the responsibilities of parenthood, particularly as his contemporaries are less than sympathetic as to the presence of a new baby at news events. After making a catastrophic *faux-pas* at a major press release, where he rashly besmirches a hot new rising talent, Ollie finds himself promptly dismissed from his job and unsure of his future. Chastising himself at having put his professional life ahead of his new duties as a parent, Ollie pledges to make his daughter his priority for the future.

Ollie makes the decision to leave the urban sprawl and relocate to New Jersey, where he and his daughter Gertie (Raquel Castro) move in with Ollie's widower father Bart (George Carlin). Initially, he plans this to be a temporary side-step, but seven years later the pair are still living there. Ollie now works for the local Works Department, following in his father's footsteps, while Gertie attends elementary school nearby. He nevertheless continues to torture himself by trying, entirely in vain, to get back into the publicity business. However, his press release gaffe has become so well-known that no agency in all of New York will take him seriously again – even all these years down the line.

One afternoon, Ollie takes his daughter to hire a video from a local rental store when he is intrigued to meet Maya Harding (Liv Tyler), one of the clerks. When she discovers that Ollie has been innocuously raiding the adult section of the store, she claims that she is currently compiling a thesis for university on the link between family men and pornography, and asks him to take part. Maya gently mocks his rental tastes until she discovers his family situation, and then is mortified by the seeming impropriety of her line of questioning. Using his video store membership details, she drops around to Ollie's home at night to apologise. He accepts, and also reluctantly agrees to meet later and get better acquainted.

Ollie takes Gertie on a trip to New York, as he has promised to get her tickets for Stephen Sondheim's musical *Sweeney Todd*, which is being staged on Broadway. She is enraptured by the

187

show, but Ollie is slightly puzzled later when she seems to prefer the comfortable homeliness of their town in New Jersey to the colourful hustle and bustle of the big city. Given his incessant determination to get back onto the New York employment ladder, Gertie's indifference towards the urban metropolis gives him pause for thought.

Back in New Jersey, Maya meets Ollie as planned at the local diner and continues to quiz him for research purposes. She is stunned to learn that he has remained celibate since the death of his wife seven years previously, and resolves to rectify this situation as soon as possible. Ollie is somewhat stupefied by Maya's forwardness, but is mesmerised enough to cooperate. However, before the pair have the chance to turn Maya's theoretical research into a practical demonstration at home, Gertie arrives early and interrupts them... as do Bart and his workmates soon afterwards. Fortunately for Ollie, everyone seems very accepting of Maya, even although Ollie himself finds her behaviour a little bewildering (though not unattractively so).

At a public meeting of the local authority, Ollie uses his oratory skills to calm an unruly group of residents whose area of the town is soon to be affected by maintenance work. His success buoys his attitude towards his professional marketability, and he decides to arrange a meeting with his old assistant during his publicity days, Arthur Brickman (Jason Biggs), who now has a successful career of his own. Arthur is determined to help his friend out of the doldrums, and manages to arrange a meeting with the head of his firm. However, this causes major friction with Gertie, who hates the thought of leaving her doting grandfather and her local school – particularly as Ollie's interview with the company falls on the same night as Gertie's upcoming school recital, which they have spent weeks together rehearsing.

Maya feigns apathy at Ollie's determination to leave his old home town, though secretly she is heartbroken at his tacit rejection of her. Bart too is hurt by his son's callousness; in spite of his steadfast support of Ollie through the years, the younger man is too captivated by the possibility of returning to his glory days to notice the upsetting effect that his dismissive attitude is having on those around him.

In spite of running the risk of missing Gertie's school recital, Ollie appears on schedule at the publicity agency in New York, only to find himself sitting in the waiting area next to the very singer-turned-actor whose career he had so disastrously snubbed seven years earlier (Will Smith, playing himself). Fortunately, Smith does not recognise him, and engages in some small-talk with Ollie to pass the time. The star voices his regret that, even with a string of huge blockbusters to his name, he still feels that he doesn't have nearly enough time to spend with his three children. The discussion ultimately brings about a profound moment of illumination for Ollie, who decides to skip the interview and race back to New Jersey in order to avoid disappointing Gertie. But will he be able to arrive back in time for the recital, and can he assuage the harm that he has caused by allowing his ambition blind him to the needs of those closest to him?

In *Jersey Girl*, we can perceive that Tyler's comedic lightness of touch had now been honed to an even greater level of refinement, thanks in part to her recent experience of whimsical portrayals in *Cookie's Fortune* and *Dr T and the Women*. The straight-talking Maya builds upon the impressive catalogue of witty characters that Tyler had breathed life into thus far. A shrewd and independent spirit, Maya is instantly memorable right from her first introduction to the viewer, and Tyler seems to take great pleasure in articulating the character's amiability, as well as her breezily unconventional views on life and love. She presents the character with a wonderfully natural playfulness, and this is no truer than in her scenes with Ben Affleck. The pair's offbeat chemistry onscreen feels very different from the rather stagy romance of *Armageddon*, and is all the more satisfying for it. Both actors seem to be much more relaxed in comparison to their previous collaboration, and allow their comic talents to come to the fore in a much more fulfilling and spontaneous manner.

Freed from the encumbrance of *Armageddon*'s high-octane action, Affleck gives a rather laid-back, thoughtful performance in *Jersey Girl*, revealing much more of his charisma and adaptability of portrayal than had been the case in Bay's film. With *Jersey Girl* – and, indeed, his many other cinematic collaborations with Kevin Smith – Affleck amply demonstrates why his performance talents remain in such high demand; he is able to move comfortably between comedy and drama, and complex fusions of the two, with considerable style. He nicely subverts the square-jawed action hero image that he had constructed for films such as *Pearl Harbor* (2001), *The Sum of All Fears* (2002) and *Daredevil* (2003), presenting Ollie as a reasonably grounded but essentially conflicted character who has a believable domestic dichotomy to deal with. His scenes with the infant Gertie are particularly touching, and say much for Affleck's versatility as an actor.

The film also contains many enjoyable supporting perform-ances, including a winning turn from George Carlin as Ollie's long-suffering father Bart. Curmudgeonly but genuinely concerned about his son and granddaughter, the ageing widower can connect meaningfully with the difficulties that Ollie is working through in his life even although the generation gap between them is apt to cause a few minor snags from time to time. The delightful Jennifer Lopez lights up the screen as Gertrude, making the most of her brief screen time to create a likeable and sassy character who seems perfectly matched with Ollie during his sharp-suited early career in the city. Praise is also more than deserved for Raquel Castro in her appearance as Gertie. Castro gives a faultlessly pitched performance as Ollie's sprightly daughter, and marks herself out as an actress with the potential for major achievement in years to come.

Kevin Smith displayed all of his usual stylistic flair in *Jersey Girl*, demonstrating his gift for inventive dialogue and show-casing his encyclopaedic knowledge of modern popular culture. Although the focus on themes such as familial relations and the conflict between ambition and personal happiness meant that the film was something of a change of pace for his directorial career, which had generally steered clear of sentimental issues in favour of ideologically issue-based subject matter, *Jersey Girl* bears many of the distinctive Smith hallmarks that his countless devotees had come to expect. His characteristic wit and affection for both New York City and New Jersey are made more than obvious throughout the film, and he is to be commended not only for the maturity of his treatment of the film's key themes, but also his steadfast refusal to provide any easy answers to his characters' concerns, beyond an acknowledgement of the fact that true family has the ability to transcend barriers and extend far beyond blood relations. The fact that Ollie and Maya's romance is ultimately left somewhat open-ended at the film's conclusion is another testament to the fact that, as in reality, not everything in life is neatly tied up in one easy move.

*Jersey Girl* performed variably amongst reviewers. Some considered Smith's unique and highly personalised style to be something of an acquired taste,[128] whereas others praised the film for its fresh take on the themes of love and the nature of the family unit (in addition to its unswerving refusal to regard these themes either too seriously or excessively flippantly).[129] To some degree, the film's critical reception may have suffered from its proximity to the previous year's screening of Martin Brest's *Gigli* (2003), a high-profile release that had also starred Ben Affleck and Jennifer Lopez, but which had performed disastrously with many critics.

For Tyler, however, her appearance in *Jersey Girl* was widely regarded as another successful performance; not for the first time in her career, some reviewers reflected that Tyler's portrayal was actually to outshine the film in which it took place.[130] Certainly, it is a very lively and uplifting performance, from Maya's somewhat irregular style of research during her early fact-finding interviews through to her energetic appearance in Gertie's school staging of a scene from *Sweeney Todd* (which, incidentally, was to feature a very charming Mockney London accent from Tyler that rivalled anyone from *Plunkett and Macleane*). Tyler had demonstrated that the massive global success she had achieved from her appearance in *The Lord of the Rings* trilogy had not fostered complacency in her approach to her acting prowess, and the sparkling performance she gives in *Jersey Girl* was to prove that not only were her comic talents continuing to diversify, but also that her general versatility as an actress was broadening ever more widely.

## FURTHER READING

Director Kevin Smith discusses *Jersey Girl*, and his approach to filmmaking in general, in a comprehensive article by Susan Wloszczyna in the 21 March 2004 issue of *USA Today*.[131] Smith also discusses the film in the context of his wider filmography in an interview with Jeff Vice in the 26 March 2004 issue of the *Deseret Morning News*,[132] and Mike Thomas in the 21 March 2004 edition of the *Chicago Sun-Times*.[133]

Tyler talks about *Jersey Girl*, and the change of pace after completing work on *The Lord of the Rings* trilogy, in an interview with Juan Morales in the Spring 2004 issue of *LA Confidential*.[134] This is also the subject of her interview with Martyn Palmer for July 2004's *Total Film* magazine.[135] She touches on the character of Maya in an article by Alun Palmer for the 1 July 2004 edition of *The Daily Mirror*.[136]

Jordan Riefe's feature on *Jersey Girl*, in which Tyler discusses the film, star Ben Affleck and director Kevin Smith, appears in the July 2004 issue of *HotDog*.[137] Tyler discusses her life at the time of the film's cinematic release with Jennifer Graham in the April 2004 issue of *Marie Claire*.[138] Her approach to her character in the film is the subject of her interview with Erin McWhirter for August 2004's *New Idea* magazine.[139]

# 15

# LONESOME JIM (2005)

*InDigEnt/ Plum Pictures*

**Director**: Steve Buscemi
**Producers**: Jake Abraham, Steve Buscemi, Daniela Soto-Taplin, Galt Niederhoffer, Celine Rattray and Gary Winick
**Screenwriter**: James C. Strouse

MAIN CAST

| | |
|---|---|
| **Casey Affleck** | Jim Roush |
| **Liv Tyler** | Anika |
| **Mary Kay Place** | Sally Roush |
| **Seymour Cassel** | Don Roush |
| **Kevin Corrigan** | Tim Roush |
| **Jack Rovello** | Ben |

*Lonesome Jim* was, in one sense, a much more modest cinematic outing for Tyler than had been the case for quite some time, as the film would see her making a welcome return to the trail-blazing independent roots of her acting career. Yet *Lonesome Jim* was a no less significant project in spite of its modest scale and budget; it was helmed by acclaimed character actor and director Steve Buscemi, whose new film was hotly anticipated by critics as well as his numerous fans. *Lonesome Jim* would share a number of themes with *Jersey Girl*, including the redemptive qualities of love and the difficulties of an unexpected return to the familial nest. However, in both approach and execution the two films were to be poles apart.

Steve Buscemi is a prolific and prominent actor both in film and on American television, having chalked up dozens upon dozens of noteworthy appearances since the early 1980s. His highly distinctive physical and vocal presence, together with his acclaimed performance style, have made him a sought-after talent in both independent and studio-led film-making. He has given significant performances in high-profile films as diverse as *Barton Fink* (1991), *Reservoir Dogs* (1992), *Pulp Fiction* (1994), *Kansas City* (1996) and *The Big Lebowski* (1998), amongst a great many others. However, in recent years Buscemi has become equally well-known as a director of independent feature films, beginning with the acclaimed *Trees Lounge* (1996), which he was also to script and star in. A low-key, intimate drama about the lives of a few regular visitors to a small local bar, the film impressed audiences and critics alike. This was followed several years later by the intense prison drama *Animal Factory* (2000), adapted by Edward Bunker from his own novel, which also caught the eye of reviewers due to its well-chosen cast and finely detailed characterisation. Thus by the time of *Lonesome Jim*'s release, commentators were watching with interest to see if Buscemi's directorial winning streak could continue into his third feature film.

Life has been troubled for aspiring young writer Jim Roush (Casey Affleck). Having left home some years previously in order to seek out success in New York City, triumph proved elusive and he found himself walking dogs for a living. Feeling that the Big Apple may not suit his sensibilities after all, Jim has finally admitted defeat and returned to live with his family in Indiana. There he is enthusiastically greeted by his parents Sally (Mary Kay Place) and Don (Seymour Cassel), though less so by his older brother Tim (Kevin Corrigan), who quietly resents Jim's *laissez-faire* attitude to working for a living and the fact that he appears to take his family for granted. His mother is delighted to welcome the prodigal son back to the nest, though Jim's father is more concerned about what he will decide to do with his life – having reached the age of twenty-seven, Jim still appears totally directionless. Even more puzzling to his parents is the fact that Jim doesn't even seem to care.

Jim goes for a wander around town at night, eventually happening upon a lively bar in the neighbourhood. Whilst drinking alone, he meets Anika (Liv Tyler), a nurse at the local hospital. He awkwardly strikes up a conversation with her, and seems a little surprised when she responds to his interest in her. Taking a shine to Jim, she invites him back to her ward at the hospital for a one-night stand. Unfortunately for Jim, his performance there is about as impressive as his writing career has been.

The next day, Jim (now even more miserable) pays a visit to the town's community centre, where Tim is the coach for an elementary school girls' basketball team. Following a match, Jim enters into a rather brutal conversation with his brother where he regrets the nature of his life and, indeed, his very existence. This soon degenerates into a nihilistic diatribe, whereby Jim points out that his brother – messily divorced and trapped in an underpaid job that he despises – should by all accounts be even more depressed than he is. Naturally, none of these observations endear him to Tim, who already has hard feelings about Jim's return to Indiana.

Soon afterwards, Jim discovers that Tim is in a coma after his car collided with a tree. According to his mother, this isn't the first time that such an 'accident' has occurred. Jim reluctantly agrees to coach the girls' basketball team while Tim is out of commission, but refuses to help Sally at the family business. Don, who is becoming infuriated with Jim's blatant apathy, pressures him into changing his mind about assisting at their metalworking factory. He is particularly adamant that Jim lend a hand due to the fact that his mother is now short-handed in the extreme. Indifferent as always, Jim agrees to help out.

Surprisingly, Jim does as he pledges, though without much enthusiasm. He continues to coach the basketball team, but only by putting as little effort or interest into the task as possible. Likewise, he rather half-heartedly assists at the factory, where he meets his Uncle Stacy (Mark Boone Jr.) – otherwise known as 'Evil' – who is one of the employees there. Jim soon discovers that Evil is running a small but lucrative narcotics exchange from his nearby trailer, though he is not so much intrigued by the news as he is more or less totally unresponsive.

Jim visits his brother in hospital. Though still in a coma, he tries in vain to communicate with him – though only to attempt to persuade him to regain consciousness and get back to work (thus saving him the trouble of assisting at the factory). He awkwardly bumps into Anika again, whom he had been studiously avoiding after their last encounter. However, Jim is somewhat dumbfounded when he finds that she is still interested in him, and they arrange a date for the weekend.

Later, Jim visits Evil to ask for some advice on how to improve his woeful sex technique. Evil regales him with some heartfelt guidance, and then asks a favour of Jim. As Evil's credit rating is so abysmal that he has been banned from opening accounts at most banks, he asks Jim if he will open an account on his behalf. When Jim asks for more details, Evil explains that he wants to purchase items by post that can only be bought by cheque, such as additions to his collection of animal skulls. Unresponsive as ever, Jim grudgingly agrees, and Evil promptly hands over a tin containing $4000 in cash.

The weekend arrives, and Jim is ready for his date with Anika. However, he is surprised when he turns up at her home only to be greeted by her son Ben (Jack Rovello), whose existence he hadn't previously known about. He decides to return to his parents' home and encourages Tim's two daughters to play with Ben on a garden trampoline belonging to the neighbours. The house now empty, Jim and Anika have a more meaningful conversation and get to know each other a little better than had been the case during their previous encounter.

Sally is elated when Tim reawakens from his coma. Tim, however, is less jubilant – he'd hoped that the car crash would have been fatal. The increasingly world-weary Don has little sympathy for his son, whom he judges to be inconsiderate and self-absorbed for even attempting suicide. Tim asks them to leave, but perks up when he meets Anika for the first time – as he points out to Jim, if even his hopeless brother can have a relationship with her then there surely must be hope for him, too.

Matters become markedly more complicated when the Drug Enforcement Agency raid the metalworking factory out of the blue and arrest Sally on suspicion of drug trafficking. Although Sally has no idea why the charge has been brought against her, the DEA explain that several packages had been sent from the factory's address which had contained narcotics, and all of them had been authorised with her signature. Don has the unenviable task of convincing the DEA that their family had no part in any such illegal activities, but Evil later admits to Jim that he had been responsible sending for the suspect parcels, and warns against him making any unwelcome testimony to the authorities.

The DEA promptly put a freeze on the Roush family business, suspecting it of being a front for drug transactions. Don is frustrated at his lack of options, and has little choice but to wait for an official judgement to be made. Jim tries to convince Evil to confess his part in the company's downfall, but the elder man won't even consider it.

Meanwhile, Tim has been transferred from hospital back to the family home. He still has two legs in plaster, and has regular visits from Anika in her professional capacity. Jim becomes jealous at the attention she is paying to his brother, even given her caring role, but she makes it clear that she doesn't appreciate his possessiveness. However, they reconcile their differences during a later discussion, where Anika begins to deduce that Jim has deeper feelings for her than his disinterested façade would at first suggest.

Sally is released from prison on bail, and tries to return her home to its usual state of domestic perfection. She meets Anika and Ben, who arrive for dinner, and seems to approve of her relationship with Jim. Jim, on the other hand, is quietly starting to formulate longer term plans for once. When they are alone together, he tries to persuade Anika to leave Indiana with him and relocate elsewhere. She considers this to be out of the question; she can't afford to move, and doesn't want to put too much distance between Ben and his natural father. Yet Jim feels that he is being stifled by his proximity to his family, and longs to make the break once again.

Jim confesses to Sally his intention to depart. She is saddened, but nonetheless tries to see Jim's viewpoint in the matter. He begins to make final preparations to get away from Indiana once more. However, with his mother's trial still pending, and his relationship with Anika hanging in the balance, everything hinges on whether Jim will face up to his responsibilities or decide to run from them once again.

*Lonesome Jim* confirmed the fact that in spite of her ever-growing worldwide fame, Tyler still appeared to be principally interested in embracing quality acting roles no matter how large or small the scale of the film that they appeared in. *Lonesome Jim* was replete with Buscemi's stylistic imprimatur, his typically acute observation of character dynamics being particularly sharp all the way throughout. This was in no small part due to a very perceptive and insightful screenplay by acclaimed writer James C. Strouse, which brings small-town Indiana to life in a very well-defined, lifelike manner. Indeed, this was reflected in the film's general atmosphere, its slight hint of claustrophobia nicely setting off Jim's feelings of being fenced in both by his family and his sense of accountability to them.

Tyler ably projects Anika's compassionate nature, often suggested through the character's satisfaction with her work in the medical sector, as well as her palpable sense of fun and cheerfulness. Anika works especially effectively in contrast with Jim – and also, to a lesser extent, Tim – both of whom make her playful gaiety all the more apparent due to their own downbeat, gloomy dispositions. Anika's optimism and gregarious exuberance, in spite of her own personal difficulties, make her the perfect romantic foil for Jim, who is ensnared in his own introverted world of existential angst. Tyler is particularly successful in demarcating the early stages of Anika and Jim's relationship. After their unfortunate first 'date', it seems manifestly clear that there is no future for the two characters, but for some reason Anika sees something in Jim that no-one else can, and decides to follow her insight accordingly. Tyler brings a touchingly sensitive quality to Anika throughout the course of the character's unconventional romance with Jim, and compliments this with a spiky wit and easy-going attitude that slowly but surely begins to chip away at the doggedly disaffected anti-hero.

*Lonesome Jim* benefits from a wonderfully misanthropic performance from Casey Affleck in the title role, and it is one which he invests with an understated and remarkably genuine pathos. Affleck (who, incidentally, is the brother of actor Ben Affleck) had previously made noteworthy appearances in films such as Morgan J. Freeman's *Desert Blue* (1998), Michael Almereyda's *Hamlet* (2000) and Steven Soderbergh's *Ocean's Eleven* (2001), but rarely had he given a performance quite so strikingly distinct as that of Jim. Affleck manages to turn a thoroughly unlikeable character into a compelling protagonist, and never skips a beat as he delineates Jim's deepening sense of misery and self-absorption. He is assisted by many finely tuned character observations along the way, such as the fact that he brings a packet of potato chips to his coma-ridden brother's bedside, disregarding the fact that he is quite patently unconscious, and then tries intently to encourage him back to wakefulness – not out of concern for Tim's health, but because his brother's revival will mean that he will no longer have to work at the family business. It is this openly narcissistic monomania that makes Jim such a fascinating character – although he is devoid of most positive aspects, he is not, in and of himself, either malicious or immoral. Rather, it would be fairer to say that he is nihilistic in nature, totally indifferent to the world around him and apathetic to the requirements and expectations of those close to him. Affleck also demonstrates some fine comic timing, such as his weirdly rambling pre-game speech to his slightly bewildered junior basketball team, which was to reveal a deeply humorous nucleus lurking beneath the film's ostensibly serious subject matter. Jim's monologue near the film's conclusion does suggest that there is still hope for the disaffected character, and Affleck carries this off with great aplomb.

The film also greatly benefited from some terrific supporting performances. Mary Kay Place puts in a splendid portrayal of the ever-cheerful Sally, her unwaveringly bright and breezy demeanour concealing genuine concern for her two thoroughly despondent sons. Her heart-to-heart with Jim, where she earnestly asks where she went wrong in raising him to have caused such misery in his life, is heart-rending in the extreme. Seymour Cassel is likewise highly effective as Jim's long-suffering father Don, who grows slowly more cynical and world-weary as the film continues. Despite his ill-disguised contempt for his sons' self-absorbed natures, Don seems to have all but given up hope that they will snap out of their gloomy melancholy and lead productive lives. Knowing that his disparagement is falling on deaf ears, he has long since resigned himself to concentrating on his own business and letting everyone else take care of theirs. Mark Boone Jr. provides strong comic relief as the drug-addled, moped-riding Evil, whilst Jack Rovello delivers a confident and polished performance as Anika's droll son Ben.

At time of writing, *Lonesome Jim* had not yet received a widespread cinematic release, having been screened only at a number of international film events across the world. Therefore, reviews of the film in the printed press are relatively few in number. However, those commentators who have had the opportunity to view *Lonesome Jim* have been largely positive about the experience, most of them praising Buscemi's directorship and the performances of the main cast.[140] This approval was mirrored at the Sundance Film Festival in 2005, where Buscemi was nominated for the prestigious Grand Jury Prize for *Lonesome Jim*.

On 14 December 2004, Tyler and her husband Royston Langdon proudly announced the birth of their new son, Milo William Langdon. Following this first addition to their family, Tyler was consequently to take a short hiatus from acting for around a year or so, not filming during the course of 2005 (although *Lonesome Jim*, which had been filmed earlier, would screen during this period). This break was to mark the conclusion of a fascinating phase of her film career, an impressive period of development which had spanned just over ten years and no less than seventeen prominent motion picture appearances. Her prolific and versatile performances had impressed the public and gained the respect of critics, assuring her the best possible foundation for the next chapter in her ever-developing career.

## FURTHER READING

Jeff Vice discusses *Lonesome Jim*'s place in the line-up for the 2005 Sundance Film Festival in his article of 16 January 2005 for the *Deseret Morning News*.[141] The film's significant position in that year's Sundance Film Festival is also discussed by Nick Roddick in an article for *The Evening Standard*'s 20 January 2005 issue.[142]

# CONCLUSION

## Liv Tyler in Modern Film and Popular Culture: The Story So Far

As we have witnessed over the course of this book, the first decade of Liv Tyler's film career has been both critically successful and popular with audiences the world over. It has seen her develop from a successful teenage model with limited acting experience into an international superstar who commands the respect of the global film industry and many critical commentators across various continents. However, her path to such acclaim was forged with more than just raw talent, excellent publicity and sheer hard work. For Liv Tyler has already become a cultural icon in her own right, and has many unique qualities which distinguish her even in an industry which has no shortage of exceptional flair and aptitude.

It seems fair to note that even if Tyler had never entered the acting profession, she would almost certainly have enjoyed some degree of fame. With father Steven Tyler, lead singer of the massively successful Aerosmith, and rock legend stepfather Todd Rundgren, she had every right to bear the oft-cited title of 'Rock Royalty'. Yet even from the beginning of her professional career in her mid-teens, she always appears to have been determined to prove herself as a distinctive talent in her own right. Her mother, well-known model and musician Bebe Buell, clearly had an enormously positive influence on the young Tyler; her obvious knowledge and experience of popular culture seems to have imbued her daughter with the kind of stamina, unpretentiousness and industrious attitude that has come to typify Tyler's approach to acting right the way through her career.

Buell's encouragement and expertise also appears evident in the time that she served as Tyler's manager during her earlier films, for their collaborative choice of features at the time was inspired. Within the course of three prolific years, Tyler had experience of a mainstream thriller (*Silent Fall*), offbeat domestic drama (*Heavy*), teen comedy (*Empire Records*) and, most crucially, her break-through role in European art-house cinema (*Stealing Beauty*). By alternating so rapidly between different genres even at this nascent stage in her career, Tyler managed to stave off any potential criticism that she possessed limited acting range (perhaps one of the most damaging assertions to point at any young performer) and instead managed to impress many commentators with the versatility of her performances.

Yet it was not only her cross-genre flexibility that brought her attention. *Heavy* and *Stealing Beauty* had both made an impact with reviewers, and the fact that Tyler was squarely in centre stage for both films (particularly the latter) augured well for her future in the industry. However, it is just as notable that *Silent Fall* and *Empire Records*, which performed variably with the critics, still managed to generate positive press for the distinctiveness of Tyler's performances. This was especially true of *Silent Fall*, which now owes much of its significance in film history to the fact that it featured Tyler's debut appearance. It seems that even from this early stage in her career, columnists were detecting that Tyler had definite star quality, and this attribute was to be greatly honed and refined in the years ahead.

So what was it about Liv Tyler that caught the imagination of so many commentators? In the aesthetic sense, one cannot deny that she is indisputably very appealing, and her uniquely striking beauty – most notably her soulful, deep blue eyes and tremendously distinctive pouting lips – is certainly one factor which has distinguished her from other more conventionally attractive actresses of her generation. But more significant is the fact that her natural good looks tend to be balanced by a profound emotional depth and penetrating intelligence (both factors being at their most evident in *Stealing Beauty*, though the latter is certainly brought to the forefront even as early as *Silent Fall*). Most noteworthy of all is the fact that although Tyler's characters sometimes form the focus of desire within a film, occasionally even personifying it, she has never once allowed herself to be objectified. Even in *Stealing Beauty*, where it could be argued that desire for Lucy Harmon (and, in turn, Lucy Harmon's longing to be desired) is absolutely central to the narrative, Tyler manages to achieve equilibrium in her portrayal of the torrid emotional forces affecting her character, because she tempers them with a discrete individuality and resolute self-determination all the way throughout.

Independence and uniqueness of personality seem to have become important to Tyler's approach to acting. It was certainly evident in the wise, slightly disenchanted Faye Dolan in *That Thing You Do!*, and was brought even more to the forefront in her portrayal of the emotionally raw Pamela Abbott in *Inventing the Abbotts*. Both of those films had showcased her ability to work in the more restrained milieu of a period setting – one feature tempered by light-heartedness, the other calling more heavily on her dramatic skills. The exciting chemistry between Tyler and Joachin Phoenix in *Inventing the Abbotts* underscored her ability to render an effective on-screen romance, and this would be used again in *Armageddon* with Ben Affleck's character AJ Frost (to lesser effect, due to her more limited screen time). Although *Empire Records* had toyed with the theme of friendship and affection, and *Heavy* and *Stealing Beauty* had both been more interested in the mechanics and nature of desire, by the late '90s Tyler was making the most of her growing ability to articulate the complexities of romantic tenderness on-screen. It was a capability well-suited to her command of emotional sensitivity.

The theme of romance would continue into *Plunkett and Macleane*, where – as Lady Rebecca Gibson – Tyler was to personify another of the themes which recur throughout her career: that of salvation. Although trapped herself by class and society, Rebecca is the very incarnation of freedom in the mind of Jonny Lee Miller's Macleane; she symbolises an escape not only from incarceration in a debtor's prison, but also from the rigid strictures and hypocrisy of pre-Enlightenment England. The film again reaffirmed Tyler's capacity for imbuing her characters with fierce independence – her defiance of Mr Chance, for instance, as well as her general disdain with the false decorum of the age. However, *Plunkett and Macleane* was also significant for displaying one of the key characteristics of the latter half of Tyler's first decade in film; the ethereal depiction of Rebecca as she appears, almost phantom-like, to Macleane at a society ball foreshadows similar directorial treatment of Tyler's characters in *Onegin* and *The Lord of the Rings*. This transcendental quality would also become significant later for other thematic reasons.

In her two collaborations with Robert Altman, *Cookie's Fortune* and *Dr T and the Women*, Tyler took full advantage of the opportunity to distinguish herself in a couple of choice character pieces. Undoubtedly, in terms of significance and screen time, she is able to do more with Emma Duvall than was the case with Marilyn, but both parts have their own particular consequence. Being cast as the practical, straight-thinking Emma allowed Tyler to demonstrate that she had more than enough ability to portray a less outwardly glamorous character in an effective way –

particularly as her performance leaves us in little doubt that Emma concealed much of her true beauty behind her ostensibly gruff exterior. Marilyn, on the other hand, presented Tyler with her first portrayal of a lesbian character, and again she did not squander the prospects that this presented. Her scenes with Kate Hudson's Dee Dee are permeated with such genuine warmth and mutual affection that the relationship between the two is never less than believable, and their chemistry is often poignant.

Tyler's appearances in Altman's films were to complete her metamorphosis from a popular teen personality into an enduring star with the ability to stay the distance of a professional film career – a gradual shift which had begun with *Stealing Beauty*, and which had continued with her parts in *Inventing the Abbotts* and *Armageddon*. The emotional maturity that Tyler had always brought to her roles was developed further in Altman's films, but was arguably even more evident in *Onegin*, perhaps her most accomplished and fully-rounded performance to date. Tyler was perfectly cast as the soulful yet despondent Tatyana Larina, and indeed she makes the role her own in such a way that it is difficult to imagine another actress working quite so effectively in conjunction with Ralph Fiennes' title character. Although the critical response to *Onegin* was slightly uneven, a majority of reviewers voiced approval of Tyler's performance, and indeed the merit that she gained in tackling so heavyweight a role – not least given the massive significance of Pushkin's work in his native Russia – meant that this historical adaptation marked a definite critical high-point in Tyler's acting career.

Tyler appeared to take some delight in playing around with her established sex-symbol status in *One Night at McCool's*, where she modifies her customary contemplative and deliberate approach to characterisation in order to portray an alluringly seductive *femme fatale* with considerable ironic glee. In many ways, *One Night at McCool's* built on *Onegin* in that it reinforced Tyler's sense of mesmeric attractiveness, which was a factor that had been emphasised early on in her career (in *Heavy* and *Stealing Beauty*) but had subsequently been played down when she had explored different aspects of romance in her numerous roles instead. This would ultimately came to the forefront again, in a very different manner, with *The Lord of the Rings* trilogy. The passionate love affair that exists between Aragorn and Arwen is central to both their story arcs, prominent in all three films, and ultimately the significance of Aragorn's long-lasting devotion to his distant lover resonates right throughout the story. Given the obvious importance of the role, it is of major credit to Tyler that she is able to believably articulate the strong emotional bonds that exist between Arwen and Aragorn, both throughout the main narrative and via flashback sequences. One of J.R.R. Tolkien's most enigmatic characters, the otherworldly presence of the Elven princess is also strongly evocative of a certain mythic quality, suggesting that – to Aragorn, at the very least – Arwen's love is a prize no less exceptional than the One Ring, and that her Evenstar jewel was replete with virtue in the same way that Sauron's Ruling Ring was full of danger and treachery.

The two roles which followed her appearances in *The Lord of the Rings* trilogy, Maya Harding in *Jersey Girl* and Anika in *Lonesome Jim*, both fostered another element of Tyler's approach to romantic performances. This aspect was the representation of a kind of emotional deliverance, dispensed via her character's wisdom and affection, to salve the dejection of the central male lead. Once again, the pivotal narrative function of this role underscored the independence and autonomy of Tyler's characters, emphasising that not only were Maya and Anika self-reliant from the male protagonist, but ultimately that the central leads would come to depend on Tyler's characters in different ways. Thus Maya and Anika utilise both their perception and self-determination to revitalise Ollie and Jim through emotional support, which Tyler expresses to good effect with a typically reflective approach to compassion and expressive sensitivity.

Therefore, at the end of the first decade of Tyler's film career, two central themes appear to have established themselves at the core of her performances. Firstly, there are the performances in which she appears as the central focus of desire, the pinnacle of others' hopes and dreams made manifest, in films such as *Heavy*, *Stealing Beauty*, *Onegin* a n d *One Night at McCool's*. These narratives stress not only Tyler's physical attractiveness, but also the affecting nature of her wide range of emotional expression. Balancing the above performances is her second main category of portrayal; that of the personification of hope, redemption or salvation in the face of hardship, peril and adversity. This is often articulated by her characters' significant position in relation to a male protagonist, and is most evident in her appearances in *That Thing You Do!*, *Inventing the Abbotts*, *Plunkett and Macleane*, *The Lord of the Rings* films, *Jersey Girl* a n d *Lonesome Jim*. These portrayals tend to lean more heavily on her ability to communicate depth of sentiment, freedom of expression, and emotional wisdom. In addition, there are roles such as that of Tatyana Larina in *Onegin* in which a combination of the above two factors are united to produce a kind of duality of purpose.

This then takes us to another intermittent characteristic of Tyler's appearances which came to be developed late in the 1990s; the establishment of an occasionally ethereal or otherworldly approach to the characters in some of her portrayals. This was true for some of *Plunkett and Macleane*, *Onegin* a n d *One Night at McCool's*, though it is perhaps most evident of all in *The Lord of the Rings* trilogy where Arwen's character is expressed – no less potently – through reflections and dreams. These diaphanous modes of depiction tended to be combined with qualities of the individual characters themselves. For instance, Lady Rebecca's distaste with the nature of her repressive and institutionally misogynistic society, combined with Macleane's breathlessly idealised view of her, combine to suggest that she is a character who transcends modern (and historical) anxieties to surpass and rise above the grim, sometimes brutal environment around her. Certainly Mr Chance, the very epitome of male chauvinist barbarity, is unable to fully subsume her will, much less seize it from her fully. Jewel Valentine in *One Night at McCool's* is different in the sense that she is largely defined by the viewpoint of other people – specifically, people who are besotted with her, due to the fact that they are projecting their own desires onto what they subconsciously perceive to be a blank psychological canvas. Tyler, of course, subverts this apparently casual sexist proclivity by instilling Jewel with a neatly-concealed strength of personality which becomes all too apparent as the film progresses. However, while Jewel's aspect is reflected through the yearning and aspirations of others, the soft focus and hazy, spectral impression of the character's quasi-dreamlike form simultaneously suggests both a tangible person and a fantasy that will always remain tantalisingly out of reach.

Tyler's performance as Tatyana Larina in *Onegin* is exceptional in the sense that her depiction is at its most ethereal when Evgeny Onegin first briefly glimpses her at the time of their first acquaintance, and then again at the end of the film when she is married to his cousin Prince Nikitin. Only when Tatyana willingly makes herself romantically available to Onegin does she appear to be entirely accessible to him; this occurs only when she has decided that she is attracted to him, and ends shortly after he so devastatingly rejects her. Thus, in this instance, her ethereality is linked to her willing availability to the protagonist rather than her perceived place in society (even although, in the end, she achieves the very pinnacle of class position).

It is ultimately as Arwen that we first see Tyler as a truly mythic beauty in the Levi-Straussian sense. For just as Tolkien had defined the Elvish race as beautiful, immortal and cultured, Arwen Undomiel is highlighted as among the most attractive of all her species, matched in aspect only by Lúthien Tinúviel, the great Elvish beauty whose grace Tolkien had written about so evocatively in *The Silmarillion*.[143] Thus Arwen's radiant appearance throughout *The Lord of the Rings* can be attributed not only to the fondness of Aragorn's memories of her, but also the stylistic contrast between the elegant, refined Elves and the much more robust and utilitarian Humans, Dwarves and Hobbits who populate Middle-earth. Arwen's ethereality is matched only by Cate Blanchett's Galadriel, who – dwelling in the ancient Elven realm of Lothlórien – has retained something of the grandeur and majesty of Middle-earth's First Age. We may surmise that, as Tolkien indicates the fact that Arwen was known to have spent time during her youth in Lothlórien, her insight gained away from Rivendell may provide some additional reason as to why she appears at times to be more radiant in aspect when compared to other Elves in the central narrative, such as Elrond, Legolas or Haldir. Interestingly, this remains true even after her transmutation into human form at the trilogy's conclusion.

Tyler's appearance in *The Lord of the Rings* alone is virtually guaranteed to assure her some degree of cinematic immortality, due to the huge popularity and cross-cultural appeal of Peter Jackson's films (and, in turn, the continuing draw of Tolkien's original masterpiece). Yet her abundant and varied appearances, and the versatility of her acting skills, strongly suggest that the best of her acting career may still be to come. Her careful choice of roles has meant that she has avoided the endless cycle of remakes and retreads which tend to be generated by Hollywood, and although her appearances in blockbusters such as *Armageddon* and *The Lord of the Rings* have hugely enhanced her public profile, she continues to select many inventive films – sometimes small in scale and modest in budget – to hone her acting skills still further, and demonstrate the growing breadth of her acting range. She also never shies away from controversial subject matter, such as the gender-related contention which was to surround *Dr T and the Women*, and it is often the case that her edgier performances in films such as *Stealing Beauty* and *Inventing the Abbotts* are the portrayals which are applauded most sincerely by the critics. Her profile has been further enhanced by the fact that in many of her most high-status projects, she tended to be the primary female character (*That Thing You Do!*, *Armageddon*, *One Night at McCool's*), which enhanced the significance of her role and served to encourage critical focus on her performance.

Additionally, Tyler is not a flamboyant performer, and is always subtle and thoughtful in her approach to characters (even when they are larger-than-life individuals, such as Jewel Valentine or Maya Harding). However, the low-key restraint of her acting style never diminishes her enthusiasm for roles, and she always appears to give a performance her all, letting her trenchant emotional intelligence shine from every new portrayal. She seems never to be afraid of trying new things, and most notably she tends not to take easy choices with her career, always pursuing roles which are of the most interest to her rather than opting for the safe options. This is what marks Tyler out as such an interesting performer – it is very difficult to pigeonhole her, as the sheer variety of her roles during her first decade in film has meant that there is rarely a common stylistic denominator beyond her trademark independence of thought and sensitivity of performance.

There is also the interesting point that Tyler has, thus far, very rarely been cast in antagonistic roles, which may be another factor in her generally-perceived likeability amongst audiences. Indeed, her two most malevolent characters – Jewel Valentine in *One Night at McCool's* and *Silent Fall*'s Sylvie Warden – both exhibit mitigating dynamics which go some way to counterbalancing their malicious actions. In the case of Sylvie Warden, her crimes stem from the fact that she herself is psychologically damaged character, and the violent actions that she engages in are a direct result of the abuse that she has suffered in early life. Jewel Valentine, on the other hand, seems to be more of an arch-materialist than genuinely villainous in nature. Although this does not excuse Jewel's immoral actions, in the context of a black comedy her characterisation is pitched very effectively. Therefore, the fact that Tyler has not yet been cast as a completely unsympathetic character may be another reason why she has become better known for her portrayals of everywoman characters, such as Faye Dolan, Maya Harding and *Lonesome Jim*'s

Anika. The effective rendering of such believable characters, often appearing in high-profile releases, corresponds with the widely-held audience perception of Tyler's public persona: both unassuming and affable.

Tyler has worked productively with celebrated veterans of the industry as well as directors who were new to feature-length films, and her success on-screen has been matched by her professionalism in the wider media. She has always performed well in interviews even from the earliest stages in her career, and numerous commentators have acknowledged her genuine friendliness and honest charm when in discussion with her. However, she has always seemed an essentially private person, even in spite of the fact that she is related to (and has bonds of friendship with) highly significant personalities from the world of film and popular music. Regardless of an eager willingness to talk openly about her roles and artistic motivation, she has quietly and carefully guarded her personal life, and seems happy to let the proficiency of her on-screen appearances speak for her instead.

Tyler has remained a popular individual with audiences and media professionals right throughout her career. In part, this is undoubtedly due to the fact that right from the outset she has worked with some of the biggest names in the international film industry, including many Academy Award winners and nominees, which has accentuated her own considerable professional significance. But the main reason why she appears to be so enduringly popular with her loyal fan-base is because, time and again, she appears to be a very genuine, down-to-earth person in an industry famed for its simulacra and heightened sensationalism. She has appeared more than happy in the past to interact with film fans at awards ceremonies and official events, often chatting candidly with them when time allows. She has also endeared herself to the public with engaging little quirks, such as an occasional tendency to kick off her designer shoes at premieres and conduct impromptu autograph sessions on the red carpet more comfortably in her bare feet.[144] It is such honest touches of unpretentiousness which continue to mark her out as a grounded and unaffected individual, full of respect for the film industry whilst never taking its pomp and ceremony all too seriously.

Tyler's thorough knowledge of fashion has led to her becoming something of a trendsetter, and today she remains a favourite of numerous high-profile designers. This has combined with a highly successful ongoing relationship with modelling throughout her life, including her hugely well-received appearances for companies such as global cosmetics giant Givenchy,[145] who thought so much of Tyler that they famously named a rose after her in mid-2005 as part of the launch of their *Very Irresistible Givenchy* Sensual Eau de Parfum.[146] Again, however, she never appears to have let her continuing status as a style icon distract her from the here-and-now of an infamously capricious industry, and away from award ceremonies and movie premieres her fashion style remains unique and inspired without ever being ostentatious.

In interviews, Tyler has often maintained that despite being voted by the public as one of the most attractive women in the media, it is those closest to her who matter more than the perceived image of her public persona.[147] This modesty may have seemed unconvincing if uttered by someone else in her position, but Tyler's general approach to other areas of her public life tends to corroborate this humility as being neither contrived nor disingenuous. Indeed, her concern for people other than herself is very evident in her dedicated support of charities, where she has made use of her massive star profile to help those in need. This is particularly true of organisations in her native New York, where she has offered encouragement for charity auctions and other fundraising events for good causes over the years. Perhaps most notably, she was appointed U.S. Fund for UNICEF Ambassador in 2003, and has actively promoted the work of that organisation to raise awareness of its various health and education programmes worldwide.

In recent years, Tyler has repeatedly expressed a desire to one day diversify into the field of popular music,[148] and her haunting vocal performance of 'Arwen's Song' in the extended edition of *The Return of the King* augurs well for the future if she does indeed decide to proceed along this path. Yet it is not only Tyler's family background that ties her to the world of music; in 2002, she herself was the subject of a highly listenable pop tribute from Dutch band The Travoltas.[149] However, in spite of her musical aspirations, Tyler has also constantly maintained a desire to remain active in the film industry for many years to come, which should come as a considerable relief to her growing army of fans.

Liv Tyler has much to be proud of at the end of her first decade in film, but it is also true to say that she has much to look forward to. Equally adept with roles in both comedy and drama, she is now an internationally-recognised star with the ability to greatly enhance the profile of a feature film by her very presence. Although she has already achieved no small measure of recognition from various different film award ceremonies, the increasing quality of her performances, her eagerness to experiment with different genres and her infectious enthusiasm for acting are all good omens for even greater success in years to come.

Liv Tyler is that rarest of rarities; a cultural icon who is a tangible human being, a superstar who is never afraid to be herself. And that's why, even now, her star is still in ascendance.

# NOTES AND REFERENCES

# CHRONOLOGICAL
# FILMOGRAPHY

## SILENT FALL (1994)

*Production Company*: Morgan Creek Productions/ Kouf/ Bigelow Productions.

*Distributor*: Warner Brothers.

*Director*: Bruce Beresford.

*Producer*: James G. Robinson.

*Co-Producers*: Lynn Bigelow, Penelope L. Foster and Jim Kouf.

*Executive Producer*: Gary Barber.

*Screenplay*: Akiva Goldsman.

*Film Editor*: Ian Crafford.

*Cinematography*: Peter James.

*Unit Production Manager*: Penelope L. Foster.

*Production Supervisor*: Todd P. Smith.

*Original Score*: Stewart Copeland.

*Production Design*: John Stoddart.

*Casting*: Joseph Middleton and Shari Rhodes.

*Art Direction*: David Bomba.

*Set Decoration*: Patty Malone.

*Costume Design*: Colleen Kelsall.

*Running Time*: 101 minutes.

*Main Cast*: Richard Dreyfuss (Jake Rainer), Linda Hamilton (Karen Rainer), John Lithgow (Dr Harlinger), J.T. Walsh (Sheriff Mitch Rivers), Ben Faulkner (Tim Warden), Liv Tyler (Sylvie Warden), Zahn McClarnon (Deputy Bear), Brandon Stouffer (Halloween Kid #1), Treva Moniik King (Halloween Kid #2), John McGee Jr. (Deputy), Ron Tucker (Forensic Detective), Catherine Shaffner (Martha).


## HEAVY (1995)

*Production Company*: Available Light.

*Distributor*: Ciné 360 Inc./ Cinépix Film Properties Inc.

*Director*: James Mangold.

*Producer*: Richard Miller.

*Line Producer*: Gretchen McGowan.

*Associate Producers*: Scott Ferguson and Jane Wright.

*Executive Producer*: Herbert Beigel.

*Screenplay*: James Mangold.

*Film Editor*: Meg Reticker.

*Cinematography*: Michael Barrow.

*Production Manager*: Trish Hofmann.
*Original Score*: Thurston Moore.
*Production Design*: Michael Shaw.
*Casting*: Todd Thaler.
*Art Direction*: Daniel Goldfield.
*Set Decoration*: Kara Cressman.
*Costume Design*: Sara Jane Slotnick.
*Running Time*: 104 minutes.
*Main Cast*: Pruitt Taylor Vince (Victor Modino), Shelley Winters (Dolly Modino), Liv Tyler (Callie), Deborah Harry (Dolores), Joe Grifasi (Leo), Evan Dando (Jeff), David Patrick Kelly (Grey Man in Hospital), Marian Quinn (Darlene), Meg Hartig (Donna), Zandy Hartig (Jean), Peter Ortel (Tony).

## EMPIRE RECORDS (1995)

*Production Company*: Monarchy Enterprises/ New Regency Pictures/ Regency Entertainment/ Warner Brothers.
*Distributor*: Warner Brothers.
*Director*: Allan Moyle.
*Producers*: Tony Ludwig, Arnon Milchan, Michael Nathanson and Alan Riche.
*Co-Producer*: Paul Kurta.
*Screenplay*: Carol Heikkinen.
*Film Editor*: Michael Chandler.
*Cinematography*: Walt Lloyd.
*Unit Production Manager*: Paul Kurta.
*Assistant Unit Production Manager*: Cecilia K. Roque
*Original Music*: Marshall Crenshaw, Vinne Dombroski, Gwar, Larry Lee, Kyle Neely, Dolores O'Riordan, Andy Patalan, Brian Reeves, Coyote Shivers, Noah Stone, Jesse Valenzuela, Robin Wilson and Mike Muir.
*Production Design*: Peter Jamison.
*Casting*: Gail Levin.
*Art Direction*: John Huke.
*Set Decoration*: Linda Spheeris.
*Costume Design*: Susan Lyall.
*Running Time*: 90 minutes.
*Main Cast*: Anthony LaPaglia (Joe Reaves), Maxwell Caulfield (Rex Manning), Debi Mazar (Jane), Rory Cochrane (Lucas), Johnny Whitworth (A.J.), Robin Tunney (Debra), Renee Zellweger (Gina), Ethan Randall

(Mark), Coyote Shivers (Berko), Brendan Sexton (Warren), Liv Tyler (Corey Mason), James 'Kimo' Wills (Eddie), Ben Bode (Mitchell Beck).

## STEALING BEAUTY (1996)

*Production Company*: Union Général Cinématographique/ Recorded Picture Company/ Jeremy Thomas
Productions/ France 2 Cinéma/ Fiction
*Distributor*: 20th Century Fox/ Fox Searchlight.
*Director*: Bernardo Bertolucci.
*Producer*: Jeremy Thomas.
*Associate Producer*: Chris Auty.
*Executive Producer*: Yves Attal.
*Screenplay*: Susan Minot.
*Story*: Bernardo Bertolucci.
*Film Editor*: Pietro Scalia.
*Cinematography*: Darius Khondji.
*Unit Manager*: Piero Sassaroli.
*Production Supervisor*: Mario Cotone.
*Original Score*: Richard Hartley.
*Production Design*: Gianni Silvestri.
*Casting*: Howard Feuer and Celestia Fox.
*Art Direction*: Domenico Sica.
*Set Decoration*: Cinzia Sleiter.
*Costume Design*: Louise Stjernsward.
*Running Time*: 113 minutes.
*Main Cast*: Sinead Cusack (Diana Grayson), Jeremy Irons (Alex), Jean Marais (Monsieur Guillaume), D.W. Moffett (Richard Reed), Stefania Sandrelli (Noemi), Liv Tyler (Lucy Harmon), Rachel Weisz (Miranda Fox), Donal McCann (Ian Grayson), Joseph Fiennes (Christopher Fox), Carlo Cecchi (Carlo Lisca), Jason Flemyng (Gregory), Anna Maria Gherardi (Chiarella Donati), Ignazio Oliva (Osvaldo Donati), Francesco Siciliano (Michele Lisca), Roberto Zibetti (Niccoló Donati), Mary Jo Sorgani (Maria), Rebecca Valpy (Daisy), Allesandra Vanzi (Marta), Leonardo Treviglio (Lieutenant).

## THAT THING YOU DO! (1996)

*Production Company*: 20th Century Fox/ Clavius Base/ Clinica Estetico Ltd.

*Distributor*: 20th Century Fox.

*Director*: Tom Hanks.

*Producers*: Jonathan Demme, Gary Goetzman and Edward Saxon.

*Associate Producer*: Terry Odem.

*Screenplay*: Tom Hanks.

*Film Editor*: Richard Chew.

*Cinematography*: Tak Fujimoto.

*Unit Production Manager*: Charles Skouras III.

*Production Supervisor*: Christa Vausbinder.

*Original Score*: Howard Shore.

*Production Design*: Victor Kempster.

*Casting*: Howard Feuer.

*Art Direction*: Dan Webster.

*Set Decoration*: Merideth Boswell.

*Costume Design*: Colleen Atwood.

*Running Time*: 108 minutes.

*Main Cast*: Tom Everett Scott (Guy Patterson), Liv Tyler (Faye Dolan), Johnathon Schaech (Jimmy Mattingly), Steve Zahn (Lenny Haise), Ethan Embry (The Bass Player), Tom Hanks (Mr White), Charlize Theron (Tina), Obba Babatundé (Lamarr), Giovanni Ribisi (Chad), Chris Ellis (Phil Horace), Alex Rocco (Sol Siler), Bill Cobbs (Del Paxton), Peter Scolari (Troy Chesterfield), Rita Wilson (Marguerite), Chris Isaak (Uncle Bob), Kevin Pollak (Boss Vic Koss), Robert Torti (Freddy Fredrickson), Chaille Percival (Diane Dane), Holmes Osborne Jr (Mr Patterson), Claudia Stedelin (Mrs Patterson), Dawn Maxey (Darlene Patterson).

## INVENTING THE ABBOTTS (1997)

*Production Company*: 20th Century Fox/ Imagine Entertainment.

*Distributor*: 20th Century Fox.

*Director*: Pat O'Connor.

*Producers*: Brian Grazer, Ron Howard and Janet Meyers.

*Executive Producers*: Jack Cummins and Karen Kehela.

*Screenplay*: Ken Hixon.

*Story*: Sue Miller.

*Film Editor*: Ray Lovejoy.

*Cinematography*: Kenneth MacMillan.
*Unit Production Manager*: Jack Cummins.
*Production Supervisor*: Marcy G. Kaplan.
*Original Score*: Michael Kamen.
*Production Design*: Gary Frutkoff.
*Casting*: Risa Bramon Garcia.
*Art Direction*: William V. Ryder.
*Set Decoration*: Kathryn Peters.
*Costume Design*: Aggie Guerard Rodgers.
*Running Time*: 110 minutes.
*Main Cast*: Liv Tyler (Pamela Abbott), Joaquin Phoenix (Doug Holt),
Billy Crudup (John Charles 'Jacey' Holt), Jennifer Connelly (Eleanor
Abbott), Joanna Going (Alice Abbott), Barbara Williams (Joan Abbott),
Will Patton (Lloyd Abbott), Kathy Baker (Helen Holt), Michael Sutton
(Steve), Alessandro Nivola (Peter Vanlaningham).

## ARMAGEDDON (1998)

*Production Company*: Touchstone Pictures/Jerry
Bruckheimer Films/ Valhalla Motion Pictures.
*Distributor*: Touchstone Pictures/ Buena Vista.
*Director*: Michael Bay.
*Producers*: Michael Bay, Jerry Bruckheimer, Gale Anne Hurd.
*Associate Producers*: Kenny Bates, Pat Sandston and Barry Waldman.
*Executive Producers*: Jonathan Hensleigh, Chad Oman and Jim Van
Wyck.
*Screenplay*: Jonathan Hensleigh and J.J. Abrams.
*Adaptation*: Tony Gilroy and Shane Salerno.
*Story*: Robert Roy Pool and Jonathan Hensleigh.
*Film Editors*: Mark Goldblatt, Chris Lebenzon and Glen Scantlebury.
*Cinematography*: John Schwartzmann.
*Unit Production Manager*: Barry Waldman.
*Production Supervisor*: Diane L. Sabatini.
*Executive Production Manager*: Liz Ralston.
*Executive in Charge of Production*: Kathy Nelson.
*Original Score*: Trevor Rabin.
*Production Design*: Michael White.
*Casting*: Bonnie Timmermann.
*Art Direction*: Lawrence A. Hubbs and Bruton Jones.
*Set Decoration*: Rick Simpson.

*Costume Design*: Magali Guidasci and Michael Kaplan.

*Running Time*: 150 minutes.

*Main Cast*: Bruce Willis (Harry S. Stamper), Billy Bob Thornton (Dan Truman), Ben Affleck (A.J. Frost), Liv Tyler (Grace Stamper), Will Patton (Charles 'Chick' Chapple), Steve Buscemi (Rockhound), William Fichtner (Colonel William Sharp), Owen Wilson (Oscar Choi), Michael Clarke Duncan (Jayotis 'Bear' Kurleenbear), Peter Stormare (Lev Andropov), Ken Campbell (Max Lennert), Jessica Steen (Jennifer Watts), Keith David (Lieutenant General Kimsey), Chris Ellis (Walter Clark), Jason Isaacs (Dr Ronald Quincy).

## PLUNKETT AND MACLEANE (1999)

*Production Company*: Working Title Films/ Arts Council of England/ Gramercy Pictures/ Stillking Films.

*Distributor*: Polygram.

*Director*: Jake Scott.

*Producers*: Tim Bevan, Eric Fellner and Rupert Harvey.

*Co-Producers*: Jonathan Finn and Natascha Wharton.

*Executive Producers*: Gary Oldman, Selwyn Roberts, Matthew Stillman and Douglas Urbanski.

*Co-Executive Producer*: Donna Grey.

*Screenplay*: Robert Wade, Neal Purvis and Charles McKeown. (Earlier Screenplay by Selwyn Roberts.)

*Film Editor*: Oral Norrie Ottey.

*Cinematography*: John Mathieson.

*Production Manager (Spain)*: Rosa Romero.

*Production Manager (Second Unit)*: Jasmin Torbati.

*Original Score*: Craig Armstrong.

*Production Design*: Norris Spencer.

*Casting*: Jessica Horáthová and Jina Jay.

*Art Direction*: Jindrich Kocí.

*Costume Design*: Janty Yates.

*Running Time*: 93 minutes.

*Main Cast*: Jonny Lee Miller (Macleane), Robert Carlyle (Plunkett), Ken Stott (Chance), Liv Tyler (Lady Rebecca), Michael Gambon (Lord Gibson), Alan Cumming (Lord Rochester), Iain Robertson (Highwayman Rob), Alexander Armstrong (Winterburn), Ben Miller (Dixon), Tommy Flanagan (Eddie), Stephen Walters (Dennis), James Thornton (Catchpole), Terence Rigby (Harrison), Christian Camargo (Lord Pelham), Matt Lucas

(Sir Oswald), David Walliams (Viscount Bilston), David Foxxe (Lord Ketch), Claire Rushbrook (Lady Estelle).


## COOKIE'S FORTUNE (1999)

*Production Company*: Elysian Dreams/ Kudzu/ Moonstone Entertainment/ Sandcastle 5 Productions.
*Distributor*: New Films International/ K2 Entertainment.
*Director*: Robert Altman.
*Producers*: Robert Altman and Etchie Stroh.
*Co-Producers*: David Levy and James McLindon.
*Executive Producer*: Willi Baer.
*Screenplay*: Anne Rapp.
*Film Editor*: Abraham Lim.
*Cinematography*: Toyomichi Kurita.
*Unit Production Manager*: Barbara A. Hall.
*Original Score*: David A. Stewart.
*Production Design*: Stephen Altman.
*Casting*: Pam Dixon Mickelson.
*Art Direction*: Richard Johnson.
*Set Decoration*: Susan Emshwiller.
*Running Time*: 118 minutes.
*Main Cast*: Glenn Close (Camille Dixon), Julianne Moore (Cora Duvall), Liv Tyler (Emma Duvall), Chris O'Donnell (Jason Brown), Charles S. Dutton (Willis Richland), Patricia Neal (Jewel Mae 'Cookie' Orcutt), Ned Beatty (Lester Boyle), Courtney B. Vance (Otis Tucker), Donald Moffat (Jack Palmer), Lyle Lovett (Manny Hood), Danny Darst (Billy Cox), Matt Malloy (Eddie 'The Expert' Pitts), Randle Mell (Patrick Freeman), Niecy Nash (Wanda Carter), Rufas Thomas (Theo Johnson), Ruby Wilson (Josie Martin).


## ONEGIN (1999)

*Production Company*: Seven Arts International/ Baby Productions/ Canwest/ Rysher Entertainment/ Starz!
*Distributor*: Samuel Goldwyn Films LLC/ GAGA Communications.
*Director*: Martha Fiennes.
*Producer*: Simon Bosanquet and Ileen Maisel.
*Line Producer*: Valery Yermolaev.

*Executive Producer*: Ralph Fiennes.
*Screenplay*: Peter Ettedgui and Michael Ignatieff.
*Story*: Alexander Pushkin.
*Film Editor*: Jim Clark.
*Cinematography*: Remi Adefarasin.
*Production Manager*: Philip Kohler.
*Production Supervisor*: Lesley Stewart.
*Post-Production Supervisor*: Miranda Jones.
*Original Score*: Magnus Fiennes.
*Production Design*: Jim Clay.
*Casting*: Mary Selway.
*Art Direction*: Chris Seagers.
*Set Decoration*: Maggie Gray.
*Costume Design*: John Bright and Chloé Obolensky.
*Running Time*: 106 minutes.
*Main Cast*: Ralph Fiennes (Evgeny Onegin), Toby Stephens (Vladimir Lensky), Liv Tyler (Tatyana Larina), Lena Headey (Olga Larina), Martin Donovan (Prince Nikitin), Alun Armstrong (Zaretsky), Harriet Walter (Madame Larina), Irene Worth (Princess Alina), Jason Watkins (Guillot), Francesca Annis (Katiusha), Simon McBurney (Triquet), Geoffrey McGivern (Audrey Petrovitch).


## DR T AND THE WOMEN (2000)

*Production Company*: Sandcastle 5 Productions/ Dr T Inc.
*Distributor*: New Films International/ Initial Entertainment Group.
*Director*: Robert Altman.
*Producer*: Robert Altman and James McLindon.
*Co-Producers*: David A. Jones, Graham King, David Levy and Tommy Thompson.
*Associate Producer*: Joshua Astrachan.
*Executive Producer*: Cindy Cowan.
*Screenplay*: Anne Rapp.
*Film Editor*: Geraldine Peroni.
*Cinematography*: Jan Kiesser.
*Unit Production Manager*: James McLindon.
*Production Supervisor*: Betsy Mackey.
*Post-Production Supervisor*: Michael Altman.
*Original Score*: Lyle Lovett.
*Production Design*: Stephen Altman.

*Casting*: Pam Dixon Mickelson.
*Art Direction*: John E. Bucklin.
*Set Decoration*: Chris Spellman.
*Costume Design*: Dona Granata.
*Running Time*: 122 minutes.
*Main Cast*: Richard Gere (Dr Travis Sullivan), Helen Hunt (Bree), Farrah Fawcett (Kate), Laura Dern (Peggy), Shelley Long (Carolyn), Tara Reid (Connie), Kate Hudson (Dee Dee), Liv Tyler (Marilyn), Robert Hays (Harlan), Matt Malloy (Bill), Andy Richter (Eli), Lee Grant (Dr Harper), Janine Turner (Dorothy Chambliss), Holly Pelham-Davis (Joanne).

## ONE NIGHT AT McCOOL'S (2001)

*Production Company*: Further Films/ October Films.
*Distributor*: USA Films/ Humax Pictures Inc.
*Director*: Harald Zwart.
*Producers*: Michael Douglas and Allison Lyon Segan.
*Associate Producer*: Veslemoey Ruud Zwart.
*Executive Producer*: Whitney Green.
*Screenplay*: Stan Seidel.
*Film Editor*: Bruce Cannon.
*Cinematography*: Karl Walter Lindenlaub.
*Unit Production Manager*: Whitney Green.
*Production Supervisor*: Sara E. White.
*Post-Production Supervisor*: Peter Mavromates.
*Original Score*: Marc Shaiman.
*Production Design*: Jon Gary Steele.
*Casting*: Juel Bestrop and Jeanne McCarthy.
*Art Direction*: David Lazan.
*Set Decoration*: Larry Dias.
*Costume Design*: Ellen Mirojnick.
*Running Time*: 93 minutes.
*Main Cast*: Liv Tyler (Jewel), Matt Dillon (Randy), Paul Reiser (Carl), John Goodman (Detective Dehling), Michael Douglas (Mr Burmeister), Reba McEntire (Dr Green), Richard Jenkins (Father Jimmy), Andrew Silverstein (Utah/ Elmo), Tim Dezarn (Detective Ertagian), Mary Jo Smith (Bingo Caller), Sandy Martin (Bingo Vendor Woman).

## THE LORD OF THE RINGS: THE FELLOWSHIP OF THE RING
(2001)

*Production Company*: New Line Cinema/ WingNut Films/ The Saul Zaentz Company

*Distributor*: New Line Cinema.

*Director*: Peter Jackson.

*Producer*: Peter Jackson, Barrie M. Osborne, Tim Sanders and Fran Walsh.

*Co-Producers*: Rick Porras and Jamie Selkirk

*Associate Producer*: Ellen Somers.

*Executive Producers*: Michael Lynne, Mark Ordesky, Robert Shaye, Bob Weinstein and Harvey Weinstein.

*Screenplay*: Fran Walsh, Philippa Boyens and Peter Jackson.

*Story*: J.R.R. Tolkien.

*Film Editor*: John Gilbert.

*Cinematography*: Andrew Lesnie.

*Unit Production Managers*: Nikolas Korda and Zane Weiner.

*Second Unit Production Managers*: Bridget Bourke and Carol Kim.

*Post-Production Supervisor*: Rosemary Dority.

*Executive in Charge of Production*: Carla Fry.

*Original Score*: Howard Shore.

*Production Design*: Grant Major.

*Casting*: Victoria Burrows, John Hubbard, Amy MacLean, Liz Mullane and Ann Robinson.

*Art Direction*: 'Peter' Joe Bleakley, Phil Ivey, Rob Otterside and Mark Robins.

*Costume Design*: Ngila Dickson and Richard Taylor.

*Running Time (Theatrical Cut)*: 178 minutes.

*Running Time (Extended Cut)*: 208 minutes.

*Main Cast*: Elijah Wood (Frodo Baggins), Ian McKellen (Gandalf the Grey), Viggo Mortensen (Aragorn), Sean Astin (Sam Gamgee), John Rhys-Davies (Gimli), Orlando Bloom (Legolas), Christopher Lee (Saruman the White), Hugo Weaving (Elrond), Liv Tyler (Arwen), Sean Bean (Boromir), Billy Boyd (Pippin), Dominic Monaghan (Merry), Ian Holm (Bilbo Baggins), Cate Blanchett (Galadriel), Marton Csokas (Celeborn), Sala Baker (Sauron), Lawrence Makoare (Lurtz), Brent McIntyre (Witch King), Mark Ferguson (Gil-Galad), Peter McKenzie (Elendil), Harry Sinclair (Isildur), Craig Parker (Haldir), David Weatherley (Barliman Butterbur), Sarah McLeod (Rosie Cotton).

**THE LORD OF THE RINGS: THE TWO TOWERS** (2002)

*Production Company*: New Line Cinema/ WingNut
Films/ Lord Zweite Productions Deutschland Filmproduktion GmbH/
The Saul Zaentz Company.
*Distributor*: New Line Cinema.
*Director*: Peter Jackson.
*Producer*: Peter Jackson, Barrie M. Osborne and Fran Walsh.
*Co-Producers*: Rick Porras and Jamie Selkirk
*Executive Producers*: Michael Lynne, Mark Ordesky, Robert Shaye, Bob
Weinstein and Harvey Weinstein.
*Screenplay*: Fran Walsh, Philippa Boyens, Stephen Sinclair and Peter
Jackson.
*Story*: J.R.R. Tolkien.
*Film Editor*: Michael Horton and Jabez Olssen.
*Cinematography*: Andrew Lesnie.
*Unit Production Managers*: Nikolas Korda and Zane Weiner.
*Second Unit Production Managers*: Bridget Bourke and Carol Kim.
*Post-Production Supervisors*: Rosemary Dority and Jonas Thaler.
*Executive in Charge of Production*: Carla Fry.
*Original Score*: Howard Shore.
*Production Design*: Grant Major.
*Casting*: Victoria Burrows, John Hubbard, Amy MacLean, Liz Mullane
and Ann Robinson.
*Art Direction*: 'Peter' Joe Bleakley, Dan Hennah, Philip Ivey, Rob
Outterside, Christian Rivers and Mark Robins.
*Set Decoration:* Dan Hennah and Alan Lee.
*Costume Design*: Ngila Dickson and Richard Taylor.
*Running Time (Theatrical Cut)*: 179 minutes.
*Running Time (Extended Cut)*: 223 minutes.
*Main Cast*: Elijah Wood (Frodo Baggins), Ian McKellen (Gandalf the
Grey/ White), Viggo Mortensen (Aragorn), Sean Astin (Sam Gamgee),
John Rhys-Davies (Gimli/ Voice of Treebeard), Orlando Bloom (Legolas),
Christopher Lee (Saruman the White), Andy Serkis (Gollum), Billy Boyd
(Pippin), Dominic Monaghan (Merry), Hugo Weaving (Elrond), Liv Tyler
(Arwen), Bernard Hill (Théoden), Miranda Otto (Éowyn), Karl Urban
(Éomer), David Wenham (Faramir), Brad Dourif (Gríma Wormtongue),
Cate Blanchett (Galadriel), Craig Parker (Haldir), Bruce Hopkins
(Gamling).

**THE LORD OF THE RINGS: THE RETURN OF THE KING** (2003)

*Production Company*: New Line Cinema/ WingNut
Films/ Lord Zweite Productions Deutschland Filmproduktion GmbH/
The Saul Zaentz Company.

*Distributor*: New Line Cinema.

*Director*: Peter Jackson.

*Producer*: Peter Jackson, Barrie M. Osborne and Fran Walsh.

*Co-Producers*: Rick Porras and Jamie Selkirk

*Executive Producers*: Michael Lynne, Mark Ordesky, Robert Shaye, Bob
Weinstein and Harvey Weinstein.

*Screenplay*: Fran Walsh, Philippa Boyens and Peter Jackson.

*Story*: J.R.R. Tolkien.

*Film Editor*: Jamie Selkirk.

*Cinematography*: Andrew Lesnie.

*Unit Production Manager*: Zane Weiner.

*Second Unit Production Managers*: Carol Kim and Brigitte Yorke.

*Production Managers*: Brendalee Hope and Robin Saxen.

*Post-Production Supervisor*: Jonas Thaler.

*Supervising Unit Production Manager*: Nikolas Korda.

*Executive in Charge of Production*: Carla Fry.

*Original Score*: Howard Shore.

*Production Design*: Grant Major.

*Casting*: Victoria Burrows, John Hubbard, Amy MacLean, Liz Mullane
and Ann Robinson.

*Art Direction*: Joe Bleakley, Simon Bright, Dan Hennah, Philip Ivey,
Christian Rivers and Mark Robins.

*Set Decoration:* Dan Hennah and Alan Lee.

*Costume Design*: Ngila Dickson and Richard Taylor.

*Running Time (Theatrical Cut)*: 201 minutes.

*Running Time (Extended Cut)*: 251 minutes.

*Main Cast*: Elijah Wood (Frodo Baggins), Ian McKellen (Gandalf the
White), Viggo Mortensen (Aragorn), Sean Astin (Sam Gamgee), John
Rhys-Davies (Gimli), Orlando Bloom (Legolas), Andy Serkis (Sméagol/
Gollum), Billy Boyd (Pippin), Dominic Monaghan (Merry), Hugo
Weaving (Elrond), Liv Tyler (Arwen), David Wenham (Faramir), John
Noble (Denethor), Bernard Hill (Théoden), Miranda Otto (Éowyn), Karl
Urban (Éomer), Bruce Hopkins (Gamling), Lawrence Makoare (Witch
King/ Gothmog), Paul Norell (King of the Dead), Cate Blanchett
(Galadriel), Marton Csokas (Celeborn), Ian Holm (Bilbo Baggins), Sarah
McLeod (Rosie Cotton).

## JERSEY GIRL (2004)

*Production Company*: Miramax Films/ Beverly Detroit/ Close Call Films/ View Askew Productions.
*Distributor*: Miramax Films.
*Director*: Kevin Smith.
*Producer*: Scott Mosier.
*Co-Producer*: Laura Greenlee.
*Line Producer*: Laura Greenlee.
*Associate Producer*: Phil Benson.
*Executive Producers*: Kevin Smith, Bob Weinstein and Harvey Weinstein.
*Screenplay*: Kevin Smith.
*Film Editors*: Olof Källström, Scott Mosier, Kevin Smith.
*Cinematography*: Vilmos Zsigmond.
*Production Manager*: Susan McNamara.
*Original Score*: James L. Venable.
*Production Design*: Robert Holtzman.
*Casting*: Diane Heery and Avy Kaufman.
*Art Direction*: Elise G. Viola.
*Set Decoration*: Diane Lederman.
*Costume Design*: Juliet Polcsa.
*Running Time*: 102 minutes.
*Main Cast*: Ben Affleck (Ollie Trinke), Liv Tyler (Maya), George Carlin (Bart Trinke), Raquel Castro (Gertie Trinke), Jason Biggs (Arthur Brickman), Stephen Root (Greenie), Mike Starr (Block), Jennifer Lopez (Gertrude Steiney), Paulie Litowsky (Bryan), Jennifer Schwalbach (Susan), Matthew Cloran (Anthony), Charles Gilbert (Sweeney Todd).


## LONESOME JIM (2005)

*Production Company*: InDigEnt/ Plum Pictures.
*Distributor*: IFC Films.
*Director*: Steve Buscemi.
*Producers*: Jake Abraham, Steve Buscemi, Galt Niederhoffer, Celine Rattray, Daniela Soto-Taplin and Gary Winick.
*Co-Producer*: Derrick Tseng.
*Associate Producers*: Saxon Eldridge, Emily Gardiner and Mandy Tagger.
*Executive Producers*: Caroline Kaplan, Jonathan Sehring, Reagan Silber,

John Sloss and Anna Waterhouse.

*Screenplay*: James C. Strouse.

*Film Editor*: Plummy Tucker.

*Cinematography*: Phil Parmet.

*Post-Production Producer*: Zennia M. Barahona.

*Post-Production Supervisor*: Emily Gardiner.

*Original Score*: Evan Lurie.

*Production Design*: Chuck Voelter.

*Casting*: Bryan Falcon, Sheila Jaffe, Jessica Smucker Falcon and Georgianne Walken.

*Art Direction*: Chuck Voelter.

*Set Decoration*: James Beaver.

*Costume Design*: Victoria Farrell.

*Running Time*: 91 minutes.

*Main Cast*: Casey Affleck (Jim), Liv Tyler (Anika), Mary Kay Place (Sally), Seymour Cassel (Don), Kevin Corrigan (Tim), Jack Rovello (Ben), Rachel Strouse (Rachel), Sarah Strouse (Sarah), Mark Boone Junior (Evil), Doug Liechty Casey (Doug the Preacher), Pam Grinstead-Angell (Stacy), Jake La Botz (Philip), Don Strouse (Neighbor).

# REFERENCES

## INTRODUCTION

1. Bebe Buell with Victor Bockris, *Rebel Heart: An American Rock 'n' Roll Journey* (New York: St. Martin's Press, 2002).

Of particular interest is Chapter 12, which deals quite extensively with Tyler's early film career.

2. For further details about Tyler's background prior to the beginning of her acting career, Jamie Diamond's excellent article 'Liv on the Edge' in the August 1999 edition of *Mademoiselle* magazine is highly recommended.

Another text which discusses the earlier years of Tyler's work in the film industry can be found in David Cavanagh's article 'Livin' Doll', which appears in the September 1996 issue of *Empire* magazine. The feature was written at the time of Tyler's critical breakthrough in Bernardo Bertolucci's *Stealing Beauty*, and gives a potted history of her life leading up to her acting career.


## 1. SILENT FALL (1994)

3. For anyone seeking information about Aerosmith and their music, a very rewarding chronicle of their work can be found in *Walk This Way: The Biography of Aerosmith*, written by Aerosmith and Stephen Davis (London: Virgin Publishing, 1998).

4. Desson Howe's review of *Silent Fall* in the 28 October 1994 edition of the *Washington Post* is representative of criticism of this kind.

5. Perhaps the most approving of all reviews at the time can be found in Peter Travers' appraisal of the film in the 3 November 1994 issue of *Rolling Stone* magazine.

6. Roger Ebert discusses Faulkner's performance in his review of the film, which appears in the 28 October 1994 issue of the *Chicago Sun-Times*.

Kenneth Turan also praises Faulkner's approach to the role in a review of *Silent Fall* in the 28 October 1994 edition of *The Los Angeles Times*.

7. Kim Lockhart, 'Cool Gene Queen', in *Sassy*, April 1995.

8. James Ryan, 'Liv Tyler', in *Details*, April 1995.

9. Malissa Thompson, 'The Real Liv Tyler', in *Seventeen*, June 1996.

10. Karen Schoemer, 'Sweet Emotion', in *Elle*, May 2001.

## 2. HEAVY (1995)

11. Barbara Shulgasser notes the subtlety of Mangold's film-making skills in her review of *Heavy* in the 12 July 1996 issue of the *San Francisco Chronicle*. Roger Ebert is also quite fulsome in his praise of the film's restraint and unconventional narrative in the *Chicago Sun-Times* review of 16 August 1996.

Duane Dudek applauds the exceptional performances on display in *Heavy*, particularly the acting skills of Pruitt Taylor Vince, in his review of 4 October 1996, which appeared in the *Milwaukee Journal Sentinel*.

12. Richard Corliss, 'One Life to Liv – But Can She Act?', in *Time*, 17 June 1996.

13. Kim Lockhart, 'Cool Gene Queen', in *Sassy*, April 1995.

14. James Ryan, 'Liv Tyler', in *Details*, April 1995.

15. Claire Connors, 'Evan Can't Wait', in *Dolly*, February 1995.


## 3. EMPIRE RECORDS (1995)

16. For a rewarding retrospective discussion of how and where *Empire Records* fits into the annals of '90s teen comedies, it is well worth checking out Nathan Rabin's review of the film's DVD release posted on 10 June 2003 to *The Onion AV Club*, the online critical review section of *The Onion* newspaper, at: <*http://avclub.com/content/node/7134*>

17. A fairly representative view of the film's critical reception on release can be found in Ken Eisner's review of *Empire Records* in the 2 October 1995 issue of *Variety* magazine.

For a somewhat less sympathetic review, Ryan Gilbey's analysis of the film in the 27 June 1996 edition of *The Independent* shines a critical light on the film's perceived shortcomings in relation to other contemporary releases.

18. Kim Lockhart, 'Cool Gene Queen', in *Sassy*, April 1995.

29. Ingrid Sischy, 'Inventing the Future', in *Interview*, April 1997.

20. James Ryan, 'Liv Tyler', in *Details*, April 1995.


## 4. STEALING BEAUTY (1996)

21. Enthusiastic criticism of *Stealing Beauty* is typified in commentary such as Hal Hinson's review in the 28 June 1996 edition of the *Washington Post*, which praises the clarity of Bertolucci's directorial vision and

commends Tyler's performance.

Another balanced, largely positive review can be found in *Rolling Stone* magazine's review of 27 June 1996, where Peter Travers is complimentary of the film's emotional resonance and Bertolucci's cinematic artistry.

Barbara Shulgasser presents a less well-disposed review in the 21 June 1996 edition of the *San Francisco Examiner*, which approves of some of the film's performances but is largely unconvinced of Bertolucci's handling of the central themes.

John Simon's extremely comprehensive assessment in the 15 July 1996 edition of the *National Review* is critical of both *Stealing Beauty* and much of Bertolucci's wider body of work, and presents a precisely argued line of reasoning to support his views.

22. *Bernardo Bertolucci: Interviews*, ed. by Fabien S. Gerard, T. Jefferson Kline and Bruce Sklarew (Jackson: University Press of Mississippi, 2000).

23. Allen Olensky, 'Tiptoeing in Tuscany', in Gerard, Kline and Sklarew, pp.235-240.

24. Graham Fuller, 'Bernardo Bertolucci's film *Stealing Beauty*', in *Interview*, July 1996.

25. David Cavanagh, 'Livin' Doll', in *Empire*, September 1996.

26. Bruce Newman, 'Directors say Tyler brings her own light to camera, action' in *The Milwaukee Journal Sentinel*, 23 June 1996.

27. Stephen Schaefer, 'Movies: Liv Tyler', in *The Boston Herald*, 24 June 1996.

28. Suzanne Lowry, 'Young pretender to Liz Taylor's throne', in *The London Telegraph*, 17 May 1996.


## 5. THAT THING YOU DO! (1996)

29. Roger Ebert's review of *That Thing You Do!* in the 4 October 1996 edition of the *Chicago Sun-Times* is generally complimentary of the film's nostalgia and the obvious enthusiasm of the main and supporting cast.

Mick LaSalle's review in the 4 October 1996 issue of the *San Francisco Chronicle* is also favourable, and ends on a note of praise for Tyler's portrayal of Faye.

Richard Harrington of the *Washington Post* is reasonably fulsome in his praise of the film in his review of 4 October 1996.

Kevin Jackson presents a detailed and largely complimentary review of *That Thing You Do!* in the 26 January 1997 issue of *The Independent*.

30. Peter Travers' review for the 22 August 1996 issue of *Rolling Stone* magazine is representative of such analysis, praising both Hanks' writing

and directing skills.

Maria Schneider's retrospective appraisal of the film, posted on 29 March 2002 to *The Onion AV Club*, is less sympathetic, identifying a lack of subtlety within the narrative in comparison with other films of the genre at the time:

*<http://avclub.com/content/node/3042>*

31. Jeff Gordinier, 'Hanks For the Memories', in *Entertainment Weekly*, 11 October 1996.

32. Anon., 'Sweet Starlet', in *Paper*, June 1996.

33. Kevin Sessums, 'Liv for the Moment', in *Vanity Fair*, May 1997.

34. Lucy Kaylin, 'All You Need is Liv: She May Be Steven's Daughter, But She's Nobody's Little Girl', in *GQ*, August 1998.

## 6. INVENTING THE ABBOTTS (1997)

35. Roger Ebert's *Chicago Sun-Times* review of 4 April 1997 is characteristic of this type of positive criticism, though he is less convinced of the film's energy and drive.

36. Walter Addiego's review in the 4 April 1997 edition of the *San Francisco Examiner* praises *Inventing the Abbotts* for its pace and elegant construction, drawing favourable comparisons with O'Connor's previous work.

Janet Maslin gives a balanced appraisal in her review of 4 April 1997 for the *New York Times*, weighing the historical accuracy of the film's production values against what she regards as a shortage of real exigency within the narrative.

Marjorie Baumgarten's review in the 4 April 1997 issue of the *Austin Chronicle* compares the film unfavourably with O'Connor's earlier *Circle of Friends*, considering the characters beyond the main and supporting casts to be superficially depicted and unconvincing.

Jonathan Rosenbaum's review for the *Chicago Reader*'s 4 April 1997 edition is much more positive, praising the film for its social relevance and for the tangible efforts of the main cast, who are paid tribute for the authenticity of their performances.

37. Sue Miller, *Inventing the Abbotts and Other Stories* (London: Phoenix, 2002).

38. Ingrid Sischy, 'Inventing the Future', in *Interview*, April 1997.

39. Kevin Sessums, 'Liv for the Moment', in *Vanity Fair*, May 1997.

## 7. ARMAGEDDON (1998)

40. Peter Travers' review for the 6 August 1998 issue of *Rolling Stone* is notably vitriolic in its criticism of *Armageddon*, and Michael Bay's direction in particular.

Bob Graham's review of the film in the *San Francisco Chronicle*'s 1 July 1998 issue is slightly more light-hearted but still stinging in its criticism, lamenting *Armageddon*'s general lack of emotional engagement.

A retrospective review of the film by Keith Phipps posted to *The Onion AV Club* on 4 April 2002 is likewise unsympathetic, considering *Armageddon* to be flawed in numerous ways and detailing these alleged faults accordingly:

<http://avclub.com/content/node/504>

41. This theme, amongst others, is picked up by Janet Maslin in her review for the 1 July 1998 issue of the *New York Times*.

42. Roger Ebert is particularly scathing about what he regarded to be *Armageddon*'s unimaginative and contrived plot devices in his review of 1 July 1998 in the *Chicago Sun-Times*.

43. This is certainly true of Marc Savlov's review in the 3 July 1998 edition of the *Austin Chronicle*, which cautiously celebrates the film's larger than life approach to large-scale action.

Maitland McDonagh's review in the July 1998 issue of *Film Journal International* also acknowledges *Armageddon*'s popular appeal, praising the professionalism of its production despite reservations about some of the film's cynicism.

44. Cindy Pearlman, '5 Minutes with... Liv Tyler', in *React*, August 1998.

45. Lucy Kaylin, 'All You Need is Liv: She May Be Steven's Daughter, But She's Nobody's Little Girl', in *GQ*, August 1998.

46. Bruce Westbrook, '*Armageddon*'s Tyler steps onto blockbuster scene', in *The Houston Chronicle*, 2 July 1998.

47. Dan Webster, 'Overblown business was booming for summer movies', in *The Spokesman Review*, 30 August 1998.

## 8. PLUNKETT AND MACLEANE (1999)

48. Stephen Holden's review of *Plunkett and Macleane*, which appears in *The New York Times*' 1 October 1999 issue, is supportive of the film's wittiness, its well-coordinated action, and many of the leading performances.

In *Film Journal International*'s review of the film in September 1999, Peter

Henn praises the film for its imaginative reworking of the conventions of the historical drama genre.

Philip Strick, writing for *Sight and Sound*'s April 1999 edition, guardedly commends *Plunkett and Macleane* for its energetic homage to different cinematic styles, but is less enthusiastic about a number of idiosyncrasies that he identifies in the plot.

49. Alexander Walker's review of the film for the 1 April 1999 edition of *The Evening Standard* is vehemently critical of what he considered to be Jake Scott's use of ostentatious directorial technique at the expense of subject matter. He is also unconvinced of the film's use of 1990s conventions in an Eighteenth Century setting, finding them to be an uncomfortable fit.

In *The San Francisco Chronicle*'s review of 1 October 1999, Mick LaSalle is critical of *Plunkett and Macleane* due to what he regarded as the unsympathetic characterisation of the central characters, and the lack of exploration of the film's true historical context.

50. For a brief but nonetheless rewarding discussion of *Plunkett and Macleane* and other British historical dramas of the late 1990s, Brian McFarlane's 'The More Things Change... British Cinema in the 1990s' is worth taking a look at. It appears in *The British Cinema Book, 2nd Edition*, edited by Robert Murphy (London: British Film Institute, 2001), pp.273-80.

51. Jamie Diamond, 'Liv on the Edge', in *Mademoiselle*, August 1999.

52. Helena Christensen, 'Liv Tyler: Interview', in *Nylon*, April 1999.

53. Elizabeth Weitzman, 'Miller time – actor Jonny Lee Miller', in *Interview*, January 1998.

### 9. COOKIE'S FORTUNE (1999)

54. Roger Ebert is fulsome in his praise of *Cookie's Fortune* in his review of 9 April 1999 for the *Chicago Sun-Times*, approving of the film's warmth and well-observed performances.

Janet Maslin's review for *The New York Times* on 2 April 1999 is similarly enthusiastic, praising Altman and screenwriter Anne Rapp for the film's alluring story and good-natured gentle comedy.

Edward Guthmann is complimentary of the eccentric characterisation of *Cookie's Fortune*, comparing the film favourably with Altman's previous work, in his review of 9 April 1999 for the *San Francisco Chronicle*.

Geoffrey Macnab is more guarded in his approval of *Cookie's Fortune* in

*Sight and Sound*'s September 1999 issue, considering the film to bear Altman's relaxed, skilful mark of authorship whilst missing his long-established note of piquancy.

John Simon is much less complimentary in his appraisal of 17 May 1999 for the *National Review*, taking issue with Altman's style in general, as well as what he regarded to be a comparative superciliousness within *Cookie's Fortune* towards the film's characters and subject matter.

55. Sheila Johnston, 'Bonny Tyler', in *The Evening Standard*, 13 August 1999.

56. Geoffrey Macnab, 'Liv and Kicking', in The *Sunday Herald*, 1 August 1999.

57. Graham Fuller, and Drew Barrymore, 'Live Tyler: Actress Liv Tyler', in *Interview*, April 1999.


## 10. ONEGIN (1999)

58. Philip French gives a strongly supportive review of *Onegin* in the 21 November 1999 issue of *The Observer*, commending both the film's quality production values and effective cinematography.

Bruce Feld's review of the film in the December 1999 issue of *Film Journal International* is similarly positive, singling out Tyler's tour-de-force performance for special praise.

Julian Graffy's review for the December 1999 edition of *Sight and Sound* is more cautiously favourable, extolling the performances of *Onegin*'s cast whilst reflecting on the likely differences in reaction between Russian audiences and viewership in the wider world.

59. In his review for the 31 March 2000 issue of the *Chicago Sun-Times*, Roger Ebert offers appreciation of the film's elaborate sophistication, but is ultimately critical of what he regarded to be the overly mannered treatment of its emotional subject matter.

Mick LaSalle is also critical in his review for the *San Francisco Chronicle*'s 3 March 2000 issue, finding *Onegin*'s pace to be considerably too purposeful for modern tastes, but remaining well-disposed towards the quality of the film's central performances.

60. Alexander Pushkin, *Eugene Onegin*, trans. by Tom Beck (Sawtry: Dedalus, 2004).

61. Christina Kelly, 'Two daddies, one love and a secret passion', in *Jane*, August 1998.

62. Cindy Pearlman, 'Don't Want to Miss a Thing', in *Chicago Sun-Times*, 18 April 1999.

63. Peter Bradshaw, 'Kith and Pushkin', in *The Guardian*, 19 November 1999.

64. Anon., 'A Fiennes family affair', in *The Evening Standard*, 18 November 1999.

65. Richard Mowe, 'Fiennes family affair proves dreams really can come true', in *The Sunday Herald*, 14 November 1999.

66. Thomas Sutcliffe, 'Profile: Ralph Fiennes – The heart of darkness', in *The Independent*, 12 February 2000.

## 11. DR T AND THE WOMEN (2000)

67. Roger Ebert is largely complimentary of *Dr T and the Women* in his review of 13 October 2000 for the *Chicago Sun-Times*, approving of the film's refusal to present any easy answers to the viewer.

Peter Henn's review of the film in the December 2000 issue of *Film Journal International* is enthusiastic about Altman's satire and energetic direction, comparing it favourably with his well-received earlier film *Short Cuts*.

Desson Howe, in the 13 October 2000 issue of *The Washington Post*, notes the enthusiasm of Altman's ensemble cast, but reflects that the film's mode of satire was becoming somewhat outdated.

In his review for the 13 October 2000 edition of *The San Francisco Chronicle*, Peter Stack praises Altman's sharp examination of modern social mores in high-society America, as well as Anne Rapp's screenplay.

Alexander Walker gives a cautiously approving review in the 5 July 2001 edition of *The Evening Standard*, noting the well-engaged talents of the film's impressive cast.

68. Peter Bradshaw gives a grim assessment of *Dr T and the Women* in his review for the 6 July 2001 issue of *The Guardian*, considering the film to be directionless and, ultimately, an all-time low in Altman's long career.

Marjorie Baumgarten is similarly unimpressed with the film in her review of 13 October 2000 for *The Austin Chronicle*, considering the narrative to be largely uninspired and the comic touches to be somewhat imprudent.

Jonathan Romney, in his review for the 8 July 2001 issue of *The Independent*, is dismayed by what he regarded to be the film's condescension towards many of its female characters, and the general superficiality of the protagonist.

John Simon delivers a damning verdict of *Dr T and the Women* in the 6

November 2000 edition of the *National Review*, criticising the film's direction, the performances of the main cast, the screenplay, and Altman's style in general.

69. Robert T. Self, *Robert Altman's Subliminal Reality* (Minneapolis: University of Minnesota Press, 2002).

70. ibid., p.144-75.

71. Lesley O'Toole, 'Liv Tyler', in *This Is London*, 19 April 2001.

72. Liv Tyler, 'Kate Hudson', in *Interview*, March 2003.


## 11. ONE NIGHT AT MCCOOL'S (2001)

73. Andy Seiler found *One Night at McCool's* to be an entertaining and amusing diversion in his review of 30 April 2001 for *USA Today*. He praises the film's swiftly-moving pace, but is less convinced about some of the comic performances.

Roger Ebert is guardedly approving of the film in his review for the 27 April 2001 issue of the *Chicago Sun-Times*, noting the finely-observed characterisation (and the way that it is viewed differently from numerous standpoints throughout the film) but judging that the narrative complexity was to stifle *McCool's* broader appeal as a comedy.

Sean Axmaker's review of 27 April 2001 for the *Seattle Post-Intelligencer* finds *McCool's* to be both energetic and good-natured, praising the film's liveliness and central performances.

74. Peter Travers' review for the 2 April 2001 issue of *Rolling Stone* finds the film's plot to be inconsistent, but praises Michael Douglas' skilful comic turn in the role of Burmeister.

Daniel Eagan is unimpressed by *One Night at McCool's* in his review of June 2001 for *Film Journal International*, finding fault with what he considered to be a flimsy plotline and considering some of the humour to be less than persuasive.

75. Karen Schoemer, 'Sweet Emotion', in *Elle*, May 2001.

76. William Thomas, 'Liv Tyler: Rock royalty is all things to all men in *One Night at McCool's*', in *Empire*, May 2001.

77. Lesley O'Toole, 'Miss Tyler is Liv-ing it Large', in *This Is London*, 19 April 2001.

78. Stephanie Trong, 'Liv Tyler: Our Favourite Houseguest', in *Jane*, April 2001.

79. Barry Didcock, 'Liv and Kisses', in *The Sunday Herald*, 29 April 2001.

80. Joshua Mooney, 'Tyler holds her own against male co-stars in

*McCool's'*, in *Chicago Sun-Times*, 11 May 2001.

81. Pamela Harland, 'Stealing Beauty: Liv Tyler on taking the spotlight in *One Night at McCool's'*, in *IF*, 27 April 2001.

82. Drew Mackenzie, 'Liv got lippy to find rock star dad', in *The Sunday Mirror*, 29 April 2001.

83. Danny Leigh, 'Too much too young?', in *The Guardian*, 19 April 2001.

84. Emma Forrest, 'Sugar and spice', in *The Daily Telegraph*, 7 April 2001.

85. Elif Cercel, 'Harald Zwart on *One Night at McCool's'*, in *Director's World*, 19 April 2001.

86. Anon., 'Screen Fright', in *The Evening Standard*, 19 April 2001.


## 13. THE LORD OF THE RINGS TRILOGY (2001-03)

87. For a short but valuable discussion of Tolkien's legacy to the fantasy genre, James Cawthorn and Michael Moorcock's *Fantasy: The 100 Best Books* (New York: Carroll and Graf, 1988), pp.161-62, is worth reading.

88. Mick LaSalle is fulsome in his praise of *The Fellowship of the Ring* in his review of 19 December 2001 for *The San Francisco Chronicle*, reflecting that the film's potent metaphors of power and desire remain ever more relevant in today's rapidly changing world.

David Hunter's review in 4 December 2001's issue of *The Hollywood Reporter* is likewise positive, praising the film's performances and dazzling special effects.

Andrew O'Hagan is very enthusiastic about the film in his review for *The Daily Telegraph's* 14 December 2001 edition, considering the film to be close to the spirit of Tolkien's books and approving of the strength of its central themes.

David Ansen found *The Fellowship of the Ring* to be both action-packed and thoughtful, commending the performances of the main cast and admiring the film's mythic resonance, in his review of 10 December 2001 for *Newsweek*.

William Arnold considered the film to be one of the best of the year in his review of 19 December 2001 for the *Seattle Post-Intelligencer*, judging its technical refinement to be far above the norm and again praising the central performances.

Claudia Puig felt that the film suffered occasional lulls in momentum, but was still largely positive in her appraisal in her review for *USA Today's* 18 December 2001 issue.

Wallace Baine is somewhat less enthusiastic in his review for the 19 December 2001 edition of the *Santa Cruz Sentinel*, considering some of the film's characterisation to be sub-par and the running length to be a trifle overlong, but still finding enough positive factors to remain hopeful for future instalments of the trilogy.

89. Philip French's review of *The Two Towers* for the 15 December 2002 edition of *The Guardian* praises the film for its earnest approach to Tolkien's saga, as well as its topicality.

The theme of contemporary relevance is continued by Mick LaSalle in the 18 December 2002 issue of *The San Francisco Chronicle*, who also voiced approval of the film's peerless special effects rendering.

Desson Howe is effusive in his admiration of the film in his review of 20 December 2002 for *The Washington Post*, where he praises the skilful combination of effective performances and finely-developed computer generated effects, and singles out the believable realisation of Gollum as one of Jackson's greatest achievements.

Carrie Rickey commends the film's immensely entertaining sense of fun in her review of *The Two Towers*, which appeared in the 18 December 2002 edition of *The Philadelphia Inquirer*. It was also one of many reviews which selected Ian McKellen's magnificent performance as Gandalf for special praise.

90. In his review for the 18 December 2002 issue of the *Chicago Sun-Times*, Roger Ebert praised *The Two Towers*' impressive cinematography and special effects, but found the film to be oddly out of step with the spirit of Tolkien's book, giving fully argued reasons for his opinion.

Sam Adams takes issue with the fact that the term 'epic' is so often applied to the trilogy, in his review in the 19-25 December issue of *The Philadelphia City Paper*. However, he is generally favourable about the qualities of *The Two Towers* itself, and admits that even if the films are not – in his opinion – truly epic themselves, they come as close as possible to achieving that goal.

91. Peter Travers is hugely admiring of *The Return of the King* in his review of 17 December 2003 for *Rolling Stone*, explaining why he considered Jackson's achievement to be an enormously impressive accomplishment in modern cinema.

In the 14 December 2003 issue of *The Observer*, Philip French praises the film's epic battles and the charm of its characterisation, considering it to be an achievement which was epic in every sense of the word.

Mick LaSalle is likewise supportive in his review of 16 December 2003 for *The San Francisco Chronicle*, approving of the overall cohesion of the film's themes as well as the timeliness of its depiction of a Manichean battle between good and evil.

Neil Norman considered *The Return of the King* to be one of the most accomplished film-making events of its time in his review of 12 December 2003 for *The Evening Standard*, drawing parallels between Tolkien's masterpiece and the myths of Arthurian legend.

In her review of 15 December 2003 for *USA Today*, Claudia Puig felt that the trilogy as whole was unprecedented both in its success and overall excellence, comparing it favourably to other cinematic epics of past years.

92. J.R.R. Tolkien, *The Lord of the Rings* (London: HarperCollins, 1992) [1968].

93. J.R.R. Tolkien, *Sauron Defeated: The End of the Third Age*, ed. by Christopher Tolkien (London: HarperCollins, 2002) [1992].

Of specific interest is Chapter 7, 'Many Partings' (pp.61-74). Arwen is also briefly mentioned in Volumes VI, VII and VIII of Tolkien's *History of Middle-earth* series.

94. Robert Foster, *The Complete Guide to Middle-earth* (London: HarperCollins, 1993) [1978], p.25.

95. J.E.A. Tyler, *The Complete Tolkien Companion* (London: Pan, 2002) [1976], p.44.

96. Paul Kocher, *Master of Middle-earth: The Achievement of J.R.R. Tolkien in Fiction* (Harmondsworth: Penguin, 1974).

Most noteworthy is Chapter 6, 'Aragorn' (pp.117-143), which discusses Arwen's character at length as part of a broader exploration of Aragorn's central role in *The Lord of the Rings*.

97. Tom Shippey, *The Road to Middle-earth*, rev. and exp. edn. (London: HarperCollins, 2005).

Perhaps the most immediately relevant part of the book in relation to this discussion is Appendix C, 'Peter Jackson's Film Versions' (pp.409-429), which offers a rewarding examination of Jackson's success in translating *The Lord of the Rings* novels to the big screen.

98. Paul Simpson, Helen Rodiss and Michaela Bushell, eds., *The Rough Guide to the Lord of the Rings* (London: Rough Guides, 2003), pp.152-53; p.155.

99. Jude Fisher, *The Lord of the Rings Complete Visual Companion* (London: HarperCollins, 2004).

100. *Peter Jackson: From Gore to Mordor*, ed. by Paul A. Woods (London: Plexus Publishing, 2005).

101. Christopher Howse and Tim Robey, 'Tolkien's ideals come shining through', in *The Daily Telegraph*, 11 December 2001.

102. Susan Wloszcznya, 'An Oscar could be waiting for *Return*', in *USA*

*Today*, 21 August 2003.

103. Duane Dudek, '*Ring* of truth', in *The Milwaukee Journal Sentinel*, 16 December 2001.

104. Sean Astin with Joe Layden, *There and Back Again: An Actor's Tale* (London: Virgin Books, 2004).

In one particularly significant section of his book, Astin reflects on Tyler's huge popularity following the release of the trilogy (p.295).

105. Dan Madsen, 'A Hopeless Romantic', in *The Lord of the Rings Fan Club Official Movie Magazine*, November 2005.

106. Bruce Kirkland, 'Elvish: The Language of Love', in *Toronto Sun*, 18 December 2001.

107. Ian Spelling, 'Elf Princess', in *Starlog*, November 2001.

108. Anon., 'J.R.R. Tolkien fanatics are an obsessive lot', in *W*, November 2001.

109. Simon Dumenco, 'Liv and Learn', in *Allure*, January 2002.

110. Kathleen Mantel, 'The Elf: Liv Tyler', in *Pavement*, January 2002.

111. Jenny Cooney Carillo, 'Liv-ing Her Role', in *Dreamwatch*, March 2002.

112. Pam Baker, 'Liv Tyler', in *The Scotsman*, 30 November 2002.

113. Simon Schwartz, 'Liv Tyler', in *Widescreen*, December 2002.

114. Anon., 'Liv in Love', in *Now*, 4 December 2002.

115. Joanna Weinberg, 'Liv's English love affair', in *The Evening Standard*, 6 December 2002.

116. Anon., 'Liv Tyler', in *Cool*, December 2002.

117. Ian Nathan, 'Arwen on Elf love... and Gollum lust', in *Empire*, January 2003.

118. Donna Walker Mitchell, 'Liv for the Moment', in *B*, May 2003.

119. Anon., 'Liv Tyler', in *OK*, December 2003.

120. Clare Goldwin, 'Liv Tyler on looks... and her gift of the gob', in *The Daily Mirror*, 22 November 2003.

121. Lisa Arcella, 'Daddy's girl: Liv Tyler gets beauty tips from pop, praise for *Rings*', in *The New York Daily News*, 3 December 2003.

122. Lynn Barker, 'Return of the Elves', in *Teen Hollywood*, 10 December 2003.

123. Anon., 'Liv Tyler and Orlando Bloom', in *One*, June 2004.

124. Josh Rottenberg, 'A Charmed Liv', in *InStyle*, February 2004.

125. Ian Spelling, 'Evenstar Farewell', in *Starlog*, March 2004.

126. Susan Wloszcznya, 'Life after Middle-earth', in *USA Today*, 13 January 2004.

127. Cindy Pearlman, '*Rings* scores $73.6 million, its stars eye future', in *Chicago Sun-Times*, 22 December 2003.

## 14. JERSEY GIRL (2004)

128. In her review for *The Times*' 17 June 2004 edition,
Wendy Ide is extremely critical of *Jersey Girl*, considering the film to be excessively treacly and emotionally unconvincing in its approach.

Peter Bradshaw is similarly unimpressed in his review of 18 June 2004 in *The Guardian*, deeming the film to be overly sentimental and rather stage-managed in its handling of its themes.

Mick LaSalle is a little more balanced in his appraisal of the film in *The San Francisco Chronicle*'s 26 March 2004 issue, acknowledging Smith's individuality of approach and distinctive humour whilst remaining critical of what he believed to be somewhat glib answers offered by the film on the issue of domestic contentment.

129. Roger Ebert enthusiastically commended *Jersey Girl* in his review of 26 March 2004 for the *Chicago Sun-Times*, praising the film's sense of fun and considering Tyler to be a flawless choice for the role of Maya.

Mike Clark is also largely favourable of the film in his review for *USA Today*'s 25 March 2004 issue, believing *Jersey Girl* to be a constructive step forward in Smith's career as a major film-maker.

130. In his review for the *Philadelphia City Paper*'s 25-31 March 2004 issue, Sam Adams considered Tyler's appearance as Maya to be a career-best performance.

Kimberley Jones is also full of praise for Tyler's portrayal in her review of 26 March 2004 for *The Austin Chronicle*, citing Tyler's spontaneous charm and effective on-screen chemistry with Ben Affleck.

131. Susan Wloszcznya, 'Kevin Smith shares the *Jersey Girl* love', in *USA Today*, 21 March 2004.

132. Jeff Vice, '*Jersey Girl* film mirrors director's life changes', in *Deseret Morning News*, 26 March 2004.

133. Mike Thomas, 'Jersey boy Kevin Smith gets personal, but not too serious', in *Chicago Sun-Times*, 21 March 2004.

134. Juan Morales, 'Liv it Up!', in *LA Confidential*, Spring 2004.

135. Martyn Palmer, 'Back to Reality', in *Total Film*, July 2004.

136. Alun Palmer, 'Gimme One of Those!', in *The Daily Mirror*, 1 July 2004.

137. Jordan Riefe, 'Liv It Up', in *HotDog*, July 2004.

138. Jennifer Graham, '10 Things I Can't Live Without', in *Marie Claire*, April 2004.

139. Erin McWhirter, 'Liv For The Moment', in *New Idea*, August 2003.

## 15. LONESOME JIM (2005)

140. Dennis Harvey is largely approving of *Lonesome Jim* in his review of 7 February 2005 for *Variety*, praising Steve Buscemi's low-key direction and the impressive performances of the main cast.

Casey Affleck's portrayal of Jim is singled out for tribute in Chris Panzner's review for *Stylus* magazine's 12 December 2005 issue, though he is critical of the fact that a film so principally concerned with failure should have such a paradoxically upbeat conclusion.

Roger Ebert gives a short but direct appraisal of *Lonesome Jim* in a review of 27 January 2005 for the *Chicago Sun-Times*, favouring the film's ambience and subtle wit.

141. Jeff Vice, '3 Sundance films directed by well-known actors', in *Deseret Morning News*, 16 January 2005.

142. Nick Roddick, 'Now the big shots are coming to town', in *The Evening Standard*, 20 January 2005.


## CONCLUSION

143. 'Of Beren and Lúthien' in J.R.R. Tolkien, *The Silmarillion*, ed. by Christopher Tolkien (London: HarperCollins, 1994) [1977], pp.194-225.

Of possible further interest is Tolkien's original epic poem which told the story of Beren and Lúthien in verse form, available to read in Volume III of The History of Middle-earth, entitled *The Lays of Beleriand*:

'The Lay of Leithian', in J.R.R. Tolkien, *The Lays of Belierand*, ed. by Christopher Tolkien (London: HarperCollins, 2002) [1985], pp.150-314.

144. Megan Neil, 'Rock-star reception for *Rings*', in *The Age*, 2 December 2003.

Anna Whitelaw, 'As the world gears up for the final film in the *Lord of the Rings* trilogy, *Return of the King*, Anna Whitelaw meets its two young stars, Liv Tyler and Orlando Bloom', in *Sain*, January 2004.

145. Cécile Guilbert, '"Very Irresistible" beauty: Liv Tyler on the chic track, with Givenchy', in *Citizen K*, June 2004.

146. Donna Freydkin, 'A Rose by Liv Tyler's Name', in *USA Today*, 23 June 2005.

Hilary Rose, 'American Beauty', in *The Australian Sunday Telegraph*, October 2004.

147. Anon., 'Liv Tyler: I'll never think of myself as beautiful', in *Grazia*, December 2005.

148. Stuart Husband, 'A breed apart', in *Sky Magazine*, November 2002.

149. The song in question, entitled 'Liv Tyler', is the second track on The Travoltas' album *Endless Summer* (Fast Music, 2002).

**SELECT BIBLIOGRAPHY**

## BOOKS AND REFERENCE GUIDES

Aerosmith, with Stephen Davis, *Walk This Way: The Biography of Aerosmith* (London: Virgin Publishing, 1998).

Astin, Sean, with Joe Layden, *There and Back Again: An Actor's Tale* (London: Virgin Books, 2004).

Baudrillard, Jean, *Simulacra and Simulation*, trans. by Sheila Faria Glaser (Ann Arbor: University of Michigan Press, 1994).

Buell, Bebe, with Victor Bockris, *Rebel Heart: An American Rock 'n' Roll Journey* (New York: St Martin's Press, 2002).

Cawthorn, James, and Michael Moorcock, *Fantasy: The 100 Best Books* (New York: Carroll and Graf, 1988)

Dyer, Richard, *Stars* (London: British Film Institute, 1992) [1979].

Ellis, John, *Visible Fictions: Cinema, Television, Video* (London: Routledge, 1989) [1982].

Fisher, Jude, *The Lord of the Rings Complete Visual Companion* (London: HarperCollins, 2004).

Foster, Robert, *The Complete Guide to Middle-earth* (London: HarperCollins, 1993) [1978].

Gerard, Fabien S., T. Jefferson Kline and Bruce Sklarew, eds., *Bernardo Bertolucci: Interviews* (Jackson: University Press of Mississippi, 2000).

Gledhill, Christine, ed., *Stardom: Industry of Desire* (London: Routledge, 1998) [1991].

Hollows, Joanne, and Mark Jancovich, eds, *Approaches to Popular Film* (Manchester: Manchester University Press, 1995).

Kocher, Paul, *Master of Middle-earth: The Achievement of J.R.R. Tolkien in Fiction* (Harmondsworth: Penguin, 1974).

Marshall, P. David, *Celebrity and Power: Fame in Contemporary Culture* (Minneapolis: University of Minneapolis Press, 1997).

Miller, Sue, *Inventing the Abbotts and Other Stories* (London: Phoenix, 2002).

Miller, Toby, and Robert Stam, eds., *A Companion to Film Theory* (Oxford: Blackwell, 2004) [1999].

Murphy, Robert, ed., *The British Cinema Book*, 2nd edn. (London: British Film Institute, 2001).

Pushkin, Alexander, *Eugene Onegin*, trans. by Tom Beck (Sawtry: Dedalus, 2004).

Rojek, Chris, *Celebrity* (London: Reaktion, 2001).

Self, Robert T., *Robert Altman's Subliminal Reality* (Minneapolis:

University of Minnesota Press, 2002).

Shippey, Tom, *The Road to Middle-earth*, rev. and exp. edn. (London: HarperCollins, 2005).

Simpson, Paul, Helen Rodiss and Michaela Bushell, eds., *The Rough Guide to the Lord of the Rings* (London: Rough Guides, 2003).

Storey, John, ed., *An Introduction to Cultural Theory and Popular Culture*, 2nd Edn. (Harlow: Pearson, 1997).

Storey, John, ed., *Cultural Theory and Popular Culture: A Reader*, 2nd Edn. (Harlow: Pearson, 1998).

Tolkien, J.R.R., *Sauron Defeated: The End of the Third Age*, ed. by Christopher Tolkien (London: HarperCollins, 2002) [1992].

Tolkien, J.R.R., *The History of Middle-earth Index*, ed. by Christopher Tolkien (London: HarperCollins, 2002).

Tolkien, J.R.R., *The Hobbit* (London: HarperCollins, 1993) [1937]

Tolkien, J.R.R., *The Lays of Beleriand*, ed. by Christopher Tolkien (London: HarperCollins, 2002) [1985].

Tolkien, J.R.R., *The Lord of the Rings* (London: HarperCollins, 1992) [1968].

Tolkien, J.R.R., *The Silmarillion*, ed. by Christopher Tolkien (London: HarperCollins, 1994) [1977].

Tolkien, J.R.R., *Unfinished Tales*, ed. by Christopher Tolkien (London: HarperCollins, 1998) [1980].

Turner, Graeme, *Understanding Celebrity* (London: Sage, 2004).

Tyler, J.E.A., *The Complete Tolkien Companion* (London: Pan, 2002) [1976].

Woods, Paul A., ed., *Peter Jackson: From Gore to Mordor* (London: Plexus Publishing, 2005).

## ARTICLES, INTERVIEWS AND REVIEWS

Adams, Sam, 'New Movie Shorts: *Jersey Girl'*, in *The Philadelphia City Paper*, 25-31 March 2004.

Adams, Sam, 'Rung Out', in *The Philadelphia City Paper*, 18-24 December 2003.

Adams, Sam, 'Straight to the Points', in *The Philadelphia City Paper*, 19-25 December 2002.

Addiego, Walter, 'An old-fashioned film with new touches', in *The San Francisco Examiner*, 4 April 1997.

Anon., 'A Fiennes family affair', in *The Evening Standard*, 18 November 1999.

Anon., 'J.R.R. Tolkien fanatics are an obsessive lot', in *W*, November 2001.

Anon., 'Liv in Love', in *Now*, 4 December 2002.

Anon., 'Liv Tyler', in *Cool*, December 2002.

Anon., 'Liv Tyler', in *OK*, December 2003.

Anon., 'Liv Tyler', in *Veronica*, December 2002.

Anon., 'Liv Tyler: I'll never think of myself as beautiful', in *Grazia*, December 2005.

Anon., 'Liv Tyler and Orlando Bloom', in *One*, June 2004.

Anon., 'Now the sister has a Fiennes triumph', in *The Evening Standard*, 8 November 1999.

Anon., 'Screen Fright', in *The Evening Standard*, 19 April 2001.

Anon., 'Seductress in a red dress', in *The Evening Standard*, 19 April 2001.

Anon., '*Stealing Beauty'*s star speaks', in *Dolly*, 1996.

Anon., 'Sweet Starlet', in *Paper*, June 1996.

Ansen, David, 'A *Ring* to Rule the Screen', in *Newsweek*, 10 December 2001.

Arcella, Lisa, 'Daddy's girl: Liv Tyler gets beauty tips from pop, praise for *Rings'*, in *The New York Daily News*, 3 December 2003.

Arnold, William, 'One *Ring* to bring them all... into the theatre', in *The Seattle Post-Intelligencer*, 19 December 2001.

Axmaker, Sean, 'Tyler the object of many desires in thriller *One Night at McCool's'*, in *The Seattle Post-Intelligencer*, 27 April 2001.

Baine, Wallace, 'Bored of the rings: Tolkien saga's first chapter lacks magic', in *The Santa Cruz Sentinel*, 19 December 2001.

Baker, Pam, 'Liv Tyler', in *The Scotsman*, 30 November 2002.

Barker, Lynn, 'Return of the Elves', in *Teen Hollywood*, 10 December 2003.

Baumgarten, Marjorie, '*Dr T and the Women'*, in *The Austin Chronicle*, 13

October 2000.

Baumgarten, Marjorie, '*Inventing the Abbotts*', in *The Austin Chronicle*, 4 April 1997.

Bradshaw, Peter, '*Dr T and the Women*', in *The Guardian*, 6 July 2001.

Bradshaw, Peter, '*Jersey Girl*', in *The Guardian*, 18 June 2004.

Bradshaw, Peter, 'Kith and Pushkin', in *The Guardian*, 19 November 1999.

Carillo, Jenny Cooney, 'Liv-ing Her Role', in *Dreamwatch*, March 2002.

Cavanagh, David, 'Livin' Doll', in *Empire*, September 1996.

Cercel, Elif, 'Harald Zwart on *One Night at McCool's*', in *Director's World*, 19 April 2001.

Christensen, Helena, 'Liv Tyler: Interview', in *Nylon*, April 1999.

Clark, Mike, '*Jersey Girl*: Feel-good fatherhood', in *USA Today*, 25 March 2004.

Condon, Eileen, 'Marriage runs rings around acting', in *The Scotsman*, 3 December 2003.

Connors, Claire, 'Evan Can't Wait', in *Dolly*, February 1995.

Corliss, Richard, 'One Life to Liv – But Can She Act?', in *Time*, 17 June 1996.

Davis, Steve, '*Cookie's Fortune*', in *The Austin Chronicle*, 16 April 1999.

Diamond, Jamie, 'Liv on the Edge', in *Mademoiselle*, August 1999.

Didcock, Barry, 'Liv and Kisses', in *The Sunday Herald*, 29 April 2001.

Dudek, Duane, '*Cookie's Fortune* a pleasant twist from Altman', in *The Milwaukee Journal Sentinel*, 9 April 1999.

Dudek, Duane, 'Director gets sentimental with *Jersey Girl*', in *The Milwaukee Journal Sentinel*, 26 March 2004.

Dudek, Duane, 'Fine performances, detail give *Heavy* its heft', in *The Milwaukee Journal Sentinel*, 4 October 1996.

Dudek, Duane, 'Grit and spectacle help *Lord* ring true: Journey begins with intimate tale', in *The Milwaukee Journal Sentinel*, 18 December 2001.

Dudek, Duane, '*Ring* of truth', in *The Milwaukee Journal Sentinel*, 16 December 2001.

Dudek, Duane, 'There's something about *McCool's* that has a familiar ring of *Mary*', in *The Milwaukee Journal Sentinel*, 27 April 2001.

Dumenco, Simon, 'Liv and Learn', in *Allure*, January 2002.

Eagan, Daniel, '*One Night at McCool's*', in *Film Journal International*, June 2001.

Ebert, Roger, '*Armageddon*', in *Chicago Sun-Times*, 1 July 1998.

Ebert, Roger, '*Cookie's Fortune*', in *Chicago Sun-Times*, 9 April 1999.

Ebert, Roger, '*Dr T and the Women*', in *Chicago Sun-Times*, 13 October 2000.

Ebert, Roger, '*Empire Records*', in *Chicago Sun-Times*, 22 September 1995.

Ebert, Roger, 'Great stories and hippies and bears, oh my!', in *Chicago Sun-Times*, 27 January 2005.

Ebert, Roger, '*Heavy*', in *Chicago Sun-Times*, 16 August 1996.

Ebert, Roger, '*Inventing the Abbotts*', in *Chicago Sun-Times*, 4 April 1997.

Ebert, Roger, '*Jersey Girl*', in *Chicago Sun-Times*, 26 March 2004.

Ebert, Roger, '*Lord of the Rings: The Fellowship of the Ring*', in *Chicago Sun-Times*, 19 December 2001.

Ebert, Roger, '*Lord of the Rings: The Return of the King*', in *Chicago Sun-Times*, 17 December 2003.

Ebert, Roger, '*Lord of the Rings: The Two Towers*', in *Chicago Sun-Times*, 18 December 2002.

Ebert, Roger, '*One Night at McCool's*', in *Chicago Sun-Times*, 27 April 2001.

Ebert, Roger, '*Onegin*', in *Chicago Sun-Times*, 31 March 2000.

Ebert, Roger, '*Plunkett and Macleane*', in *Chicago Sun-Times*, 4 October 1999.

Ebert, Roger, '*Silent Fall*', in *Chicago Sun-Times*, 28 October 1994.

Ebert, Roger, '*Stealing Beauty*', in *Chicago Sun-Times*, 28 June 1996.

Ebert, Roger, '*That Thing You Do!*', in *Chicago Sun-Times*, 4 October 1996.

Eisner, Ken, '*Empire Records*', in *Variety*, 2 October 1995.

Feld, Bruce, '*Onegin*', in *Film Journal International*, December 1999.

Ford, Ben, '*Lonesome Jim* great, but overlooked', in *The Truth*, 28 April 2005.

Forrest, Emma, 'Sugar and spice', in *The Daily Telegraph*, 7 April 2001.

French, Philip, 'It's that Gondor Moment...', in *The Observer*, 14 December 2003.

French, Philip, '*Lord of the Rings: The Fellowship of the Ring*', in *The Observer*, 16 December 2001.

French, Philip, '*Onegin*', in *The Observer*, 21 November 1999.

French, Philip, 'That's another fine myth...', in *The Observer*, 15 December 2002.

Freydkin, Donna, 'A Rose by Liv Tyler's Name', in *USA Today*, 23 June 2005.

Fuller, Graham, 'Altman's Adventures in a World of Women', in *Interview*, October 2000.

Fuller, Graham, 'Bernardo Bertolucci's Film *Stealing Beauty*', in *Interview*, July 1996.

Fuller, Graham, and Drew Barrymore, 'Live Tyler: Actress Liv Tyler', in *Interview*, April 1999.

Gilbey, Ryan, 'Dillying with the Dalai', in *The Independent*, 21 November 1997.

Gilbey, Ryan, 'Simplistic Simon', in *The Independent*, 27 June 1996.

Gilbey, Ryan, '*That Thing You Do!*', in *The Independent*, 25 January 1997.

Goldwin, Clare, 'Liv Tyler on looks... and her gift of the gob', in *The Daily Mirror*, 22 November 2003.

Gordinier, Jeff, 'Hanks For the Memories', in *Entertainment Weekly*, 11 October 1996.

Graffy, Julian, '*Onegin*', in *Sight and Sound*, December 1999.

Graham, Bob, 'Space Junk: Bruce Willis' doomsday blockbuster *Armageddon* misses the target', in *The San Francisco Chronicle*, 1 July 1998.

Graham, Jennifer, '10 Things I Can't Live Without', in *Marie Claire*, April 2004.

Guilbert, Cécile, '"Very Irresistible" beauty: Liv Tyler on the chic track, with Givenchy', in *Citizen K*, June 2004.

Guthmann, Edward, 'A Sweet, Southern *Cookie*: Great cast, script help Altman's latest sing', in *The San Francisco Chronicle*, 9 April 1999.

Guthmann, Edward, '*Heavy*'s Light Take on Life', in *The San Francisco Chronicle*, 12 July 1996.

Harland, Pamela, 'Stealing Beauty: Liv Tyler on taking the spotlight *in One Night at McCool's*', in *IF*, 27 April 2001.

Harrington, Richard, '*That Thing You Do!*: Simply Wonder-Full', in *The Washington Post*, 4 October 1996.

Harvey, Dennis, '*Lonesome Jim*', in *Variety*, 7 February 2005.

Haun, Harry, '*Jersey Girl*', in *Film Journal International*, May 2004.

Henn, Peter, '*Dr T and the Women*', in *Film Journal International*, December 2000.

Henn, Peter, '*Plunkett & Macleane*' in *Film Journal International*, September 1999.

Hinson, Hal, '*Silent Fall*', in *The Washington Post*, 28 October 1994.

Hinson, Hal, '*Stealing Beauty*: Youth and the Grace of Age', in *The Washington Post*, 28 June 1996.

Hoberman, J., 'Final Fantasy: Conclusions of grandeur', in *The Village Voice*, 15 December 2003.

Hoberman, J., 'Vice City: *Gangs of New York*; *25th Hour*; *The Two Towers*', in *The Village Voice*, 18 December 2002.

Holden, Stephen, '*Onegin*: A Cold Comeuppance in St Petersburg', in *The New York Times*, 22 December 1999.

Holden, Stephen, '*Plunkett and Macleane*: Taking From the Rich and Giving to Themselves', in *The New York Times*, 1 October 1999.

Honeycutt, Kirk, '*One Night at McCool's*', in *The Hollywood Reporter*, 19 April 2001.

Howe, Desson, 'A Towering Achievement', in *The Washington Post*, 20 December 2002.

Howe, Desson, 'Bertolucci's Shallow *Beauty*', in *The Washington Post*, 28 June 1996.

Howe, Desson, 'Scattershot Satire', in *The Washington Post*, 13 October 2000.

Howe, Desson, '*Silent Fall*', in *The Washington Post*, 28 October 1994.

Howse, Christopher, and Tim Robey, 'Tolkien's ideals come shining through', in *The Daily Telegraph*, 11 December 2001.

Hunter, David, '*The Lord of the Rings: The Fellowship of the Ring*', in *The Hollywood Reporter*, 4 December 2001.

Hunter, Stephen, 'The Femme Fatale Makes a Comedic Comeback in *One Night at McCool's*', in *The Washington Post*, 27 April 2001.

Husband, Stuart, 'A breed apart', in *Sky Magazine*, November 2002.

Ide, Wendy, '*Jersey Girl*', in *The Times*, 17 June 2004.

Jackson, Kevin, 'No sex, no drugs, and too much rock'n'roll', in *The Independent*, 26 January 1997.

Johnston, Sheila, 'Bonny Tyler', in *The Evening Standard*, 13 August 1999.

Jones, Kimberley, '*Jersey Girl*', in *The Austin Chronicle*, 26 March 2004.

Kaylin, Lucy, 'All You Need is Liv: She May Be Steven's Daughter, But She's Nobody's Little Girl', in *GQ*, August 1998.

Kelly, Christina, 'Two daddies, one love and a secret passion', in *Jane*, August 1998.

King, Barry, 'The Star and the Commodity: Notes Towards a Performance Theory of Stardom', in *Cultural Studies*, 1:2.

Kirkland, Bruce, 'Elvish: The Language of Love', in *Toronto Sun*, 18 December 2001.

Lally, Kevin, '*Cookie's Fortune*', in *Film Journal International*, March 1999.

LaSalle, Mick, '*Beauty*: It Has Nice Scenery', in *The San Francisco Chronicle*, 8 November 1996.

LaSalle, Mick, 'Down and out in New Jersey, without Jennifer Lopez by his side', in *The San Francisco Chronicle*, 26 March 2004.

LaSalle, Mick, 'Foul Police and Thieves', in *The San Francisco Chronicle*, 1 October 1999.

LaSalle, Mick, 'Hanks Does *That Thing* Quite Well', in *The San Francisco Chronicle*, 4 October 1996.

LaSalle, Mick, 'Intelligent *Onegin* Moves Too Slowly', in *The San Francisco Chronicle*, 3 March 2000.

LaSalle, Mick, '*Lord* rings true: Tolkien's epic fantasy springs to wondrous life onscreen', in *The San Francisco Chronicle*, 19 December 2001.

LaSalle, Mick, 'Mordor and mayhem: Impassioned *Lord of the Rings* follow-up pits the faithful good against realistic evil', in *The San Francisco Chronicle*, 18 December 2002.

LaSalle, Mick, 'With a little gold ring and great big dreams, Frodo and his friends make the journey and arrive at the thunderous final encounter in *Return of the King*', in *The San Francisco Chronicle*, 16 December 2003.

Leigh, Danny, 'Too much too young?', in *The Guardian*, 19 April 2001.

Lockhart, Kim, 'Cool Gene Queen', in *Sassy*, April 1995.

Lowry, Suzanne, 'Young pretender to Liz Taylor's throne', in *The London Telegraph*, 17 May 1996.

Mackenzie, Drew, 'Liv got lippy to find rock star dad', in *The Sunday Mirror*, 29 April 2001.

Macnab, Geoffrey, '*Cookie's Fortune*', in *Sight and Sound*, September 1999.

Macnab, Geoffrey, 'Liv and Kicking', in *The Sunday Herald*, 1 August 1999.

Madsen, Dan, 'A Hopeless Romantic', in *The Lord of the Rings Fan Club Official Movie Magazine*, November 2005.

Mantel, Kathleen, 'The Elf: Liv Tyler', in *Pavement*, January 2002.

Maslin, Janet, '*Armageddon*', in *The New York Times*, 1 July 1998.

Maslin, Janet, '*Cookie's Fortune*: From Altman, Salome Story with Southern Sugar and Spite', in *The New York Times*, 2 April 1999.

Maslin, Janet, '*Inventing the Abbotts*', in *The New York Times*, 4 April 1997.

McDonagh, Maitland, '*Armageddon*', in *Film Journal International*, July 1998.

McWhirter, Erin, 'Liv For The Moment', in *New Idea*, August 2003.

Miller, John J., '*Towers* Triumphant: A Tolkien return', in *National Review*, 18 December 2002.

Mitchell, Donna Walker, 'Liv for the Moment', in *B*, May 2003.

Mooney, Joshua, 'Tyler holds her own against male co-stars in *McCool's*', in *Chicago Sun-Times*, 11 May 2001.

Morales, Juan, 'Liv it Up!', in *LA Confidential*, Spring 2004.

Morris, Wesley, 'Altman's *Fortune* is telling', in *The San Francisco Examiner*, 9 April 1999.

Morris, Wesley, '*One Night at McCool's*', in *The San Francisco Chronicle*, 27 April 2001.

Morris, Wesley, '*Onegin*: All in the family', in *The San Francisco Examiner*, 3 March 2000.

Mowe, Richard, 'Fiennes family affair proves dreams really can come true', in *The Sunday Herald*, 14 November 1999.

Nathan, Ian, 'Arwen on Elf love... and Gollum lust', in *Empire*, January

2003.

Neil, Megan, 'Rock-star reception for Rings', in *The Age*, 2 December 2003.

Newman, Bruce, 'Directors say Tyler brings her own light to camera, action' in *The Milwaukee Journal Sentinel*, 23 June 1996.

Norman, Neil, 'The plot thins, but final act is breathtaking', in *The Evening Standard*, 12 December 2003.

O'Hagan, Andrew, 'If you don't like this, you don't like movies', in *The Daily Telegraph*, 14 December 2001.

O'Toole, Lesley, 'Miss Tyler is Liv-ing it Large', in *This Is London*, 19 April 2001.

Palmer, Alun, 'Gimme One of Those!', in *The Daily Mirror*, 1 July 2004.

Palmer, Martyn, 'Back to Reality', in *Total Film*, July 2004.

Panzner, Chris, '*Lonesome Jim*', in *Stylus*, 12 December 2005.

Pearlman, Cindy, 'Don't Want to Miss a Thing', in *Chicago Sun-Times*, 18 April 1999.

Pearlman, Cindy, 'Five Minutes with... Liv Tyler', in *React*, August 1998.

Pearlman, Cindy, '*Rings* scores $73.6 million, its stars eye future', in *Chicago Sun-Times*, 22 December 2003.

Phipps, Keith, '*Armageddon*', in *The Onion AV Club*, *The Onion*, 4 April 2002.

<http://avclub.com/content/node/504>

Poyser, Bryan, '*Onegin*', in *The Austin Chronicle*, 9 June 2000.

Puig, Claudia, 'Dazzling *Towers* keeps *Rings* on the right track', in *USA Today*, 17 December 2002.

Puig, Claudia, 'Middle-earth leaps to life in enchanting, violent film', in *USA Today*, 18 December 2001.

Puig, Claudia, 'With third film, *Rings* saga becomes a classic', in *USA Today*, 15 December 2003.

Quinn, Anthony, 'Cold hearts and coronets', in *The Independent*, 19 November 1999.

Rabin, Nathan, '*Empire Records*: Remix! Special Fan Edition', in *The Onion AV Club*, *The Onion*, 10 June 2003.

<http://avclub.com/content/node/7134>

Rickey, Carrie, '*Towers* advances trilogy powerfully', in *The Philadelphia Inquirer*, 18 December 2002.

Riefe, Jordan, 'Liv It Up', in *HotDog*, July 2004.

Roberts, Rex, 'Bowled Over by *McCool's*', in *Insight on the News*, 28 May 2001.

Roddick, Nick, 'Now the big shots are coming to town', in *The Evening Standard*, 20 January 2005.

Romney, Jonathan, 'A botch job by an old quack', in *The Independent*, 8

July 2001.

Rose, Hilary, 'American Beauty', in *The Australian Sunday Telegraph*, October 2004.

Rosenbaum, Jonathan, 'Prole Models', in *The Chicago Reader*, 4 April 1997.

Rottenberg, Josh, 'A Charmed Liv', in *InStyle*, February 2004.

Ryan, James, 'Liv Tyler', in *Details*, April 1995.

Savlov, Marc, '*Armageddon*', in *The Austin Chronicle*, 3 July 1998.

Schaefer, Stephen, 'Movies: Liv Tyler', in *The Boston Herald*, 24 June 1996.

Schneider, Maria, '*That Thing You Do!*', in *The Onion AV Club, The Onion*, 29 March 2002.

<*http://avclub.com/content/node/3042*>

Schoemer, Karen, 'Sweet Emotion', in *Elle*, May 2001.

Schwartz, Simon, 'Liv Tyler', in *Widescreen*, December 2002.

Seiler, Andy, 'Uneven *McCool's* a strange but frothy brew', in *USA Today*, 30 April 2001.

Sessums, Kevin, 'Liv for the Moment', in *Vanity Fair*, May 1997.

Shulgasser, Barbara, '*Heavy* carries itself with rare subtlety', in *The San Francisco Chronicle*, 12 July 1996.

Shulgasser, Barbara, '*Stealing Beauty* – A director's fantasy', in *The San Francisco Chronicle*, 21 June 1996.

Simon, John, 'Fortuna and Luna', in *National Review*, 17 May 1999.

Simon, John, '*Stealing Beauty*', in *National Review*, 15 July 1996.

Simon, John, 'Taking the Low Road', in *National Review*, 6 November 2000.

Sischy, Ingrid, 'Inventing the Future', in *Interview*, April 1997.

Spelling, Ian, 'Elf Princess', in *Starlog*, November 2001.

Spelling, Ian, 'Evenstar Farewell', in *Starlog*, March 2004.

Stack, Peter, 'Female Problems: Gere's OB/GYN delivers the laughs in Altman comedy', in *The San Francisco Chronicle*, 13 October 2000.

Stack, Peter, 'Steamy *Abbotts* Could Use Some More Invention', in *The San Francisco Chronicle*, 4 April 1997.

Strick, Philip, '*Plunkett & Macleane*', in *Sight and Sound*, April 1999.

Sutcliffe, Thomas, 'Profile: Ralph Fiennes – The heart of darkness', in *The Independent*, 12 February 2000.

Thomas, Mike, 'Jersey boy Kevin Smith gets personal, but not too serious', in *Chicago Sun-Times*, 21 March 2004.

Thomas, William, 'Liv Tyler: Rock royalty is all things to all men in *One Night at McCool's*', in *Empire*, May 2001.

Thompson, Malissa, 'The Real Liv Tyler', in *Seventeen*, June 1996.

Travers, Peter, '*Armageddon*', in *Rolling Stone*, 6 August 1998.

Travers, Peter, '*Dr T and the Women*', in *Rolling Stone*, 10 December 2000.

Travers, Peter, '*Jersey Girl*', in *Rolling Stone*, 24 March 2004.

Travers, Peter, '*Lord of the Rings: The Fellowship of the Ring*', in *Rolling Stone*, 17 January 2001.

Travers, Peter, '*Lord of the Rings: The Two Towers*', in *Rolling Stone*, 2 January 2003.

Travers, Peter, '*One Night at McCool's*', in *Rolling Stone*, 2 April 2001.

Travers, Peter, '*Silent Fall*', in *Rolling Stone*, 3 November 1994.

Travers, Peter, '*Stealing Beauty*', in *Rolling Stone*, 27 June 1996.

Travers, Peter, '*That Thing You Do!*', in *Rolling Stone*, 22 August 1996.

Travers, Peter, '*The Lord of the Rings: The Return of the King*', in *Rolling Stone*, 17 December 2003.

Trong, Stephanie, 'Liv Tyler: Our Favourite Houseguest', in *Jane*, April 2001.

Trong, Stephanie, 'Nobody's cool, tough and strong all the time', in *Jane*, February 2003.

Turan, Kenneth, '*Silent Fall*', in *The Los Angeles Times*, 28 October 1994.

Tyler, Liv, 'Kate Hudson', in *Interview*, March 2003.

Vice, Jeff, '3 Sundance films directed by well-known actors', in *Deseret Morning News*, 16 January 2005.

Vice, Jeff, '*Jersey Girl* film mirrors director's life changes', in *Deseret Morning News*, 26 March 2004.

Vice, Jeff, '*Jersey Girl* surprisingly honest, sweet', in *Deseret Morning News*, 26 March 2004.

Walker, Alexander, 'Highway Yobbery', in *The Evening Standard*, 1 April 1999.

Walker, Alexander, 'The Doctor's Delusion', in *The Evening Standard*, 5 July 2001.

Webster, Dan, 'Altman's *Fortune*', in *The Spokesman Review*, 16 April 1999.

Webster, Dan, 'Overblown business was booming for summer movies', in *The Spokesman Review*, 30 August 1998.

Weinberg, Joanna, 'Liv's English love affair', in *The Evening Standard*, 6 December 2002.

Weinstein, Wendy, '*The Lord of the Rings: The Fellowship of the Ring*', in *Film Journal International*, January 2002.

Weitzman, Elizabeth, 'Miller time – actor Johnny Lee Miller', in *Interview*, January 1998.

Westbrook, Bruce, '*Armageddon*'s Tyler steps onto blockbuster scene', in *The Houston Chronicle*, 2 July 1998.

Whitelaw, Anna, 'As the world gears up for the final film in the *Lord of the*

*Rings* trilogy, Retur*n of the King*, Anna Whitelaw meets its two young stars, Liv Tyler and Orlando Bloom', in *Sain*, January 2004.

Wloszcznya, Susan, 'An Oscar could be waiting for *Return*', in *USA Today*, 21 August 2003.

Wloszcznya, Susan, 'Kevin Smith shares the *Jersey Girl* love', in *USA Today*, 21 March 2004.

Wloszcznya, Susan, 'Life after Middle-earth', in *USA Today*, 13 January 2004.

Printed in Great Britain
by Amazon

20463279R00154